Tourism and the Anthropocene

This book brings the field of tourism into dialogue with what is captured under the Anthropocene. It explores issues and challenges which the Anthropocene may pose for tourism, and it offers significant insights into how it might reframe conceptual and empirical undertakings in tourism research. Furthermore, through the lens of the Anthropocene this book also spurs thinking about the role of tourism in relation to sustainable development, planetary boundaries, ethics (and what is framed as geo-ethics) and refocuses tourism theory to make sense of tourism's earthly entanglements and thinking tourism beyond Nature-Society. The multidisciplinary nature of the material will appeal to a broad academic audience, such as those working in tourism, geography, anthropology and sociology.

Martin Gren is Associate Professor in Tourism Studies at Linnaeus University, Sweden.

Edward H. Huijbens is a research professor at the Icelandic Tourism Research Centre, based at the University of Akureyri, Iceland.

Contemporary Geographies of Leisure, Tourism and Mobility
Series Editor: C. Michael Hall
Professor at the Department of Management, College of Business and Economics, University of Canterbury, Christchurch, New Zealand

For a complete list of titles in this series, please visit www.routledge.com.

The aim of this series is to explore and communicate the intersections and relationships between leisure, tourism and human mobility within the social sciences.

It will incorporate both traditional and new perspectives on leisure and tourism from contemporary geography, e.g. notions of identity, representation and culture, while also providing for perspectives from cognate areas such as anthropology, cultural studies, gastronomy and food studies, marketing, policy studies and political economy, regional and urban planning, and sociology, within the development of an integrated field of leisure and tourism studies.

Also, increasingly, tourism and leisure are regarded as steps in a continuum of human mobility. Inclusion of mobility in the series offers the prospect to examine the relationship between tourism and migration, the sojourner, educational travel, and second home and retirement travel phenomena.

The series comprises two strands:

Contemporary Geographies of Leisure, Tourism and Mobility aims to address the needs of students and academics, and the titles will be published in hardback and paperback. Titles include:

Routledge Studies in Contemporary Geographies of Leisure, Tourism and Mobility is a forum for innovative new research intended for research students and academics, and the titles will be available in hardback only. Titles include:

Tourism and the Anthropocene

Edited by
Martin Gren and
Edward H. Huijbens

LONDON AND NEW YORK

First published 2016
by Routledge

2 Park Square, Milton Park, Abingdon, Oxfordshire OX14 4RN
711 Third Avenue, New York, NY 10017

Routledge is an imprint of the Taylor & Francis Group, an informa business

First issued in paperback 2018

British Library Cataloguing in Publication Data
A catalogue record for this book is available from the British Library.

Library of Congress Cataloging in Publication Data
Names: Gren, Martin. | Huijbens, Edward H.
Title: Tourism and the anthropocene / edited by Martin Gren and Edward H.
   Huijbens.
Description: Abingdon, Oxon ; New York, NY : Routledge is an imprint of the
   Taylor & Francis Group, an Informa business, [2016] | Series: Routledge
   studies in contemporary geographies of leisure, tourism and mobility
Subjects: LCSH: Tourism--Environmental aspects. | Nature--Effect of human
   beings on. | Culture and tourism.
Classification: LCC G155.A1 T58947 2016 | DDC 306.4/819--dc23
LC record available at http://lccn.loc.gov/2015021355

ISBN: 978-1-138-81457-8 (hbk)
ISBN: 978-1-138-59226-1 (pbk)

Typeset in Times New Roman
by HWA Text and Data Management, London

Contents

Illustrations

Figures

Tables

Contributors

Bas Amelung is an Assistant Professor at the Environmental Systems Analysis Group at Wageningen University in the Netherlands. His research interests include the impacts of global environmental change (in particular climate change) on tourism; climate change adaptation; and polar tourism. Bas has authored more than 20 publications in scholarly journals such as *PNAS*, *Climatic Change*, the *Journal of Sustainable Tourism*, and *Tourism Management*.

Giorgio Baruchello, born in Genoa, Italy, and now an Icelandic citizen, serves as Professor of Philosophy at the School of Humanities and Social Sciences of the University of Akureyri, Iceland. His publications encompass several different areas, especially social philosophy, theory of value, and history of philosophy. Since 2005 he has edited *Nordicum-Mediterraneum* <http://nome.unak.is>, the first Icelandic scholarly journal in Nordic and Mediterranean studies.

René van der Duim studied tourism at NHTV Breda University of Applied Sciences (1972–5) and sociology at Tilburg University (1975–81). Since 1991 he has worked at the Department of Cultural Geography of Wageningen University where he now is professor. His research specifically focuses on the relation between tourism, conservation and development. He is author of articles in several scholarly journals such as *Annals of Tourism Research*, *Journal of Sustainable Tourism*, *Tourism Geographies* and has co-edited five books.

Eke Eijgelaar is Senior Researcher at the Centre for Sustainable Tourism and Transport of NHTV Breda University of Applied Sciences, the Netherlands. His main research interest concerns the monitoring and mitigation of tourism's carbon footprint, and related topics like carbon management and low- as well as high-carbon tourism such as cycle and cruise tourism. Eke has co-authored articles in the *Journal of Sustainable Tourism* and *Tourism Management*, amongst others, and published several book chapters in edited volumes.

Martin Gren has a Ph.D. in Human Geography and is Associate Professor in Tourism Studies at Linnaeus University in Sweden. He has a longstanding interest in social theory in relation to Tourism Studies and Human Geography. His current research, at the border between tourism and geography, is focused on the Anthropocene in the context of cartographic reason and geographiology. He is editor of several books, as well as author of books, original chapters and articles.

Harry Gugger is an architect and professor at the Swiss Federal Institute of Technology in Lausanne (EPFL) along with directing the Laboratoire Bâle (laba). Harry worked as a toolmaker's apprentice 1973–7 and from 1984 to 1989 he studied architecture at the Swiss Federal Institute of Technology in Zurich (ETHZ) with Flora Ruchat and at Columbia University, New York, with Tadao Ando. He received his degree in architecture at ETH Zurich in 1990. He was visiting professor at the Hochschule für Architektur und Bauwesen in Weimar in 1994. From 2000 to 2006 he was an external examiner at the AA School of Architecture in London. In 2001 he was a visiting professor at the Swiss Federal Institute of Technology in Lausanne (EPFL). In 2005 Harry became full professor for architectural design at the EPFL. In 2011 Harry Gugger transformed his laboratory into Laboratoire Bâle (laba) a satellite laboratory of the EPFL situated in Basel and dedicated to urban and architectural design. In 2010 he founded his new practice Harry Gugger Studio.

C. Michael Hall is a Professor at the University of Canterbury, New Zealand; Docent, University of Oulu, Finland; and Visiting Professor, Linneaus University, Kalmar, Sweden. Co-editor of the journal *Current Issues in Tourism* he has published widely on tourism, regional development, environmental history and change, and gastronomy. Current research focuses on walkability, wine and world heritage in Germany, Israel, Mauritius and Sweden.

Edward H. Huijbens is a geographer and scholar of tourism at the Icelandic Tourism Research Centre and professor at the University of Akureyri. Edward works on tourism theory, innovation, landscape perceptions, marketing strategies and health and well-being. He is author of articles in several scholarly journals such as *Annals of Tourism Research, Journal of Sustainable Tourism, Tourism Geographies,* has published monographs in both Iceland and internationally and co-edited four books.

Gunnar Thór Jóhannesson is an Associate Professor at the Department of Geography and Tourism, University of Iceland. His research interests are in the areas of entrepreneurship in tourism, tourism policy and destination development. He is a co-editor of *Actor-Network Theory and Tourism: Ordering, Materiality and Multiplicity* (Routledge, 2012) and *Tourism Encounters and Controversies: Ontological Politics of Tourism Development* (Ashgate, 2015). He has published his work in journals including *Tourist Studies, Tourism Geographies* and *Current Issues in Tourism.*

Erik Jönsson is a human geographer and political ecologist at the Department of Human Geography, Lund University. Erik is also a visiting scholar at the Geography Department, University of Berkeley. His work centres on future visions, planning politics and perceptions of nature(s). He has published on tourism and planning politics in journals such as *Geoforum* and *Space and Polity*, and is co-editing an upcoming anthology on political ecology in Swedish.

Britt Kramvig is an ethnographic researcher within the field of culture and planning and professor at the Department of Tourism and Northern Studies at UiT – the Arctic University of Norway. She takes on a postcolonial position inspired by indigenous, feminist and STS debates and has done ethnographic work, written and made films on a range of different topics relating to indigeneity, gender, place as well as technology and innovation. Britt insists upon working across disciplinary boundaries as people of the North perform these boundaries differently.

Berit Kristoffersen is a political geographer and post-doctoral researcher in Arctic Encounters, working at the department of Sociology, political science and community planning at UiT – the Arctic University of Norway. Berit is interested in how presence and futures are negotiated in the Arctic. How politics turns into geo-politics, how climate change is reframed as opportunistic business opportunities and how people in the north tie their identities and knowledges to the sustainability of their futures.

Bárbara Maçaes Costa is an architect and research assistant at the Laboratoire Bâle (laba) in Basel, Switzerland. Barbara graduated in 2008 from the University of Porto, faculty of Architecture, having studied under notable professors such as Álvaro Siza and Nuno Portas. She worked briefly in Copenhagen and Porto and in 2009 moved to Brussels to work for the landscape architecture office Bureau Bas Smets. At the end of 2011 she moved to Lisbon and enrolled in the Master program in Drawing at University of Lisbon Faculty of Fine-Arts, which she completed in early 2014, having specialized in Landscape Drawing. As an academic assistant for laba she is now researching spatial representation, cartography, nature writing and environmental aesthetics.

Roger Norum is postdoctoral researcher at the University of Leeds and teaching fellow in Norwegian at University College London, and a member of the HERA-funded project Arctic Encounters: Contemporary Travel/Writing in the European High North. His current work focuses on issues of sociality, transnationalism and political ecology, primarily through the lenses of migration, tourism and the global travel writing industry. Most recently, he is the co-author of *Political Ecology of Tourism: Communities, Power and the Environment* (Routledge, 2016) and *Migraciones* (Ediciones Ekaré, 2016), and he is a co-convener of Anthromob, the EASA Anthropology and Mobility Network. Roger is currently writing an English-language travel guidebook to Greenland, to be published in 2017 by Bradt.

Paul Peeters is Associate Professor at the Centre for Sustainable Tourism and Transport of NHTV Breda University of Applied Sciences, the Netherlands. Paul specializes in the impacts of tourism on the environment and specifically on climate change. His publications cover a wide range of topics, like global and regional tourism and climate scenarios, system dynamic approaches to tourism, tourism transport mode choice and modal shift, policy-making and transport technological developments.

Carina Ren is an ethnologist and associate professor at the Tourism Research Unit at Aalborg University, Denmark. Carina explores connections between tourism and other fields of the social. Through ethnographic research, she has engaged in studies on cultural innovation, the performance of branding and value-creation through events. She has co-edited two books on tourism and actor-network theory and the ontological politics of tourism and published in scholarly journals such as *Annals of Tourism Research, Tourist Studies, Ethnologia Europaea, Arctic Anthropology* and *Science Studies.*

Sverker Sörlin is professor of environmental history in the Division of History of Science, Technology and Environment at KTH Royal Institute of Technology, Stockholm, Sweden. He has written numerous books, articles, book chapters and essays on historical and contemporary uses of nature for nationalism and on the shaping of landscapes for outdoor life. He has contributed to the ongoing Anthropocene debates and been a spokesperson for the growing field of Environmental Humanities as well as a co-founder of the KTH Environmental Humanities Laboratory.

Daniel Svensson is a Ph.D. student at the Division of History of Science, Technology and Environment at KTH Royal Institute of Technology. His research, mainly in the fields of sport history and landscape history, deals with scientization of sport during the 20th century, and he also works on historical landscape perception, landscapes of sport and outdoor life, and relations between moving bodies and landscapes. Svensson has published several peer-reviewed articles and anthology chapters, and two poetry collections.

Nina Wormbs is associate professor and Head of the Division of History of Science, Technology and Environment at KTH Royal Institute of Technology. She is co-founder of the KTH Environmental Humanities Laboratory and sits on the management committee of the *Environmental Humanities Journal.* She has written on broadcasting and satellite technologies, as well as the allocation of the electromagnetic spectrum. Nina has also been an adviser to the Swedish government on media issues and sits on the board of the Nobel Museum and the Polar Research Secretariat.

Acknowledgements

First and foremost we must extend our deep gratitude to the authors whose chapters are this book. Thank you all for the hard and excellent work, and for being patient with us during the review processes! We must also thank Tyrone Martinsson for his wonderful photographs, and for being so responsive and kind to let us use them. We would further like to thank Iris Homan, an intern at the Icelandic Tourism Research Centre from Wageningen University in the Netherlands, for help and assistance in setting up the manuscript for final delivery.

The authors of Chapter 6 would like to acknowledge Reason to Return, Arctic Encounters and Arctic studies (Norwegian-Icelandic) for generous funding for fieldwork and research for this chapter.

The authors of Chapter 8 would like to acknowledge funding received from MISTRA Foundation for Environmental Research, the Swedish National Heritage Board and the Swedish Environmental Protection Agency.

Our final thanks go to Emma Travis for believing in our book proposal and Philippa Mullins for support during the whole process.

1 Tourism and the Anthropocene

An urgent emerging encounter

Edward H. Huijbens and Martin Gren

Figure 1.1 Alk Range, Hinlopen, Svalbard, August 2009 – Arrivals

©Tyrone Martinsson, published with permission

An interest in the concept of the Anthropocene has over the last years gained considerable momentum across the sciences and the humanities, but its trajectory in the tourism literature has so far been short and limited. The first attempt to engage with the Anthropocene in the context of tourism was made recently in an article by the editors of this volume (Gren and Huijbens, 2014), developed from a previous one dealing with the conceptualization of the Earth in relation to tourism (Gren and Huijbens, 2012). The aim of this book, the first of its kind, is to explore and map issues and challenges that the Anthropocene may pose for tourism studies, and how it might potentially reframe conceptual and empirical undertakings in tourism research. In this introduction we will first introduce the concept of the Anthropocene, and then provide three broad tentative themes as a brief primer for tourism's encounter with the Anthropocene. At the end we will provide an outline of the book.

Welcome to the Anthropocene

The Anthropocene is the proposed name of a new geological epoch, following the Holocene, in which humanity (the Anthropos) is being recognized as a geological force, and also one which is intimately entangled with the forces of the Earth (Oldfield *et al.*, 2014). The origins of the Anthropocene as a geological term are meticulously detailed by Castree (2014a), wherein he also states that the Anthropocene has become a 'powerfully forward facing super concept' which increasingly now frames a host of issues related to environmental change, sustainable development and various relationships between humans and non-humans in the context of geo-forces at a planetary scale.

The Anthropocene could not have been proposed if not for the recognition of the anthropogenic character of 'climate change and global environmental change ... [in] ... prior research and public debate' (Castree, 2014a, 444). Indeed, the ever growing geo-force of humanity in sculpting its earthly environment at large scale had been recognized already in the late 1800s, but then 'man' through divine decree was to become sovereign of the Earth in a new period, the *Anthropozoic,* named by the Italian geologist Antonio Stoppani (Hansen, 2013). Yet, by that time the indelible mark of the human species at a stratigraphic level was nowhere near being recognized. Since then things have changed. According to contemporary scientific knowledge, the current record levels of CO_2 in the Earth's atmosphere, fuelling global climate change and partly absorbed by the oceans, will remain stratigraphically visible for geological times to come (Zalasiewicz *et al.*, 2008). In geology, the presence and meaning of this and other stratigraphic markers are now being scrutinized and debated. At the time of writing the case is still open whether it will be possible to mark a geological epochal shift as the 'age of humans'.

Stratigraphic considerations aside, the Anthropocene has already gained considerable momentum also in the social sciences and the humanities, where the implications of humanity's collective entanglements with the Earth are explored. Johnson *et al.* (2014) identify three strands of the debate which the concept has initiated. The first deals with how the Anthropocene provides traction for environmental politics, the second how it signifies a bloated idea of humanity (the Anthropos), and the third strand how it might represent the end of humanity. The debate suggests an understanding of the Anthropocene as an uncomfortably unsettling intruder. We 'appear adrift in this new epoch, alienated not only from a world that refuses to submit to long-held conceptual frameworks, but also alienated from ourselves in relation to this strange and allegedly destructive thing called "humanity"' (p. 440) and, we might add, the Earth.

For the Earth that comes with the Anthropocene is also an unsettling intruder. In the natural science literature it is most often referred to as the 'Earth system', and that is a system which appears to be rather different from the Earth of the previous geological epoch – the Holocene which provided a relatively stable and prosperous ground for humanity. The Earth of the Anthropocene is instead unstable and filled with uncertainty and unpredictability, exemplified by the vocabulary of 'tipping points', 'global warming', 'acidification of the oceans', 'atmospheric carbon-dioxide' and 'species extinction'. Moreover, the Earth system seems to be increasingly entangled with its Anthropos and its earthly endeavours, of which the planetary environmental impacts of tourism is but one example.

The practices of climate science, and natural sciences more generally, reveal the Earth system as an elusive agency which 'talks back'. It is in a state of becoming and change, and simultaneously subjected to the geo-force of humanity. Thus revealed it is not easily captured as an object of Nature 'out there'. For example, Bruno Latour (2014, 6) wants us to recognize the Earth through James Lovelock's (1972, 2006) Gaia hypothesis, arguing that 'Gaia is another *subject* altogether – maybe also a different *sovereign*' (emphasis in original). The Greek deity personifying Earth is the alterity of our earthly entanglements resulting in the 'utter confusion between objects and subjects' (Latour, 2014, 9). Put differently, in the Anthropocene the Earth may become both a subject which underpins and makes for the Anthropos, and, at the same time, an object which is before it and may be set against its earthly undertakings. Integral to understanding the Anthropocene is thus a realization of the objective and subjective geo-agency of the Earth system, or Gaia, attuned to the way it 'talks back', and communicating this among disciplines (Oldfield *et al.*, 2014, 5).

At the most general level, the concept of the Anthropocene ushers in a host of issues about the relationship between the Anthropos and the Earth system, particularly at the planetary scale. The Anthropocene is undoubtedly a big concept, and so too are the Anthropos and the Earth system. All need to be broken down, further delineated and reconceptualized in whatever domain they are to be explored and applied. In tourism this process is only about to begin, and it is too early to tell how, and to what extent, an 'Anthropocene turn' will take place. What we can do here is to provide three broad tentative themes as a brief primer for tourism's encounter with the Anthropocene. The first deals with our place in the Anthropocene, the second with the Earth's, and the last how we may attend to both.

Tourism and the Anthropos

Although born as a geological term the Anthropocene is now also used as a concept which signifies a broad array of planetary environmental affairs. As such it may be understood as a recent addition to the sustainability discourse, particularly when used in relation to global sustainability and planetary limits and boundaries. For the Anthropos the planetary scale actualizes intergenerational responsibilities, present and future inequalities, hazards, and uncertainties. Tourism and tourists are, of course, also involved in this planetary conjuncture, not least when the traveller is considered a geo-force.

According to current scenarios there is a coming Anthropocene future of great environmental changes at planetary scale. These will include increasing global mean-temperatures, altered bio-chemical cycles, and weather extremes that become more and more difficult to predict, all with unforeseeable social and environmental consequences (see Global Weirding, 2015; IPCC, 2014). The year 2014 was the hottest ever recorded, following upon a series of record years, all post-1990s (NOAA, 2015). The changes will translate into biome and habitat relocations and alterations, possibly at scales only paralleled by five preceding events in Earth's history; in other words, alterations that eventually may even qualify as 'the sixth mass extinction' (Kolbert, 2014). Such apocalyptic sentiments have led some into a state of denial, while others have withdrawn in powerlessness, or apathy, wondering how one as a single individual member of the Anthropos can have effect, or if the time for environmental changes to transpire is simply too long for an individual lifespan. If the Anthropocene is different from other episodes of climate change, and if the problem and the solution resides in humanity as a collective geo-force, then what can or should be done?

Simon Dalby (in Johnson *et al.*, 2014, 444) argues that the Anthropocene 'is the next time, not the end time', perhaps alluding to apocalypse as 'revealing' rather than its modern meaning as 'the end'. While the project of modernity was about progress and emancipation as an escape from an archaic past, the Anthropocene becomes instead an urgent call to face a future that might already have arrived. Tempering apocalyptic visions and states of denial are part of the Anthropocene, but so is also the search for a reorientation of how planetary politics and environmental discourse can be conceived and implemented. Biermann suggests that this calls for an 'Earth system governance', which he defines as:

> the sum of the formal and informal rule system and actor networks at all levels of society that are set up to steer societies toward preventing, mitigating, and adapting to environmental change and earth system transformation.
>
> (Biermann, 2014a, 9)

An Earth system governance, under the normative context of sustainable development and planetary boundaries, would entail an 'effective institutional framework for global cooperation ... [mitigating] the human impact on planetary systems' (Biermann, 2014b, 58–9). This governance would, for example, have to address 'stranded assets' of oil firms in terms of fossil reserves that cannot be used, lest climate change keeps apace (Stenek, 2014). In terms of tourism research in the Anthropocene one could argue that Earth system governance may be aligned with:

> a research agenda on governing behaviour change in tourism mobilities, provoke and encourage further critical contemplation of the psychological

and behavioural complexities of climate change, tourism and sustainability mobility at both the individual and sectorial/institutional levels.

(Cohen *et al.*, 2014, 9)

The Anthropocene, especially for social science, also enhances a need to consider the Earth system and the Anthropos, including its subspecies of tourists, in relation to social, political, cultural and economic systems in which also tourism is firmly placed. One is the system commonly known as capitalism. Most often the assumption is that capitalism's business as usual will prevail, and also that the nation-states will continue to form the bedrock for this system (Castree, 2014b, 468). But as Klein (2014) argues, significant reordering of the global political, economic and social order will occur in the wake of planetary environmental change.

A critical contemplation of the psychological and behavioural complexities underpinning potential change or reordering also throws into sharp relief the discrepancy between the promotion of tourism development under the umbrella of sustainability in one place, and the emissions tourism generates through matter-energy transformations in other places, together with the trajectories that link them together into an earthly tourism system. Placing tourism policy and debates on, for example, high fuel-consumption at the level of tourist destinations, and a low-carbon society and green responsibilities somewhere else, does not sufficiently align tourism with issues of planetary sustainability in the Anthropocene (cf. Amelung *et al.*, 2007; Amelung and Nicholls, 2014; Hall and Higham, 2005). One Anthropocene reading suggests that changes related to the functioning of the Earth system need to be made manifest through regulatory regimes adapted to issues also at planetary scale. It is reasonable to assume that tourism cannot carry on as business as usual, but ought instead to reflect the reach of Earth system governance which includes 'effective policy coordination and integration, from local to global levels' (Biermann, 2014b, 58).

All this suggests that tourism needs also to be conceptualized as a driver of what has taken the Anthropos into the planetary environmental conditions of the Anthropocene. It needs to be understood in the context of the Anthropos, or humanity, on the move, i.e. an entire species with the growing geo-agency to transform the planet by travelling. Under the terms of the Anthropocene it seem unlikely that tourism can carry on in its modern register, that is, as a section of the Anthropos's geo-force which potentially undermines its own safe operating space by today's carbon-fuelled travelling. Various aspects of this relationship between tourism and the Anthropos are thus one key research theme that needs to be addressed in tourism's encounter with the Anthropocene.

Tourism and the Earth system

Another theme of tourism and the Anthropocene is the urgency for action and a call to return to the safe operating space of the Holocene-like conditions as fast as possible, be it by some kind of geoengineering (see Crutzen, 2006; Hamilton, 2013) or through Earth system governance. This raises questions around what kind of science should inform and guide tourism policy and planning in the Anthropocene. Some of the discussion has here been waged under what is sometimes referred to as the 'climate war'.

The war being waged has been set up between those who downplay, or flatly deny, climate science and especially the role of humans in global climate change, and those who seek to grasp it, and develop ways of mitigation and/or apprehending our means of acting on the basis of climate science (for insight into issues debated under these terms, see Sceptical Science, 2015). Seemingly plausible as two camps of an ongoing debate about scientific controversies, the ways in which this war has been waged demonstrate to us instead something rather different. Scientific controversies and public disputes on issues of climate change – what it is, to what extent it is caused by humans, how it should be studied, financed, modelled, portrayed, explained, distributed, predicted and understood – also indicate a current possible reframing from knowledge of a Nature 'out there' to an Earth of the Anthropocene which is also partly 'in here'. In the Anthropocene, the Earth humans inhabit and traverse is also the Earth which arises out of their own knowledge production and geo-forces. In other words, it is also an Earth partly of their own making.

The causes of global climate change, their effects and outcomes, are nowhere near to being completely understood, and perhaps never can be as the Earth system is an evolving dynamic system in a far-from equilibrium state of becoming in which the Anthropos itself constitutes a participating geo-force. This Earth of the Anthropocene, then, is not like the former Nature that through science could appear as a bundle of objective facts able to put an end to political disputes. It is instead an Earth transformed into an Earth system in becoming, and in the process it has shifted from the static background and instead become a dynamic part of the foreground. As incomplete as knowledge of the Earth system may be, this does not illustrate at all that climate science is being conflated with politics. Nor does it imply that the facts of climate science have become infected with the politics of values as deniers would have it. It does suggest, however, that both those who deny or dispute climate science and those who subscribe to its findings as indisputable scientific matters of fact both adhere to the same modern understanding of science according to which it must be defended and critiqued on its ability to provide unmediated facts.

Focusing on the validity of climate science knowledge claims or its ultimate truth component is therefore a side-track that leads the debate into nit-picking at science practices, amply manifest in the Climatic Research Unit email controversy of 2009. It also leads to a misguided idealization of 'climate scientists as dispassionate, objective, and neutral voices' which makes it easy 'for skeptics to dismiss the whole of climate science on evidence of their passions and politicking' (Schellenberger and Nordhaus, 2012, n.p.). But the point is, precisely, that there would be no objective knowledge of climate science without the infrastructure, the practices, the passions, perceptions, concerns, the instruments and the rest of mediations that all enable their matters of fact to be produced.

One may here note that the attitude amongst scientists is also changing. This is demonstrated in a recent interview with the climate scientist Michael Mann, famous for disseminating the 'hockey stick' figure of global warming. Therein he stated a generational shift in the attitude of scientists; 'I can't count how many postdocs and students who have told me that they see public participation as part of their roles as scientists. And that's something our generation didn't have' (Banerjee, 2013, 53). Echoing Michel Foucault and Gilles Deleuze in conversation (1977), Mann seems to realize that:

> The intellectual's role is no longer to place himself 'somewhat ahead and to the side' in order to express the stifled truth of the collectivity; rather, it is to struggle against the forms of power that transform him into its object and instrument in the sphere of 'knowledge', 'truth', 'consciousness' and 'discourse'.
>
> (Foucault and Deleuze, 1977, 207–8)

Communicating worries for the planetary future of humanity, and bringing scientists of the Anthropocene to the forefront of public debate over urgent evolving matters of concern, also raises another issue. As Chakrabarty (2009) has made clear, calling in humanity to take planetary action also begs the question of the political agency of the Anthropos. The short answer is that there is no corresponding humanity that appears as a political subject, and 'humanity seems far too slender an abstraction to carry the burden of causality' (Malm and Hornborg 2014, 65). Although the Anthropos is a constitutive geo-force in Earth system change at planetary scale, humans are involved in highly differential and uneven manners. In tourism the geo-force of the Anthropos could, for example, sometimes be delimited to those tourists who have the means to fly for leisurely purposes. In other words, also the Anthropos of the Anthropocene remains highly divided and unevenly differentiated.

> It would indeed be nice if the world were flat and non-hierarchial. Many of us have long been struggling for just such a result, and it is a vision we can easily identify with. But it is precisely the self-serving trick of neo-liberalism to assume that such a flat world is already here, hierarchy is gone, equality rules. The world may be flat for those who can afford a business class ticket to fly around it, gazing down on a seemingly flat surface, while for those gazing up at passing airplanes in Sub-Saharan Africa or the Indian countryside, the opportunity represented by London or Bombay or New York is an impossible climb to a destination visible only as mediated television or movie fantasy, if even that.
>
> (Smith, 2005, 894)

So it is that the Anthropocene can also be understood as a 'Capitalocene' (Haraway, 2014). It is in centres of globalized capital that the triggers for fossil-fuel consumption reside, and those of the affluent North carry an exponential carbon footprint as compared to those of the Sahel and the South. A consensus to act on behalf of humanity as a whole may well be wrought in an international arena or through the Intergovernmental Panel on Climate Change (IPCC), but these do not correspond with a humanity full of anthropological and geographical differences. An urgent debate is nevertheless needed on how to reduce fossil-fuel emissions, and how to possibly bridge the energy needs of future societies (see Becken, 2015). A 'Green' new industrial revolution notwithstanding, in the Anthropocene it seems that the first aim should revolve around how to create a fossil fuel-free future, what instruments should be employed to achieve this, and what changes to everyday practices and aspirations these imply. Given that 'species-thinking on climate change is conducive to mystification and political paralysis' (Malm and Hornborg, 2014, 67), action would have to recognize from where the geo-forces of planetary environmental change come.

In the context of tourism a politics of denial and scepticism have surfaced, as has the recognition of the unequal responsibilities within the Anthropos for planetary environmental change. However, as made clear by a recent rejoinder of over 50 tourism scholars, tourism research should be focused on:

> issues of adaptation, mitigation, vulnerability and resilience and the different transition trajectories that should be followed. Such areas are where debate should be focussed especially in light of issues of policy learning and flexibility, climate change governance, the role of the market, consumer behaviour, opportunity costs and development.
>
> (Hall *et al.*, 2014a, 6, see also Hall *et al.*, 2014b)

One may further argue that '[t]he geoformation of subjectivity that is at stake in the Anthropocene is a result of the capitalisation of fossil fuels' (Yusoff, 2013, 784). Adaptation, mitigation, vulnerability, resilience and planetary environmental change cannot be defined only by its causal antecedents. They are unfolding events, which the Anthropos currently is part of, and which it therefore also can influence. 'We' need to think of these events in terms of materiality and radical empiricism, progressively composing our destiny with the Earth, recognizing that 'the consequences are already there in the cause' (Latour, 2014, 11) and the primary cause is fossil fuel, especially so for tourism (Becken, 2015). Erik Swyngedouw (2013, 7) frames this composition in terms of 'egalitarian ecologies [which] are about demanding the impossible and realizing the improbable, and this is exactly the challenge the Anthropocene poses'. Issues of egalitarian ecologies will be picked up in chapters of this book, and together they illustrate one emerging theme of tourism's encounter with the Anthropocene.

Tourism and making the Anthropocene sensi/able

A final emerging theme to be addressed here in the introduction concerns the elusive, invisible or non-perceptible character of much of what we find under the Anthropocene. Tourists and non-tourists alike know from experience about the weather, but they do not directly perceive, for example, the amount of carbon-dioxide in the atmosphere. We are all crucially dependent upon various kinds of mediated knowledge, especially from the sciences, in order to comprehend and navigate the Anthropocene. As difficult as it may be to conceptualize the Anthropos as a geo-force, and turn it into an object for reasoning about planetary implications and consequences, we are also confronted with a fundamental inability, because '[t]o experience ourselves as a geophysical force, on the other hand, is impossible' (Boes, 2014, 162).

Our geo-forcefulness points to the importance of the ways by which we interlace through both perceptions and conceptions with the Earth (Huijbens and Jónsson, 2007). 'Who does the Earth think it is?' Deleuze and Guattari (1987, 39) once asked. They answered by explaining that 'God is a Lobster' whose pinchers entail a 'double articulation' by which geological, biological and social strata are formed. The first articulation refers to the materiality of a stratum, and the second concerns the expressivity of a stratum. This double articulation is the 'processes of the production of things, processes that transform states of matter, processes that enable and complicate life ... an impersonal force of contraction and dilation that characterizes events' (Grosz, 2011, 2 and 27). Although the Earth is the inherent and absolute ground for these processes, the key is that 'we do not yet know what the Earth can do' (van Tuinen, 2009, 112, quoting Peter Sloterdijk).

Nevertheless, through broadening our focus we could get more sensitively attuned to our earthly entanglements. As a consequence, an overarching Anthropocene ethical query is how to 'solicit a more profound attachment to the future of the earth' (Braun and Whatmore, 2010, 82, see also Clark, 2010; Karlsson, 2013; Yusoff, 2013; Zylinska, 2014). This attuning to the monogeism of 'the Earth as a lobster' would entail experimental living and allowing space for newly forged scientific objects such as CO_2, fossils, radioactivity, genetic mutations, toxic pesticides, and ice cores, debit cards, passports, weather, electricity, cars, planes, roads, flight routes, airports and computers. The earthly co-generation of these things and human beings can be traced, and their narratives of past and future might jolt us into reimagining environmental time across diverse scales. Exposing humanity's relationship to time, place and the agency of things that shape planetary change can surprise and startle us into new ways of thinking and feeling. It may also well be that for such a solicitation to take place in the Anthropocene, a strong and vivid political imagination is needed (Karlsson, 2013, 4).

An emerging theme of tourism and the Anthropocene is on elucidating ways in which the Earth can be made sensible through tourism practices and development. Tracing tourism's trajectories through matter movements and energy transformations will be picked up in this book, and how travelling practices and tourism development is changing the Earth, for better and for worse.

Structure of the book

All in all what these three themes of the Anthropocene amount to is possibly a new kind of individual and social ethos, an environmental ethics tied with new modes of knowledge production. Knowledge produced under the terms of the Anthropocene, where our collective force is entangled with the forces of the

Earth, is to prompt readiness to act as a constituent part of the Earth system, as fellow citizens of the land, insurgent and egalitarian (Heyd, 2007, drawing on Leopold, 1981 [1949]). Developing a particular kind of sensitivity based on reciprocity thus becomes a key word in the Anthropocene. An earthly sensitivity far removed from the Anthropos seen as steward or sovereign by divine decree, so vividly animating Earth perceptions from the Hellenistic city states, through medieval forest clearing practices, 18th-century nature orderings and the Industrial Revolution (Glacken, 1967), and modern-day Earth sciences and climate change validity debates. This type of sensibility, we argue, should allow for hospitality and the necessary proactive stance to earthly change in the Anthropocene.

Our experiential reference points are miniscule in the grand scheme of things, and perhaps a modest recognition thereto will be our only entry ticket into the Anthropocene. It is too early to tell whether the attempts to develop a durable room for the associations of humans and non-humans will enable the Anthropos to make a hospitable home for itself with Gaia.

The objective of the book is to bring the field of tourism into dialogue with the varied notions of the Anthropocene, exemplified by the three themes above. Tourism is usually either absent or very briefly accounted for in the existing Anthropocene literature, but we also believe that it has something to offer in return. For example, not only 'international travel' but also tourism in general is a constituent part of the post-war 'Great Acceleration' of consumptive practices fuelling planetary climate change. The engagements in the book reflect the current potential theoretical and practical scope of the Anthropocene, but will here be consistently related to tourism: the fate of humanity as one with the Earth, global sustainability, planetary limits and boundaries, climatically safe operating spaces, planetary environmental issues in terms of politics, science, ethics, materialities, practices and ways of being with and in the Anthropocene.

The book is divided into three sections. The book starts with three chapters placing tourism and tourists in the planetary (i.e. earthly) context of the Anthropocene, and explores how these can be understood and conceptualized as co-extensive with the Earth. The first chapter deals with the futures of tourism within a climatically safe operating space, and the second chapter with the design sensibilities in order to meet challenges of the Anthropocene at a destination level. These grander scale issues of tourism and tourists in the Anthropocene are then in the third chapter brought to bear on tourism consumption and biodiversity loss under the title 'Loving nature to death'. Issues of global sustainability and environmental ethics sustain the next three chapters dealing with tourism in the Anthropocene. The first chapter uses Actor Network Theory (ANT) to grasp tourism encounters in the 'ANThropocene', followed by a chapter contextualizing possible Anthropocene ethics for Arctic tourism. The third chapter of this section then deals with good and bad tourism by placing tourism in the context of life-valuing onto-axiology. Lastly, three chapters deal with tourism becomings in the Anthropocene. The focus is on the ways in which tourism and tourists can cultivate earthly sensibilities and attune to the Earth. The first chapter poses the question if we can move towards sustainable tourism in the Anthropocene, with the second chapter unfolding conflicts within the Anthropocene narrative through examining upscale golfing. The third part caps off with a chapter attuning us to issues and challenges of mapping tourism on the territory of Anthropocene. Thereafter a concluding chapter will summarize the arguments presented in the three parts of the book.

This book is the first of its kind to engage with tourism and the Anthropocene. We believe that the concept of the Anthropocene calls for an urgent venue for bringing together the variegated manner of tourism with planetary concerns.

References

Amelung, B. and Nicholls, S. 2014. Implications of climate change for tourism in Australia. *Tourism Management*, 41, 228–44.

Amelung, B., Nicholls, S., and Viner, D. 2007. Implications of global climate change for tourism flows and seasonality. *Journal of Travel Research*, 45, 285–96.

Banerjee, N. 2013. The most hated climate scientist in the US fights back. *Yale Alumni Magazine*, Mar./Apr., 47–53.

Becken, S. 2015. *Tourism and Oil. Preparing for the Challenge*. Bristol: Channel View Publications.

Biermann, F. 2014a. *Earth System Governance: World Politics in the Anthropocene*. Cambridge, MA: MIT Press.

Biermann, F. 2014b. The Anthropocene: A governance perspective. *The Anthropocene Review*, 1(1), 57–61.

Boes, T. 2014. Beyond whole Earth: Planetary mediations and the Anthropocene. *Environmental Humanities*, 5, 155–70.

Braun, B., and Whatmore, S. 2010. *Political Matter: Technoscience, Democracy, and Public Life*. Minneapolis, MN: University of Minnesota Press.

Castree, N. 2014a. The Anthropocene and geography I: The back story. *Geography Compass*, 8(7), 436–49.

Castree, N. 2014b. The Anthropocene and geography III: Future directions. *Geography Compass*, 8(7), 464–76.

Chakrabarty, D. 2009. The climate of history: Four theses. *Critical Inquiry*, 35, 197–222.

Clark, N. 2010. Volatile worlds, vulnerable bodies: Confronting abrupt climate change. *Theory, Culture and Society*, 27(2–3), 31–53.

Cohen, S.A., Higham, J., Peeters, P., and Gössling, S. 2014. *Understanding and Governing Sustainable Tourism Mobility: Psychological and Behavioural Approaches*. London: Routledge.

Crutzen, P.J. 2006. Albedo enhancement by stratospheric sulfur injections: A contribution to resolve a policy dilemma? *Climatic Change*, 77, 211–19.

Deleuze, G., and Guattari, F. 1987. *A Thousand Plateaus: Capitalism and Schizophrenia*. London: Continuum.

Foucault, M., and Deleuze, G. 1977. Intellectuals and power. In D.F. Bouchard (ed.), *Language, Counter-Memory, Practice: Selected Essays and Interviews*. Ithaca, NY: Cornell University Press, 205–17.

Glacken, C.J. 1967. *Traces on the Rhodian Shore: Nature and Culture in Western Thought from Ancient Timers to the End of the Eighteenth Century*. Berkeley, CA: University of California Press.

Global Weirding 2015. Global weirding video. <http://globalweirding.is/here> [accessed Jan. 2015].

Gren, M., and Huijbens, E. 2012. Tourism theory and the Earth. *Annals of Tourism Research*, 39(1), 155–70.

Gren, M., and Huijbens, E. 2014. Tourism in the Anthropocene. *Scandinavian Journal of Hospitality and Tourism*, 14(1), 6–22.

Grosz, E. 2011. *Becoming Undone: Darwinian Reflections on Life, Politics, and Art*. Durham, NC: Duke University Press.

Hall, M.C., and Higham, J. 2005. *Tourism, Recreation and Climate Change*. Clevedon: Channel View Publications.

Hall, M.C. *et al.* 2014a. No time for smokescreen skepticism: A rejoinder to Shani and Arad. *Tourism Management*, 47, 341–7.

Hall, C.M. *et al.* 2014b. Denying bogus skepticism in climate change and tourism research. *Tourism Management*, 47, 352–6.

Hamilton, C. 2013. *Earthmasters: The Dawn of the Age of Climate Engineering*. New Haven, CT: Yale University Press.

Hansen, P.H. 2013. *The Summits of Modern Man: Mountaineering After the Enlightenment*. Cambridge, MA: Harvard University Press.

Haraway. D. 2014. Anthropocene, Capitalocene, Chthulucene: Staying with the trouble. Vimeo: <https://vimeo.com/97663518> [accessed Apr. 2015].

Heyd, T. 2007. *Encountering Nature: Toward an Environmental Culture*. Aldershot: Ashgate.

Huijbens, E.H., and Jónsson, Ó.P. 2007. *Sensi/able Spaces: Space, Art and the Environment. Proceedings of the SPARTEN Conference, Reykjavík 1st–2nd June 2006*. Newcastle: Cambridge Scholars Publishing.

IPCC 2014. *Climate Change 2014. Impacts, Adaption, and Vulnerability*. New York: Cambridge University Press.

Johnson, E., *et al.* K. 2014. After the Anthropocene: Politics and geographic inquiry for a new epoch. *Progress in Human Geography*, 38(3), 439–56.

Karlsson, R. 2013. Ambivalence, irony, and democracy in the Anthropocene. *Futures*, 46, 1–9.

Klein, N. 2014. *This Changes Everything: Capitalism vs. the Climate*. New York: Simon & Schuster.

Kolbert, E. 2014. *The Sixth Extinction: An Unnatural History*. New York: Henry Holt & Co.

Latour, B. 2014. Agency in the times of the Anthropocene. *New Literary History*, 45, 1–18.

Leopold, A. 1981 [1949]. *A Sand County Almanac*. New York: Oxford University Press.

Lovelock, J.E. 1972. Gaia as seen through the atmosphere. *Atmospheric Environment*, 6(8), 579–80.

Lovelock, J.E. 2006. *The Revenge of Gaia: Why the Earth is Fighting Back – and How we can Still Save Humanity*. London: Allen Lane.

Malm, A., and Hornborg, A. 2014. The geology of mankind? A critique of the Anthropocene narrative. *The Anthropocene Review*, 1(1), 62–9.

NOAA 2015. Global analysis – December 2014. <http://www.ncdc.noaa.gov/sotc/global/2014/12> [accessed Jan. 2015].

Oldfield, F., Barnosky, A.D., Dearing, J., Fischer-Kowalski, M., McNeill, J., Steffen, W., and Zalasiewicz, J. 2014. The Anthropocene Review: Its significance, implications and the rationale for a new transdisciplinary journal. *The Anthropocene Review*, 1(1), 3–7.

Sceptical Science 2015. Global warming and climate change myths. <http://www.skepticalscience.com/argument.php> [accessed Jan. 2015].

Schellenberger, M., and Nordhaus, T. 2012. The monsters of Bruno Latour. *The Breakthrough Journal*, [e-journal] 2(Spring). <http://thebreakthrough.org/index.php/journal/past-issues/online-content/the-monsters-of-bruno-latour#> [accessed July 2014].

Smith, N. 2005. What's left? Neo-critical geography, or, the flat pluralist world of business class. *Antipode*, 37, 887–97.

Stenek, V. 2014. Carbon bubbles and stranded assets. <http://blogs.worldbank.org/climatechange/carbon-bubbles-stranded-assets> [accessed Jan. 2015].

Swyngedouw, E. 2013. The non-political politics of climate change. *ACME: An International E-Journal for Critical Geographies*, 12(1), 1–8.

van Tuinen, S. 2009. Air conditioning spaceship earth: Peter Sloterdijk's ethico-aesthetic paradigm. *Environment and Planning D: Society and Space*, 27(1), 105-118.

Yusoff, K. 2013. Insensible worlds: Postrelational ethics, indeterminacy and the (k)nots of relating. *Environment and Planning D: Society and Space*, 31(2), 208–26.

Zalasiewicz, J., *et al.* 2008. Are we now living in the Anthropocene? *GSA Today*, 18(2), 4–8.

Zylinska, J. 2014. *Minimal Ethics for the Anthropocene*. Ann Arbor, MI: Open Humanities Press.

Part I
Tourism and tourists in the Anthropocene

Figure I.1 Magdalena Bay, the burial ground at Trinity Harbour, Svalbard, July 2012 – Lurking challenges

©Tyrone Martinsson, published with permission

2 Keeping tourism's future within a climatically safe operating space

Eke Eijgelaar, Bas Amelung and Paul Peeters

Introduction

In recent decades, signs of the increasing human influence on the Earth's systems have become stronger. Paul Crutzen (see e.g. Crutzen, 2002) and others even argue that we have entered a new geological epoch: the age of man or Anthropocene. Humankind has interfered with the Earth's processes so much that the results will likely be clearly visible in the sediment layers that are currently forming. Scientific debate has shifted from discussing the justification of using the term to defining which anthropogenic signatures in the geological record fulfil the formal requirements for the recognition of such a new epoch (Lewis and Maslin, 2015). If these are fulfilled, the Holocene, with its stable and benign climate fostering humanity as we know it, is over and we have entered an epoch of human-caused change. The earthly processes that humans affect range from the global climate to local biota. Humanity has upset the climate system, primarily by burning fossil fuels. Humanity appropriates more than half the Earth's primary production and uses a large share of the Earth's land, leading to large-scale extinctions of plant and animal species as outlined by Michael C. Hall (this volume). In addition, the large-scale use of chemical fertilizers has fundamentally changed the nitrogen and phosphorous cycles. Growing populations and increasing irrigation have lowered ground water levels around the world (Ehrlich *et al.*, 2012; Rockström *et al.*, 2009). Humanity lives beyond the means that the Earth systems provide, which is not sustainable in the long run. The challenge is to reorganize society in such a way as to respect the planet's ecological boundaries. Tourism will have to do its share. In this chapter, we discuss the role of tourism in affecting the earthly processes, in particular the climate system. The chapter presents the mitigation challenge that tourism is facing, and analyses if and how tourism can meet the necessary reduction targets while remaining an economically healthy sector.

The chapter has the following structure. The notion of the Anthropocene and the related concept of planetary boundaries are introduced, then a brief history of tourism and its driving forces is sketched. The fourth section introduces the past and current trends in tourism emissions. Scenarios for future emissions are presented next, followed by an overview of mitigation options. The penultimate section sketches a handful of visions for tourism that are consistent with climatically safe operating and lastly some conclusions are drawn.

Planetary boundaries

Humanity's dominant role in shaping the Earth goes hand-in-hand with the responsibility to make human society sustainable and keep our planet habitable. Defining 'sustainable' and 'habitable', however, is not straightforward. The definition of 'sustainable' always involves some form of 'norm'. In the following there are actually two norms: we assume development to be sustainable, i.e. not having a predictable end, and we assume this to be based in natural and physical sciences. The natural cycles that humanity disrupts are closely intertwined. The major ecological, social and economic challenges that the world faces today are also closely interlinked. To make the abstract notion of sustainability more

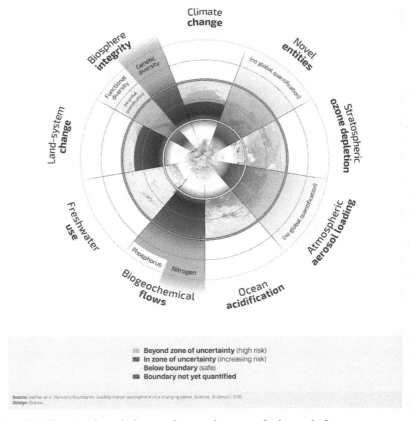

Figure 2.1 Planetary boundaries: a safe operating space for humanity?

Source: Pharand-Deschênes and Globaïa (2015). Please go to www.stockholmresilience.org/ planetaryboundaries to download the original version in colour.

concrete, Johan Rockström and others (2009) set about defining a safe operating space for humanity. Following several years of scientific scrutiny and debate (see e.g. Galaz, 2012; Lewis, 2012), this framework was further refined and updated in 2015 (Steffen *et al.*, 2015b).

The safe operating space for humanity is determined by key ecological limits that humanity needs to observe. A total of nine limits were identified, called 'planetary boundaries': climate change, biosphere integrity (made up of functional and genetic diversity), land-system change, freshwater use, biogeochemical flows (nitrogen and phosphorus cycle), ocean acidification, atmospheric aerosol loading, stratospheric ozone depletion, and novel entities. Quantifiable boundaries have not yet been established for atmospheric aerosol loading, novel entities and the functional role of biosphere integrity. In four Earth system processes – climate change, biosphere integrity (in particular genetic diversity), biogeochemical flows (both phosphorus and nitrogen), and land-system change – the proposed boundaries have been surpassed, i.e. humanity is already operating outside the safe space (see Figure 2.1).

Climate change and biosphere integrity are identified as core planetary boundaries, given their fundamental importance and potential to alter the balance of the Earth's systems (Steffen *et al.*, 2015b). Genetic diversity is critically threatened, with the current species extinction rate perhaps being 1,000 times higher than the proposed boundary value. The boundaries for climate change are an atmospheric CO_2 concentration of 350 parts per million (ppm) and an increase in top-of-atmosphere radiative forcing (RF) of $+1.0$ W m^{-2} relative to preindustrial levels. These boundaries have been surpassed: CO_2 concentrations recently crossed the 400 ppm mark and RF at $+2.3$ W m^{-2}. Radiative forcing is 'the rate of energy change per unit area of the globe as measured at the top of the atmosphere' (Rockström *et al.*, 2009, 473). Since CO_2 concentrations are fully, and RF is largely, dependent on CO_2 emissions, the term 'climatically safe operating space' can be interpreted as being a carbon budget for humanity. This is also the approach taken in this chapter. To avoid dangerous climate change and return to the climatically safe operating space, greenhouse gas emissions will have to peak and then fall between 40 and 70 per cent by 2050 (IPCC, 2014).

Tourism's great acceleration

Tourism affects many, if not all Earth system processes reflected by the planetary boundaries, but not all in similar ways or magnitude. Transport is generally considered the most problematic aspect of modern tourism in terms of its environmental impact (Peeters *et al.*, 2007).

Tourism has very old roots, dating back to the ancient Romans and beyond. For a large part of history, travelling for leisure purposes was a privilege of the elites, as it was time-consuming and costly. This changed with the advent of the railroad. Rail connections were quick, comfortable and relatively cheap, so that travelling became accessible and affordable to a larger share of society. The train trips organized by Thomas Cook in the 1850s are often considered to be the start of mass tourism (Butcher, 2003). The development of railroad networks was a direct effect of the Industrial Revolution, and in particular the steam engine. The steam engine and other types of engine allowed humankind to exploit the power of coal, natural gas and oil. Burning these fossil fuels yielded much more energy than could be produced through the physical labour of men or animals. After the Industrial Revolution, and in particular after 1850, population growth, economic development and technological innovation accelerated. A whole new kind of society emerged. Economic influence moved away from the owners of land towards the owners of capital, from the aristocracy towards the citizens. Urban areas became the centres of economic development. After the Second World War, this growth continued apace. Between 1950 and 2011, global population almost tripled, world GDP increased tenfold, and the number of patent applications almost fivefold. This post-war growth has become known as the Great Acceleration (Steffen *et al.*, 2007, 2015a).

Tourism followed a similar development path and international tourism is a recognized feature of the Great Acceleration. After the emergence of the railroad in the mid-1850s, mass tourism developed steadily, but public participation in leisure tourism remained limited. After 1950, tourism, and in particular international tourism, started developing exponentially. In 1950, around 25 million international arrivals were reported; in 2013 these were 1,087 million (UNWTO, 2014), representing a 45-fold increase or an average 6.1 per cent annual growth rate. Population growth, urbanization, the development of a middle class with rising discretionary incomes, advances in transport and communication technologies, and the rise of the phenomenon of paid holidays contributed to this exponential growth rate of international tourism. Unfortunately, global statistics ignore domestic tourism, even though domestic tourism has about five times the volume of its international counterpart (UNWTO-UNEP-WMO, 2008). Based on a modelling study (Peeters, 2013) the overall development of tourism (domestic plus international trips) might have been from 638 million in 1900 through 1,190 million in 1950 to 6,020 million in 2013: a 9.4-fold increase between 1900 and 2013.

The main share of modern-day tourism transport uses fossil fuels, in particular oil. Burning fossil fuels leads to the emission of nitrogen oxides and carbon dioxide. Nitrogen oxide emissions affect the nitrogen cycle, and may cause acidification in the region where the fuel is burned. Carbon dioxide emissions contribute to increased radiative forcing and climate change. At the same time, however, climate change has repeatedly been identified as one of the key challenges facing tourism this century (see e.g. Hall and Higham, 2005; Hall, this volume). The distribution of climates over the world is a key factor in the geographical distribution of tourism destinations and tourism flows. By changing climatic attractiveness, landscape, snow reliability, water availability and other resources, climate change transforms the competitiveness of source and destination regions alike, altering patterns of supply and demand. At the same time tourism flows (mainly air transport) are the key factor in tourism's contribution to climate change.

Gössling (2002) was the first to analyse the relevance of tourism in global environmental issues, and a research community around this topic has gradually developed since then. There is now a considerable amount of data on energy and emissions (notably Peeters *et al.*, 2007; Scott *et al.*, 2010; UNWTO-UNEP-WMO, 2008) and water (Gössling, 2015b; Gössling *et al.*, 2012), but this is not the case for land-system change and biodiversity. Eijgelaar and Peeters (2014) argue that these are the four Earth systems that tourism can most clearly be linked to. Not surprisingly they are also all vital resources for tourism. On a global level, tourism's contribution to biodiversity loss, land and water use is relatively modest. Its contribution to climate change is considerably larger, particularly when radiative forcing is taken into account. This contribution is estimated to be between 5.2 and 12.5 per cent (Scott *et al.*, 2010). Furthermore, climate change dominates tourism's environmental costs (Peeters *et al.*, 2007), and is seen as one of the major future drivers of change in tourism (Becken, 2013). In addition, CO_2 is the only stratigraphic marker discussed for a formal Anthropocene epoch start date that tourism can be linked to (Lewis and Maslin, 2015). In conclusion, tourism's main contribution to the current global environmental problems is its greenhouse gas emissions, in particular CO_2. Therefore, these emissions are the focus of this chapter.

Tourism emissions: past trends and current status

Global domestic and international tourism, including same-day trips, was estimated to contribute 5 per cent (~1,300 Megaton) of anthropogenic CO_2 emissions in 2005 (UNWTO-UNEP-WMO, 2008; Peeters and Dubois, 2010). Three-quarters of these emissions are generated by tourism transport. However, the contribution to radiative forcing is larger, notably due to secondary atmospheric impacts of aviation (see Lee *et al.*, 2010). For 2005, this 'total' contribution of tourism to global climate change is estimated to be between 5.2 and 12.5 per cent (Scott *et al.*, 2010). Tourism emissions have been growing fast, driven by the rapid increase in tourist numbers, the continuous increase in travel distance and the rising share of air transport (UNWTO-UNEP-WMO, 2008). The carbon footprint of Dutch holidaymakers can serve as an example of this development: between 2002 and 2013, CO_2 emissions produced by all Dutch domestic and international holidays increased by 16 per cent, and nearly all of that can be attributed to the increase in intercontinental holidays. Growth would have been stronger had there not been an economic recession, as the increase was already 20 per cent between 2002 and 2008 (Pels *et al.*, 2014).

Where tourism trip numbers increased with a factor of 9.4 between 1900 and 2013, the distances tourists travel increased with a factor of 88 in the same period. In 1900, 127 billion passenger-kilometres (pkm) were made, increasing to 516 billion in 1950 and 11,217 billion in 2013 (Peeters, 2013). The average distance tourists travel increased by a factor of 9.3 from about 170 km return per trip in 1900 to 1,864 km in 2013. Notwithstanding the erratic growth in number of trips and transport volumes, the increase in the average distance is characterized by an almost constant growth rate of 2.19 per cent per year. Remarkably, even the air transport revolution starting in the 1950s has not noticeably changed this growth rate, even though transport speed is known to have a major impact on the distances that people travel (Peeters and Landré, 2012).

The main problem with tourism's total greenhouse gas emissions is not so much its current 5 per cent share (UNWTO-UNEP-WMO, 2008), but its growth and future prospect. In a business-as-usual scenario, tourism sector emissions alone would exceed the 'safe' emissions budget for the entire global economy somewhere around 2050–60 (Scott *et al.*, 2010). This is shown in Figure 2.2, which depicts two absolute emissions pathways (curves A and B) for the world economy to avoid 'dangerous' climate change, i.e. more than 2°C warming in 2100 (e.g. Parry *et al.*, 2009). Curve A sees emissions peak in 2015 and decrease by 3 per cent per year, while curve B allows a later peak (in 2025) requiring a stronger, 6 per cent per year decrease after peaking. These pathways could bring the CO_2 concentration back to the planetary boundary of 350 ppm in several centuries (see above). Curve C represents an unrestricted business-as-usual pathway for tourism, including current trends in energy efficiency gains. The line intersects the emissions budget for the global economy around 2050–60. Tourism organizations, acknowledging the necessity of an emission reduction effort of their industry, have proposed aspirational goals that are consistent with those discussed above (e.g. by Parry *et al.*, 2009). The targets that best represent a collective position of the international tourism sector are those of the World Travel and Tourism Council (WTTC), who aspire for a 50 per cent

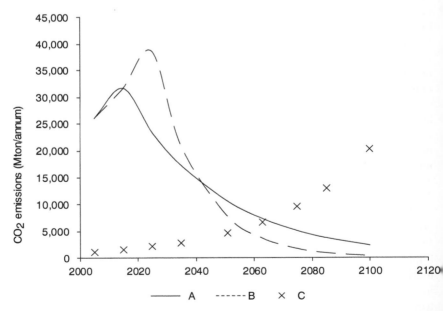

Figure 2.2 Global CO_2 emission pathways versus unrestricted tourism emissions growth

Source: Scott *et al.* (2010, 397)

emission reduction in 2035, with 2005 as a baseline (WTTC, 2009). Scott *et al.* (2010) point out that this target does not reflect current and forecasted tourism emissions development, the gap between projection and target being more than 100 per cent for 2035. The following section explores the outlook for tourism emissions in some more detail.

Scenarios for tourism and its emissions

The future is inherently uncertain and cannot be fully known in advance. Yet it is not random either, and decision-making can often benefit from exploring a number of plausible and possible futures. Scenario analysis can help us do so in a systematic way. In this kind of analysis, scenarios are logical projections based on a set of basic assumptions about relationships between socio-economic properties of the global population and some demographic and economic trends (Raskin *et al.*, 2005). Whereas they should not be seen as predictions or forecasts, scenarios may tell us something about the future.

Some tourism scenarios have been developed to inform the sector about economic developments and opportunities. These scenarios give information about numbers of trips and guest-nights and the world distribution of arrivals, but generally fail to include information about transport distances, environmental impacts and resource use, while such impacts are rather significant (Peeters *et al.*, 2007).

The World Tourism Organization published two main studies on future tourism growth in the past two decades (WTO, 2000; UNWTO, 2011). The 2000 study (WTO, 2000) was set up as a projection of the development of tourism using 1995 data as baseline. It uses socio-economic background data and develops prognoses at the (main) country geographical level. It found the number of international trips to pass the 1 billion mark in 2010, whereas it missed this by only 3 million in 2011. For 2020 it assumes a further growth at some 4.1 per cent per year to 1.56 billion international arrivals. The contribution of domestic tourism is not quantified, as earlier stated. Information about transport is only given in qualitative and anecdotal terms. Environmental impacts or resources use is also described in a qualitative way and mainly at the level of destinations, not planetary boundaries. The 2011 study takes flows between 22 regions into account and distinguishes air and surface transport (UNWTO, 2011). Global international tourism growth is estimated at an average of about 3.3 per cent per year between 2010 and 2030. This will bring total arrivals to 1.8 billion in 2030. The report also assumes the modal split to stabilize (at 52 per cent for air and 48 per cent for surface), even though it assumes the cost of surface transport to increase by 1.5 per cent per year while air transport cost would only increase by 1.1 per cent per year on average.

The volume of air transport plays a large role in tourism's impact on climate change and global fossil fuel consumption. About 90 per cent of all air transport is tourism related, omitting only commuters and the military. A portal to air transport future studies is given by the MONITOR project (German Aerospace Center (DLR), 2014). The DLR website shows a wide range of future scenarios with growth from 5 trillion pkm in 2010 to between 7 and 24 trillion in 2035.

For 2050, the three lowest projections reach between 9 and 22.5 trillion. Airbus (2014) expects almost 15 trillion pkm in 2033, while Boeing (2014) is slightly more optimistic with 15.5 trillion pkm, both close to the 'Most likely' scenario of 15.1 trillion given by the International Civil Aviation Organization (ICAO, 2014).

Though tourism and tourism transport scenarios are scarcely covered in the literature, scenarios dedicated to the relationship between tourism and climate change abound, though most are dedicated to the impact of climate change on tourism (adaptation e.g. Lise and Tol, 2002; Amelung and Viner, 2006; Nicholls and Amelung, 2008; Prideaux *et al.*, 2012). UNWTO-UNEP-WMO (2008) forms a benchmark in describing both the impacts of climate change on tourism and the impacts of tourism on the climate. The report describes an emissions scenario that takes energy efficiency gains for various elements (e.g. air transport) into account. The scenario shows CO_2 emissions to increase to about 3,000 Megaton (Mton) CO_2 in 2035 from 1,000 Mton in 2005 (see Table 2.1). In 2035, air transport emissions will have a share of 53 per cent, up from 40 per cent in 2005. In terms of radiative forcing – the main factor causing the temperature to rise – the share of aviation may vary between 70 and 84 per cent in 2035.

Other studies take a longer term view. Scott *et al.* (2010), in their business-as-usual-scenario, assume tourism's emissions to exponentially grow up to 20,000 (Mton) in 2100. In contrast, Mayor and Tol (2010b) find aviation emissions to peak at some 2,000 Mton in 2060 and decline due to a slowdown of demographic and economic growth and air transport volume growth, combined with an unrealistic view on continued fuel efficiency improvements. Contrasting scenarios are given by Owen *et al.* (2010) that show aviation emissions to increase to somewhere between 1,186 Mton and 5,067 Mton in 2100, depending on demographic and economic growth assumptions. Only the lower value is associated with a scenario peaking in 2050. In case of the higher value a growth of overall tourism emissions would most likely be in the range of 7,000 to 10,000 Mton in 2100. The overall conclusion from the scenario studies is that within the tourism sector, (air) transport

Table 2.1 Distribution of tourism emissions by sub-sector for 2005 and 2035

Sub-sectors	2005		2035	
	CO_2 *(Mton)*	%	CO_2 *(Mton)*	%
Air transport	515	40	1,631	53
Car transport	420	32	456	15
Other transport	45	3	37	1
Accommodation	274	21	739	24
Activities	48	4	195	6
Total	1,307	100	3,059	100
Total world (IPCC, 2007)	26,400			
Tourism contribution	5%			

Source: UNWTO-UNEP-WMO (2008)

causes most emissions and that it is likely these emissions will continue to grow until 2100, though the growth rate will slow down at the end of the century.

Mitigation options for staying within a climatically safe operating space

From the above it is clear that the mitigation challenge for tourism to stay within a climatically safe operating space (i.e. within the carbon budget) is huge, probably bigger than for most sectors. Tourism will need to drastically reduce its energy use. This can be achieved through technological and operational measures, and through changes in behaviour. In the following, we will outline the potential of these approaches.

Technology

Technological fix used to be the industry's mitigation favourite, even though it is acknowledged that technology alone cannot lead to absolute emission reductions, most notably in aviation (e.g. ATAG, 2014). The efficiency potential for airplanes has decreased over the last decades, and has never been able to compensate for growth in air travel (Mayor and Tol, 2010b; Peeters and Middel, 2007). Thus, aviation stakeholders are also looking at carbon trading in the medium term and a large-scale shift to biofuels in the long term for achieving climate neutral growth (ATAG, 2014). In 2050, ATAG envisages a 60 to 70 per cent reduction of emissions through biofuel use, assuming that biofuels have an 80 per cent lower carbon footprint than fossil oil-based jet fuel. Biofuels are made from geologically recent carbon fixation (as opposed to fossil fuels) in all sorts of biomass. These vary from agricultural products like grains or palm oil seeds, to biological waste (like waste fats, waste from the food industry or forestry by-products). More recently much attention is being paid to algae (Kamga and Yazici, 2014). The sustainability, economics and availability of biofuels are widely questioned (e.g. Timilsina and Shrestha, 2011; Dray *et al.*, 2012). No biofuel has yet shown competing cost with oil-based jet fuel. Even the aviation industry only expects biofuels for aviation to become price competitive in the medium term. Furthermore, some of the more promising ones, like algae, do not deliver a saving of emissions at a life cycle basis, i.e. measured from the production of the crop until its use as fuel (ICAO, 2009; Slegers *et al.*, 2011). Thus large-scale biofuel use in aviation, with subsequent emissions reduction of up to 80 per cent around 2050, appears unlikely. For the accommodation sector, energy efficiency gains are easier to achieve than for transport, all the more because energy-saving measures are often very economical, but it is tourism transport which is causing the largest absolute growth in emissions.

Staying inside a climatically safe operating space is associated with a total emission reduction of 60–90 per cent with respect to 2000 (Parry *et al.*, 2009, see also Figure 2.2). It is highly unlikely that tourism will comply with such a scenario without a reduction of (the growth of) air transport (Lee *et al.*, 2013;

Scott *et al.*, 2010). Lee *et al.* (2013) assessed aviation's ability to meet (much less drastic) emission reduction targets for 2020 (carbon neutral growth in this study) and 2050 (2005 emissions -10 per cent), and concluded that no combination of technological (including biofuels), operational and market-based measures would be enough to meet the target. Mayor and Tol (2010b) reached similar conclusions. Using a model for projecting tourist numbers and emissions, they found that international tourism emissions will grow until the middle of the 21st century, after which emissions start to fall as a result of improvements in fuel efficiency. According to Peeters and Middel (2007) these improvements may be physically unrealistic or even impossible. In any case, they come too late to keep tourism within a climatically safe operating space, even under the extreme assumption that tourism would be granted all of that space (see Figure 2.2). Peeters and Dubois (2010) conclude that 'without radical shifts, it seems impossible to find a future tourist travel system consistent with the strong CO_2 emission reductions required to avoid dangerous climate change' (p. 455). They confirm that technological improvements alone are insufficient, and that fundamental behaviour change towards low-carbon transport modes and more nearby destinations is also required.

Behaviour

Changing tourists' travel behaviour is easier said than done. Tourists are not likely to make drastic changes voluntarily and choose environmentally sustainable holidays (Juvan and Dolnicar, 2014; Hibbert *et al.*, 2013; Barr *et al.*, 2010). Many tourists, including those that accept climate change as a reality, have a limited understanding of climate change and its main causes. Confusing climate change with ozone depletion, for example, is common (see e.g. Dillimono and Dickinson, 2015), resulting in the neglect of the role of CO_2 and burning fossil fuels. In addition, the extent of tourism's contribution to total greenhouse gas emissions is not commonly known, let alone the prominent position of (air) transport in this share (McKercher and Prideaux, 2011). A poor understanding of an issue is known to reduce its perceived priority, which may explain the low priority given to climate change in general (McKercher *et al.*, 2010), and tourism's contribution to climate change in particular (McKercher and Prideaux, 2011).

Even tourists with a reasonable understanding of climate change and tourism's role often fail to connect these issues to their own travel behaviour (Hares *et al.*, 2010). They either do not consider this link or suppress it. This latter explanation is known as the attitude–behaviour gap, a widely discussed phenomenon in the recent literature on tourism and global environmental change (Hares *et al.*, 2010; Higham *et al.*, 2015; McKercher and Prideaux, 2011). The attitude–behavior gap refers to a mismatch between an individual's attitude towards environmental issues and this person's actual behaviour. This mismatch is highly context-specific as people's environmental performance is not consistent across practices (Barr *et al.*, 2011; Higham *et al.*, 2015). For instance, a person may have a very green, low-energy profile with respect to energy use at home and recycling materials, and a very high-energy profile with respect to food. The attitude–behaviour gap appears to be particularly common and persistent with respect to travelling and tourism. Tourism is now part of everyday life, and represents an arena where different identities can be practised than in other contexts at home. Travelling for leisure has become a very important aspect of people's lives, and one to which they attach great value. Travel, and in particular air travel, has come to be seen as a right and a symbol of freedom (Burns and Bibbings, 2009). The large perceived benefits of travelling may explain the heavy resistance to altering travel behaviour (Becken, 2004; McKercher *et al.*, 2010). A 'lack of awareness of tourism's impact relative to day-to-day behavior, feelings of disempowerment and an unwillingness to make significant changes to current tourism behavior' was found by Miller *et al.* (2010, 627). Higham *et al.* (2015) note an almost complete disregard among tourists of their responsibility to alter their air travel behaviour. Even the uptake of carbon offsetting schemes is low, at 1–10 per cent of tourists (Mair, 2011; McLennan *et al.*, 2014; Eijgelaar, 2011).

Those tourists who are willing to change their behaviour face additional problems. First of all, assessing the climate implications of travel options is challenging and time-consuming. For example, there is little harmonization in the assumptions and scope of carbon calculators, so that they yield widely divergent results (Juvan and Dolnicar, 2014). As a result, tourists are confronted with confusing and uncertain information and find it difficult to identify the most sustainable travel options. Secondly, there are structural barriers to sustainable, slow tourism. In a Nigerian context, Dillimono and Dickinson (2015) discern four: reliability, availability, safety and speed. Unsustainable travel is generally cheaper and more easily available than sustainable forms of travel (Gössling *et al.*, 2014).

There is virtual consensus on the need to alter tourism behaviour in a fundamental way, but there are divergent views on how to achieve that most effectively. Barr *et al.* (2011) advocate a bottom-up approach by means of social marketing, i.e. the use of conventional marketing instruments to promote behaviour that is more desirable. They argue that more radical policy measures are bound to fail if individuals' attitudes are not changed first. In contrast, authors such as Higham *et al.* (2015) argue that voluntary behaviour change in the context of (air) travel is highly unlikely. They point to the need for meaningful industry measures and strong governmental policies (Gössling *et al.*, 2014; Higham *et al.*, 2015). In this view, behaviour will follow once measures that are more stringent have been put in place.

Behavioural change, and in particular a reduction of air travel, would have large environmental benefits. It would also affect the pattern of tourist arrivals, with negative impacts for some countries and benefits for others (Scott *et al.*, 2010). For example, distance restrictions would cause about half of all the countries in the world to have an increase in arrivals, with the other half experiencing a loss, while total arrivals would not change much globally. Least developing countries might suffer more than they gain (Peeters and Eijgelaar, 2014). In principle, adversely affected (developing) countries can be compensated through the pricing of aviation emissions (Keen *et al.*, 2012; Pentelow and Scott, 2011).

Several studies have investigated the merits of mitigation options for tourism (Dubois *et al.*, 2011; Peeters and Dubois, 2010; UNWTO-UNEP-WMO, 2008; Scott *et al.*, 2010). Using a back-casting approach – a scenario methodology that tries to find pathways to a desired future state (e.g. a certain reduction of emissions) – and maximizing the tourism economy, Peeters and Dubois (2010) show that two major 'solutions' exist for four different global economic and background scenarios. Either tourism keeps the modal split between car and other surface/water forms of transport at its current level (mainly car) and reduces global flying to the volume of the 1970s, or it chooses to massively shift from car to rail and coach transport, while maintaining 2005 volumes of air transport. The desired future assumed an absolute reduction of emissions by some 70 per cent in 2050 with respect to 2005 emissions. An often mentioned objection against such strong reductions of air transport is the idea that specifically developing countries, whose main economy sometimes is long-haul tourism, would suffer most (e.g. many examples in Lipman *et al.*, 2012). However, Peeters and Eijgelaar (2014) clearly show that a reduction of air transport would not specifically hit developing countries, and would indeed also benefit many (mainly larger) developing countries. Reducing distances does not much affect the global number of tourist trips, but mainly its distribution between source markets and destinations (as shown based on a systems approach in Peeters and Landré, 2012; Peeters, 2010, 2013). This means that non-remote developing countries, which are home to the majority of poor people, may even gain by reduced travel distances because outbound tourism is reduced and both domestic and neighbouring country tourism is enhanced (Peeters and Eijgelaar, 2014).

Long-term visions of tourism

But what measures or policies would be needed to create the large modal shift (from car to rail) and a zero growth of aviation needed to keep tourism within planetary carbon budgets? Urry (2010: 205) refers to many examples of what he coins as 'such neo-liberal exemplars of excess', such as the large investments in ever bigger cruise ships which are 'which are floating gated communities again organized around consuming to excess' (p. 205). Clearly the tourism industry itself is driven in the wrong direction from within. So some strong government interference seems inevitable. Several studies have looked at taxes or inclusion of aviation in emission trading (Anger, 2010; Hofer *et al.*, 2010; Rothengatter, 2010; Mayor and Tol, 2010a). The general outcome is that emissions will be reduced at very low ratios only. However, all these studies assume very low taxes/carbon costs, or taxes that are imposed within single isolated countries, meaning a strong leakage of the effect due to the international character of aviation. Most of these studies fail to recognize an emission trading system that enforces the significant emission reduction needed to stay within a safe operating space. Global 'safe' emission trading would increase carbon cost from the 'ineffective' levels of $10 ton CO_2 resulting in a chance of less than 30 per cent of staying below the 2°C warming dictated by the planetary boundary, up to between $100 and $1,000/ton CO_2 for achieving 70 per cent or more probability to stay within the planetary boundary (Rogelj *et al.*, 2013). Carbon costs of this order of magnitude will affect transport volumes more significantly (Dray *et al.*, 2012). Effective frameworks would include taxing high-carbon while supporting low-carbon transport modes, and developing infrastructure aimed at inducing modal shifts (Gössling *et al.*, 2014). In particular, investments in rail infrastructure will be needed (Westin and Kågeson, 2012). In addition, the tourism sector needs to innovate and develop low-carbon tourism products (Peeters *et al.*, 2009; Gössling, 2015a) and slow tourism (Lumsdon and McGrath, 2010).

Conclusion

This chapter assessed the place of tourism in a climatically safe operating space for humanity. The notion of a safe operating space has become relevant because of humanity's large and increasing influence on the Earth's life-supporting processes in the Anthropocene. Tourism's place in humanity's safe operating space turns out to be uncomfortable and challenging. While the climatically safe operating space (annual carbon budget) will be shrinking fast, tourism keeps on growing rapidly. Tourism emissions are increasing even faster than arrivals, as distances travelled increase and the modal split shifts towards air travel. If the current trend continues, tourism will consume the world's entire 'safe' carbon budget within 40 years (see Figure 2.2), a clearly unsustainable prospect. Technological progress is already factored in, but by no means fast enough to balance demand growth.

Research and development may be further intensified, by aiming at maximum energy efficiency in all transport and accommodation facilities. But even then, the emissions savings will not be enough to compensate for growth in demand and achieve a 60–70 per cent cutback in absolute emissions. A radical change in behaviour is required too, realizing such a change is very challenging. Substantial voluntary changes are unlikely, among others because of tourism's connotations of freedom and enjoyment; tourists' limited understanding of the climate change issue, and lack of attractive sustainable alternatives. In addition, policies aimed at behavioural change are highly unpopular. Tourism transport would likely become more expensive, in particular flying. There is no way around it, though: reducing distances and air travel is the number one condition for moving tourism back into a climatically safe operating space.

References

Airbus 2014. *Flying on Demand: Global Market Forecast 2014–2033*. Paris: Airbus S.A.S.
Amelung, B., and Viner, D. 2006. Mediterranean tourism: Exploring the future with the Tourism Climatic Index. *Journal of Sustainable Tourism*, 14, 349–66.
Anger, A. 2010. Including aviation in the European emissions trading scheme: Impacts on the industry, CO_2 emissions and macroeconomic activity in the EU. *Journal of Air Transport Management*, 16, 100–5.
ATAG 2014. Our climate plan. <http://aviationbenefits.org/environmental-efficiency/aviation-and-climate-change/our-climate-plan/> [accessed Nov. 2014].

Barr, S., Gilg, A., and Shaw, G. 2011. 'Helping people make better choices': Exploring the behaviour change agenda for environmental sustainability. *Applied Geography*, 31, 712–20.

Barr, S., Shaw, G., Coles, T., and Prillwitz, J. 2010. 'A holiday is a holiday': Practicing sustainability, home and away. *Journal of Transport Geography*, 18, 474–81.

Becken, S. 2004. How tourists and tourism experts perceive climate change and carbon-offsetting schemes. *Journal of Sustainable Tourism*, 12, 332–45.

Becken, S. 2013. Shapers and shifters for the future of travel and tourism. In J. Leigh, C. Webster and S. Ivanov (eds), *Future Tourism: Political, Social and Economic Changes*. Abingdon, Oxon: Routledge, 80–91.

Boeing 2014. *Current Market Outlook 2014–2033*. Seattle, WA: Boeing Commercial Airplanes.

Burns, P.M., and Bibbings, L.J. 2009. The end of tourism? Climate change and societal changes. *21st Century Society*, 4, 31–51.

Butcher, J. 2003. *The Moralisation of Tourism: Sun, Sand ... and Saving the World?* London: Routledge.

Crutzen, P.J. 2002. Geology of mankind. *Nature*, 415, 23.

Dillimono, H.D., and Dickinson, J.E. 2015. Travel, tourism, climate change, and behavioral change: Travelers' perspectives from a developing country, Nigeria. *Journal of Sustainable Tourism*, 23, 437–54.

Dray, L.M., Schäfer, A., and Ben-Akiva, M.E. 2012. Technology limits for reducing EU transport sector CO_2 emissions. *Environmental Science and Technology*, 46, 4734–41.

Dubois, G., Ceron, J.P., Peeters, P., and Gössling, S. 2011. The future tourism mobility of the world population: Emission growth versus climate policy. *Transportation Research Part A: Policy and Practice*, 45, 1031–42.

Ehrlich, P.R., Kareiva, P.M., and Daily, G.C. 2012. Securing natural capital and expanding equity to rescale civilization. *Nature*, 486, 68–73.

Eijgelaar, E. 2011. Voluntary carbon offsets a solution for reducing tourism emissions? Assessment of communication aspects and mitigation potential. *European Journal of Transport and Infrastructure Research*, 11, 281–96.

Eijgelaar, E., and Peeters, P. 2014. The global footprint of tourism. In C.M. Hall, A. Lew and A. Williams (eds), *The Wiley-Blackwell Companion to Tourism*. Chichester, Sussex: John Wiley & Sons, 454–465.

Galaz, V. 2012. Environment: Planetary boundaries concept is valuable. *Nature*, 486, 191.

German Aerospace Center (DLR) 2014. MONITOR digest on air transport future studies. <http://monitorportal.dlr.de/en/web/guest/scenarios> [accessed Dec. 2014].

Gössling, S. 2002. Global environmental consequences of tourism. *Global Environmental Change*, 12, 283–302.

Gössling, S. 2015a. Low-carbon and post-carbon travel and destinations. In C.M. Hall, S. Gössling and D. Scott (eds), *The Routledge Handbook of Tourism and Sustainability*. Abingdon, Oxon: Routledge.

Gössling, S. 2015b. New performance indicators for water management in tourism. *Tourism Management*, 46, 233–44.

Gössling, S., Peeters, P., Hall, C.M., Ceron, J.P., Dubois, G., Lehmann, L.V., and Scott, D. 2012. Tourism and water use: Supply, demand, and security. An international review. *Tourism Management*, 33, 1–15.

Gössling, S., Peeters, P., Higham, J.E.S., and Cohen, S.A. 2014. New governance models for behaviour change in tourism mobilities: A research agenda. In S.A. Cohen, J.E.S. Higham, P. Peeters and S. Gössling (eds), *Understanding and Governing Sustainable*

Tourism Mobility: Psychological and Behavioural Approaches. Abingdon, Oxon: Routledge.

Hall, C.M., and Higham, J. 2005. *Tourism, Recreation and Climate Change: International Perspectives.* Clevedon: Channelview Publications.

Hares, A., Dickinson, J. and Wilkes, K. 2010. Climate change and the air travel decisions of UK tourists. *Journal of Transport Geography,* 18, 466–73.

Hibbert, J.F., Dickinson, J.E., Gössling, S., and Curtin, S. 2013. Identity and tourism mobility: An exploration of the attitude–behaviour gap. *Journal of Sustainable Tourism,* 21, 999–1016.

Higham, J., Reis, A., and Cohen, S.A. 2015. Australian climate concern and the 'attitude–behaviour gap'. *Current Issues in Tourism,* online first.

Hofer, C., Dresner, M.E., and Windle, R.J. 2010. The environmental effects of airline carbon emissions taxation in the US. *Transportation Research Part D: Transport and Environment,* 15, 37–45.

ICAO 2009. Comparison of life cycle GHG emissions from select alternative jet fuels, CAAF/09-IP/6. *Conference on Aviation and Alternative Fuels.* Rio de Janeiro: ICAO.

ICAO 2014. *2013 Environmental Report: Destination Green.* Montreal: ICAO.

IPCC 2014. Summary for policymakers. In O. Edenhofer *et al.* (eds), *Climate Change 2014, Mitigation of Climate Change. Contribution of Working Group III to the Fifth Assessment Report of the Intergovernmental Panel on Climate Change.* Cambridge and New York: Cambridge University Press.

Juvan, E., and Dolnicar, S. 2014. The attitude–behaviour gap in sustainable tourism. *Annals of Tourism Research,* 48, 76–95.

Kamga, C., and Yazici, M.A. 2014. Achieving environmental sustainability beyond technological improvements: Potential role of high-speed rail in the United States of America. *Transportation Research Part D: Transport and Environment,* 31, 148–64.

Keen, M., Perry, I., and Strand, J. 2012. *Market-Based Instruments for International Aviation and Shipping as a Source of Climate Finance.* Washington, DC: World Bank.

Lee, D.S., *et al.* 2010. Transport impacts on atmosphere and climate: Aviation. *Atmospheric Environment,* 44, 4678–4734.

Lee, D.S., Lim, L.L., and Owen, B. 2013. *Bridging the Aviation CO_2 Emissions Gap: Why Emissions Trading is Needed.* Manchester: Manchester Metropolitan University.

Lewis, S.L. 2012. We must set planetary boundaries wisely. *Nature,* 485, 417.

Lewis, S.L., and Maslin, M.A. 2015. Defining the Anthropocene. *Nature,* 519, 171–80.

Lipman, G., DeLacy, T., Vorster, S., Hawkins, R., and Jiang, M. (eds) 2012. *Green Growth and Travelism: Letters from Leaders.* Oxford: Goodfellow Publishers.

Lise, W., and Tol, R.S.J. 2002. Impact of climate on tourist demand. *Climatic Change,* 55, 429–49.

Lumsdon, L.M., and McGrath, P. 2010. Developing a conceptual framework for slow travel: A grounded theory approach. *Journal of Sustainable Tourism,* 19, 265–79.

McKercher, B., and Prideaux, B. 2011. Are tourism impacts low on personal environmental agendas? *Journal of Sustainable Tourism,* 19, 325–45.

McKercher, B., Prideaux, B., Cheung, C., and Law, R. 2010. Achieving voluntary reductions in the carbon footprint of tourism and climate change. *Journal of Sustainable Tourism,* 18, 297–317.

McLennan, C.J, Becken, S., Battye, R., and So, K.K.F. 2014. Voluntary carbon offsetting: Who does it? *Tourism Management,* 45, 194-198.

Mair, J. 2011. Exploring air travellers' voluntary carbon-offsetting. *Journal of Sustainable Tourism,* 19, 215–30.

Mayor, K., and Tol, R.S.J. 2010a. The impact of European climate change regulations on international tourist markets. *Transportation Research Part D: Transport and Environment*, 15, 26–36.

Mayor, K., and Tol, R.S.J. 2010b. Scenarios of carbon dioxide emissions from aviation. *Global Environmental Change*, 20, 65–73.

Miller, G., Rathouse, K., Scarles, C., Holmes, K., and Tribe, J. 2010. Public understanding of sustainable tourism. *Annals of Tourism Research*, 37, 627–45.

Nicholls, S., and Amelung, B. 2008. Climate change and tourism in Northwestern Europe: Impacts and adaptation. *Tourism Analysis*, 13, 21–31.

Owen, B., Lee, D.S., and Lim, L. 2010. Flying into the future: Aviation emissions scenarios to 2050. *Environmental Science and Technology*, 44, 2255–60.

Parry, M., Lowe, J., and Hanson, C. 2009. Overshoot, adapt and recover. *Nature*, 458, 1102–3.

Peeters, P. 2010. Tourism transport, technology, and carbon dioxide emissions. In C. Schott (ed.), *Tourism and the Implications of Climate Change: Issues and Actions*. Bingley, Yorks.: Emerald.

Peeters, P.M. 2013. Developing a long-term global tourism transport model using a behavioural approach: Implications for sustainable tourism policy making. *Journal of Sustainable Tourism*, 21, 1049–69.

Peeters, P., and Dubois, G. 2010. Tourism travel under climate change mitigation constraints. *Journal of Transport Geography*, 18, 447–57.

Peeters, P., and Eijgelaar, E. 2014. Tourism's climate mitigation dilemma: Flying between rich and poor countries. *Tourism Management*, 40, 15–26.

Peeters, P., and Landré, M. 2012. The emerging global tourism geography – an environmental sustainability perspective. *Sustainability*, 4, 42–71.

Peeters, P.M., and Middel, J. 2007. Historical and future development of air transport fuel efficiency. In R. Sausen, A. Blum, D.S. Lee, and C. Brüning (eds), *Proceedings of an International Conference on Transport, Atmosphere and Climate (TAC); Oxford, United Kingdom, 26th to 29th June 2006*. Oberpfaffenhoven: DLR Institut für Physic der Atmosphäre, 42–47.

Peeters, P., Gössling, S., and Lane, B. 2009. Moving towards low-carbon tourism: New opportunities for destinations and tour operators. In S. Gössling, C.M. Hall, and D.B. Weaver (eds), *Sustainable Tourism Futures: Perspectives on Systems, Restructuring and Innovations*. New York: Routledge, 240–257.

Peeters, P., Szimba, E. and Duijnisveld, M. 2007. Major environmental impacts of European tourist transport. *Journal of Transport Geography*, 15, 83–93.

Pels, J., Eijgelaar, E., de Bruijn, K., Dirven, R., and Peeters, P. 2014. *Travelling Large in 2013: The Carbon Footprint of Dutch Holidaymakers in 2013 and the Development since 2002*. Breda: NHTV Breda University of Applied Sciences.

Pentelow, L., and Scott, D.J. 2011. Aviation's inclusion in international climate policy regimes: Implications for the Caribbean tourism industry. *Journal of Air Transport Management*, 17, 199–205.

Pharand-Deschênes, F., and Globaïa 2015. *Planetary Boundaries: A Safe Operating Space for Humanity*. Stockholm: Stockholm Resilience Centre.

Prideaux, B., McKercher, B., and McNamara, K.E. 2012. Modelling a tourism response to climate change using a four stage problem definition and response framework. *Asia Pacific Journal of Tourism Research*, 18, 165–82.

Raskin, P., Monks, F., Ribeiro, T., van Vuuren, D., and Zurek, M.B. 2005. Global scenarios in historical perspective. In S.R. Carpenter, P.L. Pingali, E.M. Bennett and M.B. Zurek (eds), *Ecosystems and Human Well-Being: Scenarios*, vol. 2. Washington, DC: Island Press, 35–44.

Rockström, J., *et al.* 2009. A safe operating space for humanity. *Nature*, 461, 472–5.

Rogelj, J., McCollum, D.L., Reisinger, A., Meinshausen, M., and Riahi, K. 2013. Probabilistic cost estimates for climate change mitigation. *Nature*, 493, 79–83.

Rothengatter, W. 2010. Climate change and the contribution of transport: Basic facts and the role of aviation. *Transportation Research Part D: Transport and Environment*, 15, 5–13.

Scott, D., Peeters, P., and Gössling, S. (2010). Can tourism deliver its 'aspirational' greenhouse gas emission reduction targets? *Journal of Sustainable Tourism*, 18, 393–408.

Slegers, P., Wijffels, R., Van Straten, G., and Van Boxtel, A. 2011. Design scenarios for flat panel photobioreactors. *Applied Energy*, 88, 3342–53.

Steffen, W., Broadgate, W., Deutsch, L., Gaffney, O., and Ludwig, C. 2015a. The trajectory of the Anthropocene: The great acceleration. *The Anthropocene Review*, 2, 81–98.

Steffen, W., Crutzen, P.J., and McNeill, J.R. 2007. The Anthropocene: Are humans now overwhelming the great forces of nature? *Ambio*, 36, 614–21.

Steffen, W., *et al.* 2015b. Planetary boundaries: Guiding human development on a changing planet. *Science*, 347. doi: 10.1126/science.1259885.

Timilsina, G.R., and Shrestha, A. 2011. How much hope should we have for biofuels? *Energy*, 36, 2055–69.

UNWTO-UNEP-WMO 2008. *Climate Change and Tourism: Responding to Global Challenges*. Madrid: UNWTO-UNEP.

UNWTO 2011. *Tourism towards 2030: Global Overview*. Madrid: UNWTO.

UNWTO 2014. *UNWTO World Tourism Barometer January 2014*. Madrid: World Tourism Organization.

Urry, J. 2010. Consuming the planet to excess. *Theory, Culture and Society*, 27, 191–212.

Westin, J., and Kågeson, P. 2012. Can high speed rail offset its embedded emissions? *Transportation Research Part D: Transport and Environment*, 17, 1–7.

WTO 2000. *Tourism 2020 Vision*, vol. 7. *Global Forecasts and Profiles of Market Segments*. Madrid: World Tourism Organization (WTO).

WTTC 2009. *Leading the Challenge on Climate Change*. London: World Travel and Tourism Council.

3   Undoing Iceland?

The pervasive nature of the urban

Edward H. Huijbens, Bárbara Maçães Costa and Harry Gugger

Introduction

This chapter follows the work that the Basel-based studio laba (Laboratoire Bâle, Federal Institute of Technology Lausanne) carried out on Iceland during the academic year of 2014–15, with the aim of creating a 'territorial constitution' for the industries of the island. The Swiss group of researchers and architects base their analysis on the premise that nature has become artificial through the growing pervasiveness of the urban and the increasingly cultural quality of nature resulting from growing conservation efforts, and ultimately that planet Earth is a human product. Indeed one of the markers of the Anthropocene is the ever growing pace of urbanization and the growing percentage of the world's population living in urban centres. Globally 54 per cent of the world's population resided in urban areas in 2014. In 1950, 30 per cent of the world's population was urban, and by 2050, 66 per cent of the world's population is projected to be urban (United Nations, 2014).

The chapter seeks to displace the urban as a fixed point of reference in juxtaposition to the rural or, in this specific undertaking, the wilderness landscapes of Iceland. Grosz's (2011) book *Becoming Undone* inspires us to think through how this undoing is inherent in the practices of making a North Atlantic cold water island destination with its vast wilderness areas (Jóhannesson *et al.*, 2010) into an attractive option for international travelers. Moreover, through undoing the urban/wilderness dyad and its imbrication with the ordering practices of tourism in constituting a destination, an ontology of vibrant material becoming emerges (Bennett, 2010). With this ontology we will release Iceland from a static position, or an understanding often all too easily appropriated by marketing media and representing the island as dead or thoroughly instrumentalized, 'feed[ing] human hubris and our earth-destroying fantasies of conquest and consumption' (Bennett, 2010, p. ix).

In Iceland, the only urban centre houses two-thirds of the total population and functions as the gateway for almost all international and domestic tourism in the country. As elsewhere Iceland's growing pace of urbanization, engulfing the previously stable typologies of 'city' and 'countryside' into a whole new myriad of hybrid conditions, has posed the artificiality of nature as a precondition of life on Earth: a 'world' of domesticated nature and wild urbanization. If the Neolithic Revolution gave birth to 'the city', then the Industrial Revolution gave birth to 'the urban', and if the first altered the natural environment, then the second abolished the concept of nature altogether. In this context, having lost its sublime adversary (nature) and its supreme subject (the human as centre of the world), designing human environments becomes a less humanist task but also a more ecological one, because it becomes less about violent colonization of 'nature' and more about a mediated dialogue of equals (Gugger and Costa, 2014). This absolute reduction forces a humbling (and humiliating) decentring of the human, who can no longer be 'the measure of all things' (Clark, 1969, ch. 4, referring to Leon Battista Alberti). This grievous realization is crucial if we are to move beyond climate-change denial and accept that the age of the Anthropocene is a time for post-anthropocentric (speculative) realism (Morton, 2013a). Naturally, it is still important to make room for the human, as nature becomes an artefact, and the Anthropocene should not become a further instrument for the cynical forces of urban (economic) expansionism. If completely devoid of its humanity, place is reduced to banal space or entertaining event, and designing is reduced to the generic, ready-made container. But a certain degree of abstraction can be an opportunity for openness. Designing in the Anthropocene is not about denying humanity its place on Earth, on the contrary: it is about extending our privilege to non-humans and expanding our perception of reality beyond the principle of correlationism, 'which requires humans to be one ingredient in everything that exists' (Harman, 2009, 126). 'If a tree falls in a forest and no one is around to hear it, does it make a sound?' (Berkeley, 1710) Where classical idealism would have argued that it does not, because reality always requires human perception, a post-anthropocentric worldview, such as speculative realism, would suggest that the sound's existence does not require human validation. 'There does not exist a forest as an objectively fixed environment: there exists a forest-for-the-park-ranger, a forest-for-the-hunter, a forest-for-the-botanist, a forest-for-the-wayfarer, a forest-for-the-nature-lover, a forest-for-the-carpenter, and finally a fable forest in which Little Red Riding Hood loses her way' (Agamben, 2004, 41). To this 'infinite variety of perceptual worlds' (Agamben, 2004, 40) or as Jakob von Uexküll famously called them, *Umwelts*, speculative realism would add 'the forest-for-the-spider, the forest-for-the-spider-web, the forest-for-the-tree, and last but not least, *the forest-for-the-forest*. Even if it could exist on its little ownsome [sic], a forest would exemplify how *existence just is coexistence*' (Morton, 2013b, 113, emphasis in original).

Ultimately, it is the Earth that is made artefactual and we need to understand how we can frame our responsibility towards it through designing tourist destinations. Bruno Latour, who could also be considered as 'one of the most important map-makers of the Anthropocene' (Gren this volume) refers to this Earth as Gaia and argues that 'Gaia should not be considered an applied theory, it is a matter that vibrates in all sorts of different mediums' (Latour, 2014, 69).

The task at hand for humans is to find a more horizontal representation of the relation between human and nonhuman actants in order to be more faithful to the style of action pursued by each.

(Bennett, 2010, 98, see also Grosz, 2011, 16)

The design principles and methods of the Laboratoire Bâle (studio laba) aim to be true to the style of action pursued by the Earth and us together. How to make sense of matter vibrating in different mediums comes down to the ways in which we do our 'philosophizing, storytelling and art-making [which] function as inevitable *technical* prostheses for a human engaged in the theorization of matter' (Zylinksa, 2014, 136). Making room for design in the Anthropocene, for us, is thus imperative, not least when it comes to tourism.

This chapter will proceed in three parts before drawing some conclusions and take-home messages in terms of tourism and the Anthropocene. First an understanding of the Anthropocene allowing for humans, temporality and the Earth is presented together with the ways in which these are imbricated through a focus on its three core constituents; the Anthropos, the Cene and the Earth. The second part theorizes the materialist take of the chapter, and how the urban/wilderness dyad can be unhinged. Part three of this chapter undoes the pervasive nature of urbanism in terms of Icelandic wilderness as a key tourism resource. Finally these aspirations will be inflected in the earthly take on the Anthropocene drawn up in the preceding sections to establish the ways of understanding destinations in terms of their continual undoing in times of the Anthropocene.

Urbanization, the Anthropocene and the Earth

The growing number of people living in urban centres is one of the markers of the Anthropocene represented in the numerous graphs presented in the original formulation of the concept (Steffen *et al.*, 2011, 851). The paradigm of urbanization represents to Cerdá:

> the condition of limitlessness and the complete integration of movement and communication brought about by capitalism, which Cerdà saw as the unprecedented 'vast swirling oceans of persons, of things, of interests of every sort, of a thousand diverse elements' that work in permanent reciprocity and thus form a totality that cannot be contained by any previous finite territorial formations such as the city.
>
> (Aureli, 2011, 9)

'Cittá diffusa' (Secchi), 'metapolis' (Ascher), 'postmetropolis' (Soja), 'global city' (Sassen), 'space of flows' (Castells), 'generic city' (Koolhaas) are all recently invented concepts that name and define the new kind of urban phenomena that have come to asymmetrically permeate the globe. While each has its own particular standpoint, they all address (directly or by implication), the demise of the humanist city (Eisenman, 1984, 9) and that of its analogous dichotomy, city/ wilderness. In Iceland, Reykjavík the capital in the south-west corner of the island has grown disproportionally compared to the rest of the country in the post-war years and has been designed to accommodate cars over people. The city now houses two-thirds of the total population of Iceland and over half of its surface area is covered with asphalt (Iceland Academy of the Arts, 2009). The city is also the key gateway for tourists entering Iceland, a vast majority of whom are there for its pristine nature and wilderness areas. Yet the city is not a flipside of the rural. Engulfed by 'junkspace' (Koolhaas, 2004), city-as-object and rural-as-background no longer exist; what is left now is an ambiguous and hybrid condition that has no genetic code and is impossible to describe in typological terms.

In the Anthropocene the majority of humanity live in an urban-industrialized civilization but at the same time people often presume that our real home is in the wilderness, in that 'Nature' with capital N driving so many to travel the globe. The trouble with this belief (which does not lack religious overtones) is that nature quietly expresses and reproduces the very values that it pretends to reject: it acts like a landmark in the desert, which by its state of exceptionality ends up perpetuating and endorsing the banality and sameness of that very desert. The classical city wall drew the limit between the two worlds, with the cultural object in the foreground, contained and framed against the backdrop of wilderness. The industrial (modern) city blurred and irreparably damaged this once-stable opposition. The social polis merged with the bucolic arcadia in infinite, site-specific combinations and bred a succession of 'transgenic landscapes' (Domingues, 2011, 39) that we now generally refer to as 'the urban'. The territory lost friction and changed in more or less awkward ways to the point at which 'the urban' itself became a kind of all-pervading (mostly chaotic) cultural background – one might say, a kind of nature.

> Air, water, wood: all are enhanced to produce … a parallel Walden, a new rainforest. Landscape has become Junkspace, foliage as spoilage: Trees are tortured, lawns cover human manipulations like thick pelts … sprinklers water according to mathematical timetables.
>
> (Koolhaas, 2004, 170)

The lack of genetic code and the impossibility of describing the urban in typological terms recognizes that indeed '[t]he earth can be infinitely divided, territorialized, framed' (Grosz, 2008, 17). Undoing the city-as-object and rural-as-background leaving only an ambiguous and hybrid condition creates confusion on the face of it, yet one that

> allows contemporary theorists, activists and designers to develop problem formations adequate to the politics of hypercomplexity that inhabit our postnatural inhabitations on the earth.
>
> (Turpin, 2013, 10)

The urban and the Anthropocene

To start with a problem formation of the Anthropocene, the term can be divided into three interrelated constituents i.e. the *Anthropos*, the *Cene* and the *Earth*. The last of these three is invisible in the Anthropocene concept, but arguably what it is all about. The Earth needs to be included since the Anthropocene denotes a geological epoch. Moreover, it is also the very mapping of the relationship between the Earth and the Anthropos which is at stake under the terms of the Anthropocene, and the planetary consciousness it entails. Consequently, it shall come as no surprise that the Anthropos has attracted some close scrutiny among geologists as outlined in the introduction to this volume. What the geologists study is how the *Anthropos* is actually able to provide a 'marker' for signifying and identifying strata in the geological record, but the conceptual ramifications are succinctly summed by Rowan stating that the Anthropocene is:

> not simply a disputed designation in geological periodization but a philosophical event that has struck like an earthquake, unsettling the tectonic plates of conceptual convention.
>
> (Rowan in Johnson and Morehouse, 2014, 447)

The Anthropos have indeed changed the functioning of the Earth system, precipitating new conceptual conventions that do not need proof in geological strata *per se* for their legitimacy.

The second part of the concept of the Anthropocene is the Cene, a common word-forming element in geology. Drawing on its Greek and Latin etymology, the Anthropocene is a 'lately done or made, new, young' geological period, epoch, or age in the geological timescale. If officially accredited such a status it would succeed the Holocene, the previous interglacial period of the last 11,000 years or so. It is here of outmost importance to note that the Anthropocene has not only ushered in the possibility of a new geological epoch. In terms of temporality one of the most fundamental messages amplified through the concept of the Anthropocene is that the geological timescale of the Earth and the historical one of the Anthropos can no longer be conceived of as clearly differentiated and mutually exclusive, as once they were. A basic tenet of geological science used to be that 'human chronologies were insignificant compared with the vastness of geological time; that human activities were insignificant compared with the force of geological processes' (Oreskes, 2007, 93, see also Sigvaldason, 1994). This is no longer the prevailing understanding, as often illustrated by the phenomena of climate change or what used to be called 'global warming'. For example, a claim often made is that the Anthropos has to drastically reduce its carbon emissions within the timescale of less than three decades in order to avoid more than 2°C increase in global atmospheric mean temperature.

This is nothing but a truly astonishing folding of the agencies and temporalities of the Anthropos and the Earth. What used to be understood and researched as a distinct climate residing far away in geological time, slowly ticking in the natural solitary register of the Earth, has become something in which the historical temporality of the Anthropos itself is imbricated. According to Morton: 'The end of the world has already occurred. We can be uncannily precise about the date on which the world ended. ... It was in April 1784, when James Watt patented the steam engine, an act that commenced ... the inception of humanity as a geophysical force on a planetary scale' (2013a, 7). The focus can also be put on the 'Great Acceleration' of the 1950s. Whatever the precise natal dates may be, the overall message is that the Anthropocene is overlapping with the present or recent time of the Anthropos, in short; modernity. In the words of Morton; 'we are no longer able to think history as exclusively human, for the very reason that we are in the Anthropocene' (Morton, 2013a, 4). In a similar vein Chakrabarty contends that the 'geologic now of the Anthropocene has become entangled with the now of human history' (Chakrabarty, 2008, 212).

However one chooses to understand the concept of the Anthropocene, it is evident that it is able to function as a fixed point for engagements across the sciences and between disciplinary domains ranging from architecture to anthropology, geology to grammatology. As its usage is not restricted to a single disciplinary domain with its internal logics, it can also be distinguished as a transdisciplinary concept. Perhaps the growing momentum of the interest in the concept of the Anthropocene is a sign of it being born in an Earth-world and delivered to an Anthropos in wait for such a transdisciplinary concept orienting ordering practices of the Anthropos. As for the Earth, its invisibility in the concept of the Anthropocene is understandable in geology, but rather unfortunate in the context of social science in general and tourism in particular. For social theorizing and tourism practices it is actually the Earth that poses the greatest challenge when it comes to getting a grip on the Anthropocene or visiting any destination.

The studio laba point of departure is that the Earth in the age of the Anthropocene is an artefact – Spaceship Earth, an artificial object travelling through time and space and steered by Earthiens (Fuller, 1969). A recurrent theme of the Anthropocene is certainly the need to consider the intertwined relationship between the Anthropos and the Earth at planetary scale, yet 'no form of life lives on the earth per se' (Grosz, 2008, 46). The Anthropos inhabit territories, which are part of larger surroundings and eventually 'terra-tories', but do not become territory unless constituted. In this braided (dis)unity of the Earth and the Anthropos, geo-forces are placed at the centre of descriptive and analytical concern. These general implications and challenges of the Anthropocene will eventually have to play out also in tourism, be it international travel or at the level of individual destinations, i.e. how territories are constituted for tourism purposes and the key consideration here resides in the practices of design and ultimately architecture.

All design, but especially architecture, colonizes space for human appropriation, defining a boundary of domination set against a background of wilderness and chaos (Grosz, 2008). The undoing of the pervasiveness of today's many phenomena of urbanization becomes our departure point for understanding design practices in the Anthropocene. The epitome of the urban-industrialized world we live in and the rapid urbanization of Iceland, is the city. The classical city contained the agglomeration of civilized inner public spaces segregated from the outer (extramural) countryside. The urban centres of the Anthropocene are vast swirling oceans of persons, of things, of interests of every sort, of a thousand diverse elements that vibrate through and with us in constituting itself, wilderness, tourism destinations and ourselves. Allowing the elements to be expressed through design is the technical prostheses of architecture in the Anthropocene.

The problem of life is the problem of design

> For some time we may have thought that the U-bend in the toilet was a convenient curvature of ontological space that took whatever we flush down into a totally different dimension called Away, leaving things clean over here Now we know better: instead of the mythical land Away, we know the waste goes to the Pacific Ocean or the wastewater treatment facility. . . . There is no Away on this surface, no here and no there.
>
> (Morton, 2013a, 31)

The mythical land Away is also the objective of so many tourists, getting away from the hassle of everyday life in the urban. The urban centres of the Anthropocene as junkspace open an understanding of the intertwined relationship between the Anthropos and the Earth at planetary scale. The imbrication of us with everything prefigured by the pervasiveness of the urban shows how there is no escaping the Earth, yet life is not *on* the Earth but *of* the Earth. Life constitutes territories, terratories, tiny insides 'but where the artificial conditions for the deployment of life forms are fully provided and paid for' (Latour, 2009, 143).

Understanding the making of these artificial conditions and their undoing is what life is about. 'The becoming of life is the undoing of matter' (Grosz, 2011 54), at the same time as 'the problem of life is the problem of design' (Grosz 2011, 173). Discharging the urban as fixed and representable in juxtaposition to wilderness, or the rural, allows for a 'turbulent material imagination' (Anderson 2014, 138), one wherein explicitly drawing on matter's vibrancy through and with us 'things matter not because of how they are represented but because they have qualities, rhythms, forces, relations, and movements' (Stewart, 2011, 445). At the same time, it is imperative to recognize that 'the concepts that [Earth] creates, that come to populate the ground that holds it up from within, are the inevitable means of fleshing out this full immanent ground' (Gasché, 2014, 21).

The elements of the Earth, the miniscule and matter in its vibrancy highlight 'the contemporary importance of our immersion within materially complex and fragile balances of earth, air, water, and fire' (Jackson and Fannin, 2011, 436). Immersion in the material makes space for Earth in our repertoire, yet at the same time hitches 'the issues of earthly volatility to that of bodily vulnerability' (Clark, 2010, p. xx) Concomitantly however this bodily vulnerability is not one of the individual. As much as matter quavers and shifts, so does the individual, as Grosz argues:

> These becomings are individuations, processes of the production of things processes that transform states of matter, processes that enable and complicate life ... a life that is individuated but no longer individual ... the unity of being even while affirming its fundamentally differentiating forces.
>
> (Grosz, 2011, 2, 38, 41)

The geo-forces of the Anthropos are differentiating forces, ones that transform the state of matter and us with it, through processes of individuation which Simondon (1992, 300) described as:

> a partial and relative solution, manifested in a system that contains latent potentials and harbours a certain incompatibility with itself; an incompatibility due at once to the forces in tension as well as to the impossibility of interactions between terms of extremely disparate dimensions.

The processes of undoing are thus generative and '[i]n this strange, *vital* materialism, there is no point of pure stillness, no indivisible atom that is not itself aquiver with virtual force' (Bennett, 2010, 21 and 57, emphasis in original). The material thus conceived is thus an internalization of heterogeneous entities that through their multiple interactions acquire emergent properties, i.e. the potential to create new and qualitatively different relations (Protevi and Bonta, 2004). Consequently, the Anthropos entails an understanding of subjectification in which both human and inhuman geo-forces are incorporated. As Bennett (2010, 11) claims by citing Margulis and Sagan (2000, 49) '[w]e are walking, talking minerals'. This geo-subjectification is also exemplified by Yusoff:

> The extension of the social into the strata inadvertently produces new modes of subjectification that are geologic, thereby rendering social forces (and the 'bodies politic' of society) as composed, at least in part, of inhuman forces.
> (Yusoff in Johnson and Morehouse, 2014, 452)

This suggests that designing territories, or any tourism destination, has to rely on numerous methods and experiments that are being devised in order to grasp this incorporation of inhuman forces and the braiding of the human social subject with geo-forces.

Mixing literary inspirations and theoretical considerations thereof Klingan *et al.* (2014) provide for an exposé of the constantly shifting qualities of the material, presenting new positions on the forms that knowledge takes within the Anthropocene, focusing on the elemental and miniscule. Klingan *et al.* (2014) focus on grains, rays and vapours and how geo-forcing activities effectively alter the Earth System dynamics, redistributing sediments, currents, and rays towards unknown configurations. Allowing room for the elemental and miniscule in design is about attunement – an open-ended comportment and ecological sensibility. An illustration is offered by J.M.W. Turner's impressionistic painting *Rain, Steam and Speed*, which portrays urban infrastructures dipped in sunset light and industrial mist.

Getting attuned to and knowing these emergent forms is currently being experimented with through, for example, *A Matter Theatre* curated by Katrin Klingan, Ashkan Sepahvand, Christoph Rosol and Janek Müller, the University of Wisconsin-Madison Nelson Institute's 2014 *Anthropocene Slam* and Latour's *Gaia's Global Circus*. These three have in common experimenting with methods to address the limited repertoire of concepts and sensibilities the Anthropos possesses to make sense of its own imbrication with the Earth as a geo-logical being who shares its distributed agency with the forces of the Earth. For the Anthropos with its non-human agency and geo-forces, life does not only mean to live on the Earth, but also of and through its agency and forces. The challenge becomes not only to map the Anthropos in terms of non-human agency and geo-forces but also how to explicitly theorize this earthly Anthropocene existence.

Constituting a territory for the Anthropos, carving out destinations for tourism purposes relies then on matters of concern and design, as the problem of life is the problem of design.

Design in the Anthropocene

As territories get constituted and the Earth is made artefactual through undoing the urban we need to understand how we can frame our responsibility towards it through designing tourist destinations. Destination development in Iceland is the concern of this section and the way in which the studio laba approached the making of a territorial constitution for Icelandic industries, amongst them tourism. The group aimed to imagine a formal language for architecture that goes beyond the aesthetics of nature, and an industrial aesthetics that goes beyond its classical opposition to nature. Tourism in Iceland invests heavily in nature and what is conceived of as the natural.

> Tourism in Iceland is characterized by the strong interest tourists show in gazing at, playing in and enjoying nature. It involves travel to the various natural attractions, such as mountains, glaciers, volcanoes, lava fields, geysers, sand fields, rivers, waterfalls, a varied coastline and a vast wilderness area in the central Highlands.
> (Sæþórsdóttir, 2010, 29, see also Sæþórsdóttir *et al.*, 2010)

Gazing at, playing in and enjoying nature places us as conscious cultural beings against the world of natural things: civilized artificiality versus original wilderness. This idea of 'artificiality' has its root in the Latin word *artificium*, which means 'art, craft or skill' and eventually also acquired the meaning of 'inauthenticity', thereby coming to encompass the common associations of 'truth' with nature and 'deceit' with culture. However, nature in the sense of something non-artificial, unaltered by human activity, hardly exists anymore. Even those places we call nature reserves or national parks (maintained in order to preserve fragile ecosystems and biodiversity) are paradoxically artificial, since the act of conservation itself can only ever result in something man-made. Design (biotech agriculture, plastic surgery, beach resorts, rural tourism, greenhouse tomatoes, hypo-allergenic cats) makes so-called nature take on an artificial authenticity. Preserved/protected nature is always a sanitized, tamed and overall more human-friendly version of the real thing – a domesticated, hypernatural version that is little other than culture in disguise. Ironically, the more we learn to control nature, the less nature we have, and the more we change nature, the more complex, strange and unknowable it appears.

In Iceland, the illusion of nature – that virgin wilderness of ebony lava fields and slushy moss – still remains, as vividly portrayed in tourism marketing and tourist perceptions of the island. But there are cracks in the 'real'. We can't unknow what we know, and out on the highlands, the melted snow and 'the sunshine on one's shoulders is a reminder that man has cracked the ozone, that, thanks to us, the atmosphere absorbs where once it released' (McKibben, 2011, 297) and the flaming red glow on the horizon is a warning that melting ice caps are making the land rise faster, possibly provoking increased volcanic eruptions which shut down flights and spew ash in the European air.

In light of these ontological paradoxes, the studio laba group aim for a language that lets 'the creative faculty imagine what is to be known' as the poet Percy Shelley so eloquently put it, imagining an 'ecology without nature' (Morton, 2007), directly corresponding with earthly formulations of the Anthropocene: Gaia or Earth system. This is a post-anthropocentric territory to be imagined, where tourism infrastructures might become beautiful landmarks, and human impact might be seen as a responsible act of cultivation rather than an embarrassing damage to so-called 'pristine wilderness'. Therein buildings interact with climate and its changes, collaborating, as Robert Smithson (1996) put it, with geology's entropy and the massive scale of the territory. Within this destination reimaging, there is the chance to re-establish an integral non-aggressive relationship with living ecological cycles, where 'development could tend toward a sensuous culture … [and] socially necessary labour would be diverted to the construction of an aesthetic rather than a repressive environment, to parks and gardens rather than highways and parking lots, to the creation of areas of withdrawal rather than massive fun and relaxation' (Marcuse, 1969, 90).

Contrary to most mainstream environmentalism, ecology is not about the smaller scale, the smaller footprint, the more authentic, and the search for a kind of back-to-the-roots originality. Ecology is forcing us to face compulsive interdependence and coexistence and this forces us to zoom out, and look beyond each of our private backyards: 'the best environmental thinking is thinking big – as big as possible, and maybe even bigger than that, bigger than we can conceive' (Morton, 2012, 20). But thinking big not only in terms of space but also as Turpin (2013, 4) asks: have things always been done, thought or produced this way, are they thought done or produced in different ways in different places and can different ways of thinking, doing and producing be conceived for the future?

Ecology requires more (responsible) human involvement, not less. Having this in mind, studio laba's academic structure for architectural production has the core goal of incorporating 'nature' into architecture, that is, of including the scale of the landscape into the scale of the design object in a way that blurs the limit between the two. The method employed by the studio aims at slowing down the process of architectural design and invites students to think big, and include the territory in their intervention plot, overcoming the classical opposition between the humanist domestic inside and the wild outside left for domination and contemplation. As difficult as this may be, because

> ecological thought is difficult: it involves becoming open, radically open – open forever, without the possibility of closing again. Studying art provides a platform, because the environment is partly a matter of perception. Art forms have something to tell us about the environment, because they can make us question reality. ... Reframing the world, our problems, and ourselves is part of the ecological project. This is what praxis means – action that is thoughtful and thought that is active.
>
> (Morton, 2012, 8–9)

Therefore, architectural production *per se* lasts for the students at studio laba one semester, but it is preceded by another full semester of researching that has the goal of producing a Territorial Constitution for Icelandic industries. This pre-study is called the Territorial Analysis and it is structured as follows:

- My Place: The designer is asked to interpret and represent their initial feeling towards the selected region in an intuitive and highly personal way.
- The Archives: The designer gathers, collects and compiles data, facts and figures about the selected region and then organizes it in the form of a reference wall.
- The Reading: The designer is to obtain a geographical understanding of the facts gathered, in correlation with the physical morphology of the selected region, with emphasis on cartography. As the word suggests, the reading is not intended to be neutral but rather already a construction, a critical framing and selection that reveals judgement and narrative.
- The Form: The designer finds an articulation between landscape systems and territorial programmes and proposes a spatial figure that clarifies, organizes and enhances existing conditions.
- A Territorial Constitution: The designer creates a road map providing a logical set of guiding rules which allow for an appropriate long-term development of the selected region.

The articulation between the first semester of Territorial Analysis and the second semester's Architecture Project is achieved in the intermediate exercise Feasibility Study, where each student must pick out a site and programme, in articulation with its immediate and large-scale context, through a suitable design concept.

The method outlined by the studio laba group is destination design in the spirit of Bennett's (2010) example of metal:

> The desire of the craftsperson to see what a metal can *do*, rather than the desire of the scientist to know what a metal is, enabled the former to discern *a* life in metal and thus, eventually to collaborate more productively with it.
>
> (Bennett, 2010, 60, emphasis original)

Note that Bennett's (2010) aim is not to downplay science, arguably a privileged vantage point to life's intrigues as her Darwin examples make clear. The focus is on the practices of design and architecture animating the Earth and demystifying nature as the anthropocentric ideal and focusing on ecology, opposed to the modernist abstraction which drove the progressive transformation of the organic human body into the machine, mirroring the way in which industry turned the figure of the worker into 'mere appendage of flesh on a machine of iron' (Marx, 1906, 462).

The abstract ecology of artefactual Earth

From the crafts developed through metallurgy to the refining of fossil fuels to plastic bags, humanity has demystified nature to an ever greater extent. A Styrofoam cup will take about 500 years to degrade. Radioactive waste deposited beneath mountains has an average harmful life expectancy of about 100,000 years (for it can endure between 10,000 and one million years), three times longer than the time spanning back to the Chauvet cave paintings executed by Palaeolithic humans. At the beginning of the 19th century, the world's population was 1 billion, but it is now seven times that, and by 2050 it is predicted to surpass 9 billion. Atmospheric CO_2 concentration has more than doubled since 1950. Human debris dumped in the oceans has been accumulating in patches known as the Pacific trash vortex. Polymer plastic (found, for instance, in the common plastic shopping bag) does not biodegrade as much as degrade, breaking down into increasingly smaller pieces (microplastics) until it eventually enters the food chain.

We live in an age of ecological panic masked under the cynicism of ideological denial (Žižek, 2011). In the scheme of the five stages of grief, after denial follow anger, bargaining and depression, until we eventually reach the point of acceptance. Tourist perceptions and marketing strategies in Iceland are in fact grieving the death of the idea of nature and the loss of our anthropocentric worldview. About two hundred years of modern industry have drastically changed 'Nature's garden' into a polluted, less biodiverse, CO_2 induced greenhouse. However, the 'artifactualization' of nature started many centuries earlier, when Earth 'shifted from pristine and untracked wilderness to mapped and deeded and cultivated land' (McKibben, 2011, 297). Nature was long gone by the time Romanticism resuscitated its ghost:

The ghost of 'Nature', a brand new entity dressed up like a relic from the past age, [is] haunted by the modernity in which it was born. ... Modern thinkers had taken for granted that the ghost of Nature, rattling its chains, would remind them of a time without industry, a time without 'technology,' as if we had never used flint or wheat. But in looking at the ghost of Nature, modern humans were looking in a mirror. In Nature, they saw the reflected, inverted image of their own age – and the grass is always greener on the other side. ... Nature was an ideal image, a self-contained form suspended afar, shimmering and naked behind glass like an expensive painting. ... Nature was a special kind of private property, without an owner, exhibited in a specially constructed art gallery. The gallery was Nature itself, revealed through visual technology in the eighteenth century as 'picturesque' – looking like a picture.

(Morton, 2012, 5)

Modernism has been the history of Western culture's progressive path towards abstraction – from Courbet, to Cézanne, to Picasso; from Kandinsky, to Rothko, to Frank Stella; from Brancusi, to Sol LeWitt, to Robert Smithson. This pattern in the visual arts was a response to, and a reflection of, the growing abstraction of social relations within modern industrial society. 'To abstract' comes from the Latin *abstrahere*, literally 'to draw away from', which means to uproot something out of its totality, in order to define generic frameworks rather than specific (concrete) solutions. Abstraction was, in fact, the grand project of modernity: to detach thinking from tradition and myth and seek a universal rationale that is both generic and all-inclusive.

'Abstract art does not appeal to the emotions but to the mind' (Smithson, 1996, 337–8). It shies away from representation of ideology and/or of the subjective pathos of the author, becoming what Umberto Eco (1969) called an 'Open Work', that is, a work of art whose meaning is somewhat indeterminate and incomplete, and thus admits a myriad of contingent interpretations (from performer or viewer) without fear of adulteration (Eco, 1989, 4). Abstraction produces forms with flexible, indeterminate content.

And then, correspondingly, modern industrial society was also the process through which the formal city dissipated into the abstract process of urbanization 'the generic habitat of absolute individualism' (Aureli *et al.*, 2007, 33), based on the ideology of incommensurability and infinite growth propelled by constant movement and production. Urbanization presupposes the fundamental substitution of politics with economics as a mode of city governance and at the same time 'human association shifts from the political space of the city to the economic space of the house' (Aureli, 2011, 13). Interestingly, the word 'economy' has its root in *oikonomia* (from *oikos* 'house' and *nemein* 'manage'), which literally means 'household management'. This underlying affiliation of the concept of urban (supposedly the common sphere) with the dimension of the house (the private space of the individual) is an idiosyncratic paradox of our current times.

Ludwig Hilberseimer synthesized this ethos by affirming that cities should be projected through the coordination between its two diametrically opposite extremes: the economic forms of production and the individual inhabitable capsule. His 1926 project for the Hochhausstadt (High-Rise City) reveals this by endlessly repeating the same generic building type along an abstract grid The result is a hybrid of blocks and slabs in which all civic activities, such as production, living, and commerce, are superimposed rather than zoned in different locations. Hochhausstadt is a city of anywheres where movement, change and flexibility are its motors and architecture has been reduced to pure abstraction: the lack of formal hierarchy stands for the lack of social hierarchy and representation The city is reduced to its reproductive conditions (Aureli, 2011). In similar ways

Hilberseimer's proposal for the Chicago Tribune building, in 1922, proposed an empty building, where architecture was reduced to envelope and furniture, and the plan of a ready-made industrial structure. Hilberseimer realized and drew upon the fact that both material and immaterial production followed the same industrial logic and industrial Earth is 'a world that no longer depends on the "real" or "natural" time or space' (Halley, 1991, 56–60). Things like electric lighting, air conditioning, the division of labour or communication technologies have contributed to make 'abstraction the hallmark of our experience of space and architecture, or lack thereof' (Aureli *et al.*, 2010, 56). Networks, landscapes, globalization, junkspace, cittá diffusa, metapolis, postmetropolis, global city, space of flows, generic city … All of these concepts resonate a certain aesthetics of industrialization, evoking an ideological praise for infinity achieved through endless repetition and non-compositional seriality.

Artificiality is a product of the pervasiveness of industry on Earth, and its formal aesthetic result is abstraction. Abstraction has its good and bad points. On the pessimistic side, it entails the problem of removal of authorship, and of lack of a specific meaning or message. On the positive side, its lack of authorship can suggest a sense of commonality, where the abstract object can be seen as the result of collective production. Furthermore, viewed as an 'Open Work' abstraction can be the device through which architecture becomes a background, switching places with 'nature' and the non-human world. In other words, abstraction can be the aesthetic through which domesticated design objects abdicate their role as significant anthropocentric landmarks and symbols of land colonization, and become minimalist background sculptures, which enhance and interact with the geological design of mountains, glaciers, volcanoes, lava fields, geysers, sand fields, rivers, waterfalls and other earthly places of our own making, extracted from matter. In this sense design 'is the excess of matter that is extracted from it to resonate for living beings … it is the way that the present most directly welcomes the future' (Grosz, 2011, 189 and 191).

Conclusion

Making room for a particular type of design of and for the Anthropocene, is for us imperative, not least when it comes to tourism, design which 'establishes territory out of the chaos that is the earth' (Grosz, 2008, 11).

Indeed the Earth is one made artefactual, through processes of design but at the same time we need to engage and be sensitized by this fact. The growing number of people living in urban centres is one of the markers of the Anthropocene. These urban centres are engulfed by 'junkspace' (Koolhaas, 2004) where city-as-object and rural-as-background no longer exist. The Earth takes the place of former Nature, but it does not provide the truth or stable background – it is in an unpredictable state of becoming, rendering attempts at design as acts of responsibility. What is left now is an ambiguous and hybrid condition that through processes of framing can be made abstract in order to be generative of design.

In the light of such ambiguity, one might propose the replacement of the urban/ wilderness dyad with that of controllable vs. autonomous, whereby wilderness would be that which we can control and the urban all that we cannot (Mensvoort, 2006). According to this new classification, greenhouse tomatoes and nature reserves would belong to the cultural category, while computer viruses, traffic jams and 'the urban' (in all its pervasive autonomous anarchy) would be considered natural.

The acceptance of the reality of climate change requires this same kind of speculation. We live in an environment that we can only understand vicariously and partially, and of which we are cause and effect. The non-human world can no 'longer [be] excluded or [dismissed as] merely decorative features of [our] social, psychic, and philosophical space' (Morton, 2013a, 22). The environment is no longer a background, and to this design should respond with a commitment to openness, extending the responsibility of design to more than just our immediate comfort and needs. The Earth thus becomes a cultivated responsibility, rather than an outside leftover dimension, or a primordial womb to which one could escape (laba, 2014, 11) and tourism, that fundamentally humanist activity of cultural exchange and exposure, can go beyond mere entertainment and become a place of hospitable confrontation and coexistence (Levinas, 1998).

The design principles of the studio laba manifest the ways in which concerns for industry and tourism destination development in particular can be framed. Bennett (2010, 99) argues that in order to grasp the Earth in its vibrancy some degree of anthropomorphism is needed. At the end of the day designing destinations is about what constitutes to us matters of concern. Our intentions play a role, yet are not the only decisive elements at play. Bennett (2010) asks us to loosen 'the connections between efficacy and the moral subject' (p. 32), broaden the range of places to look for sources of change (p. 37), and transform our relations with mute objects 'into a set of differential tendencies and variable capacities' (p. 108). This means placing the design question on each of our shoulders as to what assemblages to associate with and/or extricate from. The problem of life is the problem of design and this problematization averts our attention sideways, seeing causality as emergent and recognizing the alien quality of our own flesh (Bennett, 2010, 112, see also Grosz, 2011, 32, 85). These are the imperatives of the Anthropocene, where 'life is an elaboration out of matter' (Grosz, 2011, 31), and design needs to allow it to become expressive, intensive and resonate to become more than itself (Grosz, 2008, 4).

The territorial constitution of Icelandic industries is to be rendered through 'ecology without nature' with the Laboratoire Bâle (studio laba) methods. Their aim is to allow the elaboration of matter to become intensified through reading and learning from the territory and the collective perception of the way the Anthropos is placed within the world. By expanding the field of architectural design of destinations into territorial studies and undoing Iceland through unhinging the urban as a point of departure, the city as home becomes part of the architectural object of a tourism destination. Inversely, the aesthetics of Nature – geysers and waterfalls – is what precludes our understanding of the Earth in the age of the Anthropocene and the ways in which it has become globally dominated by urban exploitation. Seeing the two in opposition, the urban and wilderness, precludes the emergence of territory through the unpredictable state of becoming of the Earth.

In sum, to design a tourism destination in the Anthropocene with ecological sensibilities necessary for ethical practices one needs to critically assess one's own cultural background and its influence on the perception and understanding of the site under consideration, filter relevant information and use comparative references, identify territorial forms that reflect cultural issues of history, governance, economy and type and understand the long-term phasing and timing of planning. The key emphasis of design in the Anthropocene is to play with paradoxes and cultivate and foster sensibilities and attunement with more than human worlds. 'To put it bluntly, my conatus will not let me "horizontalize" the world completely' (Bennett, 2010, 104), but abrogating the urban as a fixed point of reference in juxtaposition to the wilderness landscapes of Iceland is a first step.

References

Anderson, B. 2014. *Encountering Affect: Capacities, Apparatuses, Conditions*. Aldershot: Ashgate Publishing.

Agamben, G. 2004. *The Open: Man and Animal*. Stanford, CA: Stanford University Press.

Aureli, P.V. 2011. *The Possibility of an Absolute Architecture*. Cambridge, MA: MIT Press.

Aureli, P.V. *et al*. 2010. *Rome: The Centre(s) Elsewhere*. Rotterdam: NAi.

Aureli P.V. *et al*. 2007. *Brussels Manifesto*. Rotterdam: NAi.

Bennett, J. 2010. *Vibrant Matter: A Political Ecology of Things*. Durham, NC: Duke University Press.

Berkeley, G. 1710. *A Treatise Concerning the Principles of Human Knowledge*. Mineola, NY: Dover Publications.

Chakrabarty, D. 2008. The climate of history: Four theses. *Critical Inquiry*, 35, 197–222.

Clark, K. 1969. *Civilization*. London: BBC Books.

Clark, N. 2010. *Inhuman Nature. Sociable Life on a Dynamic Planet*. London: Sage.

Domingues, Á. 2011. *Vida no Campo*. Porto: Dafne Editora.

Eco, U. 1989. *The Open Work*. London and Cambridge, MA: Harvard University Press.

Eisenman, P. 1984. Editor's introduction. In A. Rossi (ed.), *Architecture of the City*. Cambridge, MA: MIT Press, 3–11.

Fuller, R.B. 1969. *Operating Manual for Spaceship Earth*. Baden: Lars Müller Publishers.

Gasché, R. 2014. *Geophilosophy: On Gilles Deleuze and Felix Guattari's What Is Philosophy?* Evanston, IL: Northwestern University Press.

Grosz, E. 2008. *Chaos, Territory, Art: Deleuze and the Framing of the Earth*. New York: Columbia University Press.

Grosz, E. 2011. *Becoming Undone. Darwinian Reflections on Life, Politics, and Art*. Durham, NC: Duke University Press.

Gugger, H., and Costa, B.M. 2014. Urban-nature: The ecology of planetary artifice. *San Rocco: Ecology*, Winter 2014(10), 32–40.

Halley, P. 1991. Abstraction and culture. *Tema Celeste*, Autumn, 56–60.

Harman, G. 2009. *Prince of Networks: Bruno Latour and Metaphysics*. Melbourne: Re.press.

Iceland Academy of the Arts, 2009. *Reykjavíkurgreining* (Reykjavík Analysis). Reykjavík: Iceland Academy of the Arts.

Jackson, M., and Fannin, M. 2011. Letting geography fall where it may – aerographies address the elemental. Guest editorial. *Environment and Planning D: Society and Space*, 29, 435–44.

Johnson, E., and Morehouse, H. 2014. After the Anthropocene: Politics and geographic inquiry for a new epoch. *Progress in Human Geography*, 38(3), 439–56.

Jóhannesson, G.Þ., Huijbens, E., and Sharpley, R. 2010. Icelandic tourism: Past directions – future challenges. *Tourism Geographies*, 12(2), 278–301.

Klingan, K., Sepahvand, A., Rosol, C., and Scherer, B.M. (eds) 2014. *Textures of the Anthropocene: Grain, Vapor, Ray*. Cambridge, MA: MIT Press.

Koolhaas, R. 2004. *OMA Content*. Cologne: Taschen.

Iaba 2014. *Industrial Landscape: A Territorial Constitution for Iceland*. Basel: Iaba.

Latour, B. 2009. Spheres and networks. Two ways to interpret globalization. *Harvard Design Review*, 30(spring/summer), 138–44.

Latour, B. 2014. Bruno Latour. Interview with Camila Marambio. *Miami Rail* (winter), 68–71.

Levinas, E. 1998. *Otherwise than Being: or, Beyond Essence*. Pittsburgh, PA: Duquesne University Press.

Marcuse, H. 1969. *An Essay on Liberation*. Boston, MA: Beacon Press.

Margulis, L. and Sagan, D. 2000. *What is Life?* Berkeley, CA: University of California Press.

Marx, K. 1906. *Capital*, vol. 1. New York: Dover.

McKibben, B. 2011. From the end of nature. In B. McKibben (ed.), *The Global Warming Reader*. New York: OR Books, 293–8.

Mensvoort, K. van 2006. Real nature is not green. <http://www.nextnature.net/2006/11/ real-nature-isnt-green> [accessed Aug. 2014].

Morton, T. 2007. *Ecology without Nature: Rethinking Environmental Aesthetics*. Cambridge, MA: Harvard University Press.

Morton, T. 2012. *The Ecological Thought*. Cambridge, MA: Harvard University Press.

Morton, T. 2013a. *Hyperobjects: Philosophy and Ecology After the End of the World*. Minneapolis, MN, and London: University of Minnesota Press.

Morton, T. 2013b. *Realist Magic: Objects, Ontology, Causality*. Ann Arbor, MI: Open Humanities Press.

Oreskes, N. 2007. The scientific consensus on climate change: How do we know we are not wrong? In J.F.C. Dimento and P. Dougham (eds), *Climate Change: What does it Mean for Us, our Children, and our Grandchildren?* Cambridge, MA: Cambridge University Press, 65–99.

Protevi, J., and Bonta, M. 2004. *Deleuze and Geophilosophy*. Edinburgh: Edinburgh University Press.

Sæþórsdóttir, A. 2010 Planning nature tourism in Iceland based on tourist attitudes. *Tourism Geographies*, 12(1), 25–52.

Sæþórsdóttir, A.D., Hall, C.M., and Saarinen, J. 2011. Making wilderness: Tourism and the history of the wilderness idea in Iceland. *Polar Geography*, 34(4), 249–73.

Sigvaldason, G.E. 1994. Náttúrusýn jarðfræðings (Nature in the eyes of a geologist). In R.H. Haraldsson and Th. Árnason (eds), *Náttúrusýn. Safn greina um siðfræði og náttúru*. Reykjavík: University of Iceland's Center for Ethics, 287–92.

Simondon, G. 1992. The genesis of the individual. In J. Caryand and S.Z. Kinter (eds), *Incorporations*. New York: Urzone, 297–319.

Smithson, R. 1996. The pathetic fallacy in esthetics. In J. Flam (ed.), *Robert Smithson: The Collected Writings*. Los Angeles, CA: University of California Press, 337–8.

Stewart, K. 2011. Atmospheric attunements. *Environment and Planning D: Society and Space*, 29, 445–53.

Steffen, W., Grinevald, J., Crutzen, P., and McNeill, J. 2011. The Anthropocene: Conceptual and historical perspectives. *Philosophical Transactions of the Royal Society A*, 369, 842–67.

Turpin, E. (ed.) 2013. *Architecture in the Anthropocene: Encounters among Design, Deep Time, Science and Philosophy*. Ann Arbor, MI: Open Humanities Press.

United Nations 2014. *World Urbanization Prospects: The 2014 Revision. Highlights*. New York: United Nations.

Žižek, S. 2011. *Living in the End of Times*. London and New York: Verso.

Zylinska, J. 2014. *Minimal Ethics for the Anthropocene*. Ann Arbor, MI: Open Humanities Press.

4 Loving nature to death

Tourism consumption, biodiversity loss and the Anthropocene

C. Michael Hall

Introduction

Thinking about tourism and the Anthropocene raises significant theoretical and practical issues with respect to the agency of tourism and dualities such as human: natural and debates as to whether humans and human systems are separate from or part of 'natural' systems. This is not just an academic debate as it frames understandings of the effects of individual and collective actions. However, the present chapter takes the position, undoubtedly not shared by all, that while such debates are integral to theorizations of the Anthropocene and understanding how biodiversity loss may be stemmed, the conscious decisions by human beings that lead to the loss of landscapes and the extinctions of other species demands an understanding of agency that still leads to a separation between the natural and the unnatural, if not humans and the other. Humans and their institutions have the conscious capacity to 'do other' and not trash the planet and cause the extinction of other species. Nature (the non-human world) as far as we know does not. Therefore, tourism certainly is a biophysical force. However, fundamentally it is a human or social one that is affected by and in turn affects the environment in which it occurs.

Environmental change and the extinction of species are natural processes (Lande, 1998). However, what is 'unnatural' is that the current rate of loss is now higher than what it has been for tens of thousands if not millions of years. According to the Secretariat of the Convention on Biological Diversity (CBD, 2010, 9), 'There are multiple indications of continuing decline in biodiversity in all three of its main components – genes, species and ecosystems.' The likely result is a biostratigraphic signal that marks the combination of human induced extinctions, global species migrations, and the widespread replacement of indigenous vegetation with often exotic agricultural monocultures (Cox, 2004; Zalasiewicz *et al.*, 2008).

Tourism as a socio-economic activity is a significant contributor to environmental change and well illustrates the increasingly problematic entanglement of humans and nature in the Anthropocene. Trying to assess tourism's 'impacts' is difficult because tourism both influences and is influenced by biodiversity and notions of the natural. The dominant metaphor of human impacts on the natural world is derived from a material realist ontology (Hall, 2013) which 'has come to frame our thinking and circumscribe debate about what constitutes explanation' (Head, 2008, 374). In terms of tourism or tourist impact on the environment this understanding is problematic. It places emphasis on the moment(s) of collision between two separate entities (e.g. the 'impact' between tourism and the environment), thereby favouring explanations and methods that depend on immediate correlation in time and space (Weyl, 2009). Moreover, it therefore circumscribes our understanding of 'impact' to the detriment of the search for other mechanisms of connection and causation rather than simple correlation (Head, 2008). As will be discussed below this is a major issue for assessing the effects of tourism as many of its most problematic influences on biodiversity may take a number of years before they become apparent.

The emphasis on the moment(s) of impact also assumes a stable environmental baseline (Hall and Lew, 2009), which as we know with respect to environmental change is not the case over longer time periods. It also assumes an experimental method in which only one variable is changed (Head, 2008), an approach that is clearly inappropriate for understanding complex and dynamic socio-environmental systems. However, perhaps most influential is the way in which the term 'tourism impacts' or 'tourist impacts' ontologically positions tourism and tourists as 'outside' the system under analysis, as outside of nature (or whatever it is that is being impacted) (Hall and Lew, 2009). This is ironic given that research on global climate and environmental change demonstrates just how deeply entangled tourism is in environmental systems (Gössling and Hall, 2006a; Hall and Saarinen, 2010; Hall, 2013). Yet the metaphor remains in widespread use, creating a significant explanatory divide between humans and nature and requiring the conflation of bundles of variable processes under headings like 'human', 'climate', 'environment' and 'nature' (Head, 2008). These dichotomous explanations with their veneer of simplicity and elegance gloss over their underlying assumptions. As Head (2008, 374) explains, 'the view that causality is simple takes many more assumptions than the view that it is complex'.

Conflating these bundles and placing tourism 'inside' the system being analysed raises fundamental questions when understanding and influencing trends as well as the ethical relationships between tourism and the environment (Hall, 2013). This latter point is extremely significant for biodiversity given the supposed virtues of ecotourism and other forms of nature-based tourism for environmental conservation (e.g. see Christ *et al.*, 2003). However, the 'aggressive faith' of many agencies in market solutions to environmental problems (Brockington *et al.*, 2008), including the development of nature-based tourism, has allowed capitalism to identify, open and colonize new spaces in nature (Duffy and Moore, 2010). There is nothing new in the relationship between capitalism and conservation – the first national parks were, after all, created because they were worthless for other commercial activities such as agriculture, forestry or mining but could assume an economic value on the basis of their aesthetic picturesque qualities for tourism (Frost and Hall, 2009). But what is 'new' is the vast scope of the ecotourism project by which the tourism derived economic values of particular ecosystem services, i.e. the commodification of ecosystem services as part of the green economy, are reified as justifications for biodiversity conservation and the extent to which this is regarded as somehow being ethically based (Hall, 2014). Such reflections provide the basis for a more critical assessment of tourist consumption of biodiversity.

This chapter therefore argues that it is not just enough to measure or describe biodiversity loss and tourism's role within it, as important as this is, but also to look at the science of the Anthropocene and global environmental change and way in which the 'solutions' to such change are constructed. Such an approach does not mean that the chapter takes the position that biodiversity loss and global environmental change do not exist, rather it contends that the current anthropogenic factors behind biodiversity loss – and hence what should be a focus of response – are social rather than 'natural' artefacts or, to put it another way, they are only 'natural' in the sense that they increasingly appear as outcomes inherent to neoliberal capitalist modes of consumption (Büscher and Arsel, 2012; Dempsey, 2013; Fuentes-George, 2013; Sullivan, 2006). As a social force and process tourism must therefore be integral to any understanding of global environmental change (Gössling and Hall, 2006a). Often despite, and in some cases perhaps because of, the very good intentions of those who seek to use tourism as a conservation tool, tourism is deeply embedded within processes of human-driven species loss that look set to become Earth's sixth great extinction event (Chapin et al., 2000; Ceballos et al., 2010; Hall, 2010a, 2010b). Tourism therefore reflects the wider complexity of the couplings between human and natural systems that vary across space, time and organizational units (Liu et al., 2007).

The chapter first describes the overall scale of biodiversity loss before examining the various interrelationships between tourism and biodiversity and some of the temporal and spatial issues involved in analysing impact. It then proceeds to discuss in closer detail some of main categories by which tourism's effect on biodiversity can be understood. The chapter ends by discussing perhaps the most significant of these, biological exchange, although perhaps an even deeper view of time that incorporated evolutionary processes would note tourism's role in the artificial selection of species.

The scale of biodiversity loss

In October 2014 the international media carried a report that the global wild animal populations had declined in absolute numbers by 52 percent in the previous 40 years. Populations of freshwater species had suffered an even worse fall of 76 per cent. The figure came from a Zoological Society of London (ZSL) and World Wildlife Fund (2014) report that found that there were half as many mammals, birds, reptiles, amphibians and fish in 2010 as there were in 1970. The report's 'Living Planet Index' tracks more than 10,000 vertebrate species populations from 1970 to 2010. Although the finding was based on incomplete data, only 181 of the 3,038 species investigated came from low-income countries, what was notable was 'while there are those who argue about whether the precise figure is accurate, there seem to be few who doubt the general trend' (BBC, 2014). Similarly, the fourth iteration of the global biodiversity outlook of the Secretariat of the Convention on Biological Diversity, also published in October 2014, reported that progress with respect to government implementation of measures to reduce biodiversity loss was poor.

> in most cases ... progress will not be sufficient to achieve the targets set for 2020, and additional action is required to keep the Strategic Plan for Biodiversity 2011–2020 on course ... Extrapolations for a range of indicators suggest that based on current trends, pressures on biodiversity will continue to increase at least until 2020, and that the status of biodiversity will continue to decline.
>
> (CBD, 2014, 10)

> Despite individual success stories, the average risk of extinction for birds, mammals and amphibians is still increasing ... Genetic diversity of domesticated livestock is eroding, with more than one-fifth of breeds at risk of extinction and the wild relatives of domesticated crop species are increasingly threatened by habitat fragmentation and climate change.
>
> (CBD, 2014, 14)

Major transformations have also occurred at biome scale. Ellis *et al.* (2010) identified that in 1700 nearly half of the terrestrial biosphere was wild, without permanent human settlements or substantial land use. Most of the remainder (45 percent) was in a semi-natural state with limited agricultural use and settlements. By 2000, the opposite was true, with the majority of the biosphere utilized by agriculture and settlements, less than 20 percent was semi-natural and only a 25 percent left as wilderness. According to Ellis *et al.* (2010) anthropogenic transformation of the biosphere during the Industrial Revolution resulted about equally from land-use expansion into wilderness areas and intensification of land use within semi-natural biomes (see Goldewijk *et al.*, 2011, for an alternative dating of biotic change).

Current estimates put the extinction rate at 100–1,000 times greater than the natural background level (Pimm *et al.*, 1995, 2014; Mace *et al.*, 2005), and the rate is projected to increase tenfold more this century (Mace *et al.*, 2005; Barnosky *et al.*, 2011; Ceballos *et al.*, 2010; Pimm *et al.*, 2014). The five principal pressures directly driving biodiversity loss – habitat change, overexploitation, pollution, invasive alien species and climate change – are all factors to which tourism is a significant contributor (Hall, 2010a), and 'are either constant or increasing in intensity' (CBD, 2010, 9). Given this situation it therefore becomes urgent to assess tourism's short- and long-term role in biodiversity conservation and loss as a marker of the Anthropocene and global environmental change.

Tourism and biodiversity

According to Christ *et al.* (2003, 41), 'Biodiversity is essential for the continued development of the tourism industry', although there is 'an apparent lack of awareness of the links – positive and negative – between tourism development and biodiversity conservation'. Tourism is usually regarded as a utilitarian anthropocentric or economic justification for valuing biodiversity, particularly with its long recognized role in the creation of national parks and protected areas as well as helping to conserve charismatic mega-fauna, such as dolphins, elephants, gorillas, lions, orang-utan, rhinoceros, tigers and whales (Leader-Williams and Dublin, 2000); charismatic mega-flora, e.g. California Redwoods, Joshua Tree (Hall *et al.*, 2011), and specific landscapes and ecosystems, such as barrier reefs, which may be significant attractions in their own right (e.g. Fennell, 1999; Hall and Boyd, 2005; Balmford *et al.*, 2009; Buckley, 2009; Frost and Hall, 2009).

The commodification of nature as spectacle by tourism is clearly integral to nature-based tourism, where representations of, and connection to, places, people and causes has long been mediated through commodified images (Brockington and Duffy, 2010; Igoe, 2010). However, as discussed below, commodification via tourism is also integral to the creation of many of the protected areas that are supposedly essential to biodiversity conservation. Igoe *et al.* (2010, 502) argue that in consuming these images tourists are given 'the romantic illusion that they are adventurously saving the world', while the deleterious ecological impacts of these very purchases, particularly their carbon emissions and ecological footprint, and the lifestyles they require, are ignored or 'neatly erased' (Brockington and Duffy, 2010, 472) in the dominant discourses of ecotourism.

> By focusing consumers' attention on distant and exotic locales, the spectacular productions . . . conceal the complex and proximate connections of people's daily lives to environmental problems, while suggesting that the solutions to environmental problems lay in the consumption of the kinds of commodities that helped produce them in the first place.
>
> (Igoe *et al.*, 2010, 504)

One of the paradoxes facing an assessment of tourism contribution to biodiversity loss as a marker of the Anthropocene is that, although tourism may benefit biodiversity conservation via the maintenance of 'protected' natural areas, many of the factors linked to biodiversity loss such as land clearance, pollution and climate change are also related to tourism development (Gössling and Hall, 2006a; Gössling *et al.*, 2010). Tourism therefore provides both positive and negative contributions to biodiversity conservation (Table 4.1) (Hall, 2006b). Unfortunately, the full evaluation of the contribution of tourism to conservation is hindered by insufficient consideration of the spatial and temporal scales and connections at which effects occur (Hall and Lew, 2009).

As Table 4.1 indicates, many of the usually described positive benefits of tourism for biodiversity and natural ecosystems are relatively immediate. The difficulty is that most positive assessments of the benefits of tourism (e.g. Christ *et al.*, 2003) rest on it being a better economic alternative than other development options, such as forest clear felling or conversion of land to agriculture, and do not recognize a number of the longer term negative contributions of tourism that are not immediately captured in impact assessments. These include tourism acting as a means of artificial selection, for example, because it provides a utilitarian focus on conserving charismatic species that possess public relations and tourism value above other species that do not have such attraction. Tourism's contribution to climate change and the introduction of alien species also constitutes a long-term effect on biodiversity that is not usually accounted for in terms of tourism impact. The specific loss of ecosystems and species as a result of tourism-related development tends to occur in amenity areas such as the coast, although even here long-term change is likely to come as much from ecosystem fragmentation as from direct ecosystem change (e.g. Gibson *et al.*, 2013). Some of these contributions to environmental change and biodiversity loss are discussed in more detail below.

As noted above, it has long been recognized that extinction and colonization of habitats is an ongoing process. But just as importantly it has also been recognized that without human interference such processes tend to lead to a relative equilibrium between extinction and immigration over the long term while the habitat remains in a steady state. Globally, habitat conversion exceeds habitat protection by a ratio of 8:1 in temperate grasslands and Mediterranean biomes, and 10:1 in more than 140 ecoregions (Hoekstra *et al.*, 2005). Human influences, including the role of tourism as a factor in development, are changing this balance with respect to both extinction and the introduction of new species at a rate that is making it extremely difficult, if not impossible, for new equilibria to be established (Hall, 2010c). Although tourism rarely directly kills off species, tourism-related developments and land use contribute to species range contraction and extinctions through habitat loss and fragmentation, often through processes of resort development and tourism urbanization. Such processes are spatially and geographically distinct, being related to high natural amenity areas such as the coast where coastal ecosystems are subject to tourism and resort developments, land clearance and wetland loss. Airold and Beck (2007) estimated that every day between 1960 and 1995, a kilometre of European coastline was developed, with most countries estimating losses of coastal wetlands and seagrasses exceeding 50 per cent of the original area, with peaks above 80 per cent for many regions. Many European coastal habitats have been lost or severely degraded, and it is estimated that only a small percentage of the European coastline (< 15 per cent) is in 'good' condition (Airoldi and Beck, 2007).

Europe provides some of the best data for tourism-related habitat loss. Focusing on coastal zones, 22,000 km^2 of Europe's coastal zone is estimated to be covered in concrete or asphalt, with artificial surfaces increasing by almost 1,900 km^2 between 1990 and 2000 alone (Airoldi and Beck, 2007). Approximately two-thirds of the Mediterranean coastline is urbanized, exceeding 75 per cent in the regions with the most developed industries (Hall, 2006a). Airoldi and Beck (2007)

Table 4.1 Positive and negative contributions of tourism to biodiversity conservation

	Time scale in which impact is identified	Comments
Usually regarded as positive		
• An economic justification for biodiversity conservation practices, including the establishment of national parks and reserves (public and private)	Short to long-term	Provides for the conservation of certain landscapes and associated ecosystems, usually with overall low utilitarian values for exploitative economic development, e.g. agriculture, forestry.
• A source of financial and political support for biodiversity maintenance and conservation	Short-term	Dependent on ongoing tourist and industry interest, also contributes to the ongoing neoliberalization of nature by which value is primarily accrued in economic terms rather than with respect to the intrinsic value of nature.
• An economic alternative to other forms of development that negatively impact biodiversity and to inappropriate exploitation or harvesting of wildlife, such as poaching	Short-term	Generally short-term as conservation actions are only maintained while tourism is more economically attractive than other options. Should conditions change other options will dominate.
• A mechanism for educating people about the benefits of biodiversity conservation	Short to long-term	May have immediate impact on environmental behaviour but long-term maintenance of that behaviour is unknown.
• Potentially involves local people in the maintenance of biodiversity and incorporating local ecological knowledge in biodiversity management practices	Short-term; longer-term unknown	May have immediate impact on environmental behaviour but long-term maintenance of that behaviour in the face of other economic alternatives is unknown
Portrayed as both positive and negative		
Focus on charismatic mega-fauna and flora	Short- and long-term	Focus on individual species may fail to appreciate broader ecological significance of ecosystems though may assist specific species to survive in short-term. May be regarded as a form of artificial selection by which species with some attributes (e.g. 'cuteness') are favoured to survive over others

Usually regarded as negative

• Outside of national parks and reserves contributes to the fragmentation of natural areas and a reduction in their size	Long-term	Can lead to isolation of gene pools and species loss. Also provides greater opportunities for introductions of invasive species.
• Contributes to changes in ecosystem conditions, particularly ecosystems in high value amenity areas such as the coast and alpine areas, as well as more localized effects such as trampling	Short to long-term	Direct contributor to ecosystem change and loss, e.g. replacement of dune systems or wetlands with golf courses. Ecosystem loss will directly affect some plant and animal species.
• Is a major vector for the introduction of exotic species and diseases. In some cases introductions may be deliberate, e.g. for hunting, fishing or aesthetic reasons.	Short to long-term	Some disease introductions may have immediate impact. The effects of the introduction of competing exotic species usually take years to be fully appreciated but can lead to significant long-term ecosystem change.
• Is a significant contributor to climate change	Long-term	The effects of climate change will be experienced over centuries
• The presence of tourists can lead to changes in animal behaviour	Medium-term	Animals will modify behaviours to avoid tourists, or in the case of feeding potential respond to them
• Consumptive tourism such as hunting and fishing if poorly managed can lead to species loss	Long-term	Hunting and fishing may act as a form of artificial selection in evolutionary terms; over-exploitation will also affect gene pools

Source: after Hall 2010a

suggest that more than 50 per cent of the Mediterranean coasts are dominated by concrete with more than 1,500 km of artificial coasts, of which about 1,250 km has been developed for harbours, marinas and ports. They also suggest that industrial and tourism-related urban development of industry have taken up to 90 per cent of the coastline in some regions (including the French Riviera, Athens, Barcelona, Marseille, Naples, the north Adriatic shorelines). Over 25 years ago Jeftic *et al.* (1990) suggested that tourist developments occupied 42 per cent of the entire Spanish coast, rising to 58 per cent in Catalonia. In Cyprus 95 per cent of the tourism industry is located within two kilometres of the coast. At the turn of the 21st century over 43 per cent of the Italian coastline was completely urbanized, 28 per cent partly urbanized and less than 29 per cent was free of construction. There are only six stretches of the Italian coast over 20 km long that are free of construction and only 33 stretches between 10 and 20 km long. Similar rates of coastal urbanization are also to be found elsewhere in the Mediterranean (Hall, 2006a). Tourism also contributes to habitat loss and fragmentation via its ecological footprint in terms of resource requirements and pollution and waste (Gössling and Hall, 2006a, 2006b; Gössling *et al.*, 2015).

Tourism and biological invasion

The introduction of alien species into an environment is a major influence on biodiversity that is associated with tourism because of the capacity of tourists and the infrastructure of tourism to act as carriers of exotic species. Since the 17th century, invasive alien species have contributed to nearly 40 per cent of all animal extinctions for which the cause is known (CBD, 2006). It is estimated that approximately 480,000 species have been accidentally or deliberately introduced to locations that lie beyond the natural limits of their geographic range (Pimentel *et al.*, 2001). Many of these species have been extremely beneficial, for example with respect to food production. However, alien species have also led to major economic losses (Vilà *et al.*, 2010; Heikkilä, 2011). Pimentel *et al.* (2001) estimate that non-native species invasions in the United States, the United Kingdom, Australia, South Africa, India, and Brazil cause more than US$314 billion per year in damages. In the United States alone Pimentel *et al.* (2005) estimate that invading alien species cause losses adding up to almost US$120 billion per year. In a study of the socio-economic parameters influencing plant invasions in Europe and North Africa Vilà and Pujadas (2001a) found that the density of naturalized species was moderately positively correlated to the number of tourists that visit a country ($r = 0.49$). Vilà and Pujadas (2001b, 399) also found that, 'Mediterranean basin countries such as France, Italy and Spain that receive many tourists are the ones with the highest density of alien species. Contrary to our expectations the correlation between the density of alien plants and the percentage cover of protected land was positive.'

Tourism contributes to biological invasion in three main ways (Hall and Baird, 2013):

1   By providing a justification for the planned introduction of new species or the reintroduction of species to their former range.

2   By being a vector for unplanned biological invasion.

3   By disturbing habitat and therefore making it easier for invasive species to become established.

The socio-economic benefits of tourism activities, such as hunting, fishing and landscape 'improvement' have long provided a reason for the introduction of exotic species. For example, desirable sport fish species, such as salmon and trout, have been deliberately introduced to locations outside of their natural range in order to enhance recreational fishing opportunities (Arismendi and Nahuelhual, 2007), usually with little or no consideration of indigenous fauna and flora (Gillespie, 2001). For example, the rainbow trout (*Oncorhynchus mykiss*) is one of the most widely introduced fish species in the world and, as of 2003, had been introduced into 82 countries (Cambray, 2003). Although highly prized as a sports fish and for eating, from an environmental perspective introduction of rainbow trout has led to hybridization, disease transmission, predation and competition with native species (Dunham *et al.*, 2004). Such sport fishing species, as Cambray (2003, 217) notes, 'have become part of the global consumer society'. Even though fishing for such species may represent an example of nature-based tourism, it does not contribute to the conservation of the indigenous biodiversity of regions outside of the introduced species natural range.

In an examination of tourism-related species introduction pathways into the Nordic region, Hall *et al.* (2010) identified numerous species that had potentially been introduced as a result of tourism activities, such as cruise ships (Drake and Lodge, 2007). These included 169 species introduced via ballast water and sediments, 29 by hull fouling, 172 by transport, 24 for hunting and 21 for angling or sport. Even given the potential for double counting between countries in the region, such figures highlight tourism's role as a vector or even justification for species introductions (Hall, 2011a).

Increased mobility perhaps serves as one of the greatest contributions of tourism to introduction of exotic fauna and flora. Species have always moved, whether via the action of wind, other species or flotsam. However, the number, speed and distance of species mobility has gone hand-in-hand with changes in human mobility (Hall, 2010a). Given the increased travel distances undertaken by people each year as indicated in many long-distance travel surveys (Gössling *et al.*, 2009), the likelihood of species being introduced in areas outside of their normal range has also increased. As Tatem *et al.* (2012, 1818) observed, 'The global air network enables many of the world's most isolated and diverse ecosystems to become connected and aids the movement of organisms, including disease vectors, to new habitats where they can become damaging invasive species, economically and healthwise.' Such issues are not usually factored in to the usual assessments of the value of tourism for biodiversity conservation, even though the threat of introduction of disease or invasive species is recognized in natural science (Hall, 2007). Indeed, the disassociation from issues of production that often characterizes contemporary consumption of nature-based tourism (as well as much academic commentary) means that consumer satisfaction and even the consumption experience may be unencumbered by 'reality' (Borgmann, 2000). However, in examining and enlarging the understanding of the consumption of nature-based tourism in both a spatial and temporal context, it is possible to problematize the extent to which tourism actually contributes towards the maintenance of biodiversity.

Increased movement of species is only one part of successful biological exchange. For a species to become established it will also require a suitable habitat. For this to occur the micro- and/or macro-environmental conditions may need to change. Tourism's role in environmental change therefore means that it is implicated at both of these spatial scales, at the macro level via climate change and at the micro level via processes of tourism development. Within short time scales habitat disturbance is best understood in terms of direct human activities such as infrastructure construction (Morgan and Carnegie, 2009) or overuse, e.g. high levels of trampling as in some coastal dune systems (Doody, 2012). However, if using longer time scales then the role of tourism related change in habitat loss and disturbance are critical as Anthropocenic markers. This is particularly significant for locations in which climate change is the most rapid, such as alpine and high latitude regions (Hall, 2015).

Tourism, climate change and biodiversity

Tourism also affects biodiversity through its contribution to climate change, to which it contributes approximately 8 per cent of the effects of emissions, and consequent effects on habitats and species (UNWTO–UNEP–WMO, 2008; Scott et al., 2010; Hall et al., 2011). Significantly the emissions from tourism are predicted to increase in the foreseeable future in absolute terms as the continued growth of international and domestic travel and tourism and aviation substantially exceeds any expected efficiency gains (Gössling et al., 2013).

Substantial research has been undertaken on the implications of climate change for species geographic ranges which has typically sought to model the relationships between climate and distribution, in relation to such issues as habitat fragmentation and loss (Travis, 2003), species distribution, pests and disease (Walther et al., 2009), and the establishment and development of protected areas in such a way that they 'can accommodate the changes in species distributions that will follow from climate change' (Gaston, 2003, 181). The implications are immense. For example, approximately 80 per cent of Canada's national parks are expected to experience shifts in dominant vegetation under scenarios of double levels of CO_2 while analysis of vegetation response to climate change in Yellowstone National Park region suggests regional extinctions and the emergence of communities with no current analogue (Hannah et al., 2002).

Some tree species already exhibit movement towards higher latitudes and higher altitudes (Beckage et al., 2008). For example, in the 20th century uphill migration of treelines in Scandinavia has been observed on the order of 150–200m

(Kullman, 2004). Some ecosystems that have either very limited distribution, as at the top of mountain ranges, or are potentially subject to extremely rapid change, such as some coastal ecosystems, are likely to have little or no capacity to move. This may be significant for niche nature-based tourism products based in vulnerable environments. In the case of Australia for example this would include such significant tourism areas as the tropical and temperate rainforests as well the relatively low-lying alpine areas in south-east Australia and the Stirling and Porongup Ranges in western Australia (Hughes, 2003). In eastern Australia the rainforests of the North Queensland Wet Tropics are a World Heritage Site that is under substantial threat from climate change (Steffen *et al.*, 2009). The region is dominated by mountain ranges up to 1,600m, with altitude being the strongest environmental gradient affecting species composition and patterns of biodiversity (Williams, 2009). These mountain forests contain the highest numbers of endemic species in the Wet Tropics. With climate change cloud forests and other highland rainforests types are predicted to become greatly reduced in area and more fragmented across the Wet Tropics. Anything greater than a 2°C temperature increase (so-called 'safe' climate change) will lead to dramatic declines in species distribution, with some completely losing their current climatic environment. To put it crudely, there is nowhere left for them to go.

However, while there has been academic (Scott *et al.*, 2012) and, to a limited extent, institutional interest in supporting research on the interrelationships between tourism and climate change (UNWTO–UNEP–WMO; World Economic Forum, 2009), there has not been a corresponding level of interest with respect to tourism's role in biodiversity conservation and loss (Hall, 2010a; IUCN World Commission on Protected Areas, 2012).

Conserving biodiversity: national parks and reserves

One of the few positive indicators with respect to biodiversity conservation is the protection of areas of conservation value. According to the Secretariat of the Convention on Biological Diversity, a target of

> conserving 17 per cent of terrestrial areas by 2020 is likely to be met globally, although protected area networks remain ecologically unrepresentative and many critical sites for biodiversity are poorly conserved. The element to protect 10 per cent of coastal and marine areas is on course to be met in coastal waters, although open ocean and deep sea areas, including the high seas, are not well covered. Inadequate management of protected areas remains widespread.
>
> (CBD, 2014, 14)

As noted above, tourism, and ecotourism in particular, has provided a short-term economic rationale for the establishment of national parks and reserves that serve to conserve species and habitats (Loureiro *et al.*, 2012; Teelucksingh and Watson, 2013; Bayliss *et al.*, 2014).

The global conservation estate has grown enormously since the first UN List of Protected Areas was published in 1962 with 9,214 protected areas covering an area of 2.4 million km². The 2003 edition listed 102,102 sites covering 18.8 million km². 'This figure is equivalent to 12.65 percent of the Earth's land surface, or an area greater than the combined land area of China, South Asia and Southeast Asia' (Chape *et al.*, 2003, 21). Of the total area protected it is estimated that 17.1 million km² constitute terrestrial protected areas, or 11.5 per cent of the global land surface, although some biomes, including lake systems and temperate grasslands, remain poorly represented. Marine areas are also significantly under-represented in the global protected area system, with an estimated 0.5 per cent of the world's oceans included in protected areas (Chape *et al.*, 2003). Nevertheless, the present size of the global conservation estate exceeds the IUCN's earlier target of at least 10 per cent of the total land area being set aside for conservation purposes (CBD, 2014), although there are clearly substantial variations between both countries and biomes in terms of the actual area set aside (Chape *et al.*, 2003). It has been suggested that the IUCN's target has been dictated more by political considerations than biological science (Soulé and Sanjayan, 1998). Rodrigues and Gaston (2001, 2002) observed that the minimum area needed to represent all species within a region increases with the number of targeted species, the level of endemism, and the size of the selection units. They concluded that

- no global target for the size of a network is appropriate as those regions with higher levels of endemism and/or higher diversity will correspondingly require larger areas to protect such characteristics;
- a minimum size conservation network sufficient for capturing the diversity of vertebrates will not be sufficient for biodiversity in general, because other groups are known to have higher levels of endemism (see also Gaston, 2003); and
- the 10 per cent target is likely to be grossly inadequate to meet biodiversity conservation needs.

Studies of species–area relationships suggest that 30 to 50 per cent of a given community or ecosystem type needs to be conserved to maintain 80 to 90 per cent of the species (Soulé and Sanjayan, 1998). However, in their analysis of the conservation deficits for the continental USA Dietz and Czech (2005) noted that even 30 to 50 per cent may not be enough to sustain species in the long term, with research indicating that there is no single threshold value that can be broadly applied to conserve all species (Fahrig, 2001; Garda *et al.*, 2010).

It should also be noted that the areas set aside as protected areas in most countries have historically been those with relatively low biological diversity that would make them suitable for agricultural and timber production (Hall, 1992; Frost and Hall, 2009), although they may still contain rare and endangered species. This means that reserve selection has usually been biased towards locations that are otherwise undesirable for commercial use (Joppa and Pfaff, 2009), a situation referred to by Hinds (1979) as the 'cesspool hypothesis' and Runte (1973) and Hall

(1989, 1992) as the 'worthless lands hypothesis' of national park and protected area establishment. The issue of protected areas being primarily allocated to residual areas, those places that are remote or unpromising for extractive activities, has also been noted in the establishment of marine reserves (Devillers *et al.*, 2014). The creation of national parks is a good example of how tourism does not offer a neat solution to conservation and environmental problems. Instead, it can be understood as a tool of capital to commodify nature for direct and indirect consumption. Since the early to mid-19th century the Romantic understanding of nature has been integral to the construction of landscape and nature for tourist consumption. Landscapes and national parks are cultural products that are employed by capital to attract mobile visitors to experience an idealized nature in which environmental processes have often been severely affected by human activity. In the contemporary context tourism relation to protected areas has been extended and deepened through neoliberal capitalism, defining and giving economic value to the 'services' ecosystems provide for humans (Brockington and Duffy, 2010; Dempsey and Robertson, 2012). However, for the vast majority of tourists and, arguably, for the many researchers that have sought to argue the value of ecosystem services as a justification for biodiversity conservation, the irony of such an approach has been missed. Given that capital and its activities has been identified as a major driver in the consumption of biodiversity, why then should biodiversity be conserved for tourism if, in reality, the higher values it is meant to provide are actually illusory and dependent on extremely narrow interpretations of relations between tourism and the environment?

The way that tourism acts to provide an economic value for nature is integral to the way that neoliberalism is fundamentally concerned with 'the financialisation of everything' (Harvey, 2005, 33). The problem with the rhetoric of valuing nature and tourism's contribution to biodiversity conservation under these terms is that industry and government promotion of nature-based tourism and ecotourism in particular as being a form of ethical consumption only focuses on the immediate purchase of economic services and short-term effects. 'It presents us only with market solutions, win–win solutions (or win–win– win and more), ethically traded commodities, saved nature, wholesome communities, integrated landscapes, sustainable development, cleansed reputations and secure conservation brands' (Brockington and Duffy, 2010, 481). When wider considerations such as the implications of tourism development for habitat loss and the mobility of tourists for emissions and invasive species are brought to bear, the consumption of natural capital may be anything but ethical.

Therefore, potentially one of the values of recognizing the environmental politics of the Anthropocene is that it may open up new tensions between the promises of neoliberal capitalism and the realities of human destruction of the natural environment, including as a result of tourism, at hitherto unknown scales. As Zalasiewicz *et al.* (2010, 2231) recognized 'It has the capacity to become the most politicized unit, by far, of the Geological Time Scales and therefore to take formal geological classification into uncharted waters'. Importantly, the new debates that the Anthropocene may bring must not be 'just' geological and natural science based but must instead appreciate and engage the conditions that led to such change. This includes not only tourism as an industry in a direct sense, and the effects it has had, but, perhaps even more importantly, recognizing that tourism is a major conduit for the commodification and neoliberalization of nature and the subsequent environmental losses that this brings.

Yet such an approach represents a major challenge to the way that much research on tourism and the environment is presented as well as the science of the Anthropocene itself as it causes us to rethink notions of impact as they have often been laid out. If the physical properties of biodiversity conservation and loss, as significant as they are, are treated in isolation from the surrounding social relations, this serves to conceal, normalize and thereby reproduce those unequal social relations that led to such loss in the first place (Demeritt, 2001). This does not mean that natural science understandings of the Anthropocene and tourism's role in environmental change, as discussed above, are without value. Instead, to gain an understanding of how tourism actually contributes to change in the Anthropocene it is necessary to move beyond narrow technical and reductionist approaches that embrace only some forms of knowledge and assumptions at the expense of others. This would include, for example, framing the problem of change in terms of alternatives, and no less relevant approaches, such as the structural imperatives of the capitalist economy that drive emissions, species exchange and biodiversity loss (Wainwright, 2010).

Loving nature to death?

The loss of biodiversity at gene, species and ecosystem levels is one of the most significant aspects of global environmental change. It is both a significant biostratigraphic marker of the Anthropocene as well as major long-term challenge for human well-being, given the extent to which biodiversity underpins the global economy and human welfare (Martens *et al.*, 2003; CBD, 2014). However, it has arguably not received the same attention in either public debate or tourism research as climate change, another dimension of global environmental change with which it is deeply interrelated (Scott *et al.*, 2012). Biodiversity, or at least the existence of certain charismatic species and ecosystems, is significant as an attraction for 'ecotourism' and 'nature-based tourism'. Nevertheless, the extent to which tourism contributes towards biodiversity loss through tourism urbanization, habitat loss and fragmentation and contribution to climate change is also dramatic and, arguably, makes attempts to paint a picture of tourism as an environmentally benign industry increasingly problematic (Hall, 2010a).

Undoubtedly, tourism can make a contribution to the conservation and maintenance of biodiversity but, in reality long-term success stories are few and far between and are generally isolated to individual species and relatively small areas of habitat rather than a comprehensive contribution to biodiversity conservation. Although tourism has led to biodiversity maintenance at a local level in some instances, the global picture is one in which tourism, like many other industries that have a large ecological footprint and lead to clearance of natural areas, is not necessarily a net contributor to biodiversity conservation once consideration of impact occurs over broader spatial and temporal scales (see Table 4.1), especially with respect to the contribution of emissions to climate change and the role of tourism as a vector for invasive species (Hall, 2015).

In business and policy terms the environmental impacts of tourism are usually only dealt with in narrow spatial and temporal scales. The big picture is usually only addressed by academics or as part of foresight efforts to envisage futures in 30 to 50 years' time, although even here the primary drivers are usually economic and strategic rather than conservation oriented. The failure of tourism to successfully balance its demands on the natural environment, or what can be termed from an ecological economics perspective as natural capital, also described as 'steady-state tourism' (Hall, 2009), is nothing new, and arguably underlies much thinking on sustainable tourism (Hall, 2011b). For example, although the concept of scarcity rent influenced much of earlier thinking with respect to the value of ecotourism, derived measures such as reducing access to desirable environment or wildlife in the face of high demand and charging more for the experience while reducing environmental impacts, have often foundered on cultural and political values that have historically favoured access (Hall, 2006b). Indeed, for most of their history national parks agencies have actively sought to encourage visitation so as to meet the recreational component of their mandate and to create a political environment supportive of national parks (Runte, 1973, 1997; Hall, 1992; Frost and Hall, 2009). Vicarious appreciation, even via the increasing possibilities of virtual consumption, does not appear sufficient to save species and their habitats; direct consumption of the spectacle of nature is therefore actively encouraged via tourism as a means of generating economic value for something that is otherwise valueless in direct monetary terms. Unfortunately, in the face of growing permanent and temporary populations and personal mobility, the consequences of increased access and mobility is becoming problematic for many conservation authorities, with their 'resolution' being found in the adoption of more market-oriented approaches to park and protected area management, which inevitably means embracing tourism – as a commercial enterprise – even more closely.

Yet, arguably, the commercial imperatives of tourism and its drivers appear not to be open to question. Despite evidence as to the long-term contribution to environmental change as a result of biological exchange, emissions or habitat change, the focus of policy-makers and much of academia stays on business as usual. The difficulties for widening the debate with respect to how tourism contributes to biodiversity loss as a marker of the Anthropocene however is that the appeals of formal quantitative evaluation methods, as opposed to more critical positionings, are social and political as much as technical and scientific. Just as significantly, as Demeritt (2001) suggests, it also makes them more credible from a public perspective of 'objective' natural science, 'insofar as adherence to rigidly uniform and impersonal and in that sense "procedurally objective" … rules limits the scope for individual bias or discretion and thereby guarantees the vigorous (self-)denial of personal perspective necessary to make knowledge seem universal, trustworthy and true' (Demeritt, 2001, 324). In addressing the

Anthropocene it becomes imperative to understand not just how the markers of environmental change are constructed but, more importantly, the ways in which tourism's relationships to the biological and physical environment are constructed and commoditized and the long-term implications this has for biodiversity and natural capital.

References

Airoldi, L., and Beck, M.W. 2007. Loss, status and trends for coastal marine habitats of Europe. *Oceanography and Marine Biology: An Annual Review*, 45, 345–405.

Arismendi, I., and Nahuelhual, L. 2007. Non-native salmon and trout recreational fishing in Lake Llanquihue, southern Chile: Economic benefits and management implications. *Reviews in Fisheries Science*, 15(4), 311–25.

Balmford, A., Beresford, J., Green, J., Naidoo, R., Walpole, M., and Manica, A. 2009. A global perspective on trends in nature-based tourism. *PLoS Biol*, 7(6), e1000144.

Barnosky, A.D., *et al.* 2011. Has the Earth's sixth mass extinction already arrived?. *Nature*, 471(7336), 51–7.

Bayliss, J., *et al.* 2014. The current and future value of nature-based tourism in the Eastern Arc Mountains of Tanzania. *Ecosystem Services*, 8, 75–83.

BBC 2014. Small data: Have we lost half the world's animals? *BBC News Magazine Monitor*, 6 Oct.

Beckage, B., Osborne, B., Gavin, G.G., Pucko, C., Siccama, T., and Perkins, T. 2008. A rapid upward shift of a forest ecotone during 40 years of warming in the Green Mountains of Vermont. *Proceedings of the National Academy of Sciences*, 105, 4197–4202.

Borgmann, A. 2000. The moral complexion of consumption. *Journal of Consumer Research*, 26, 418–22.

Brockington, D., and Duffy, R. 2010. Capitalism and conservation: The production and reproduction of biodiversity conservation. *Antipode*, 42, 469–84.

Brockington, D., Duffy, R., and Igoe, J. 2008. *Nature Unbound: Conservation, Capitalism and the Future of Protected Areas*. London: Earthscan.

Buckley, R. 2009. Evaluating the net effects of ecotourism on the environment: A framework, first assessment and future research. *Journal of Sustainable Tourism*, 17, 643–72.

Büscher, B., and Arsel, M. 2012. Introduction: Neoliberal conservation, uneven geographical development and the dynamics of contemporary capitalism. *Tijdschrift voor economische en sociale geografie*, 103(2), 129–35.

Cambray, J.A. 2003. Impact on indigenous species biodiversity caused by the globalisation of alien recreational freshwater fisheries. *Aquatic Biodiversity, Developments in Hydrobiology*, 171, 217–30.

CBD, Secretariat of the Convention on Biological Diversity 2006. *Global Biodiversity Outlook 2*. Montreal: SCBD.

CBD, Secretariat of the Convention on Biological Diversity 2010. *Global Biodiversity Outlook 3*. Montreal: Secretariat of the Convention on Biological Diversity.

CBD, Secretariat of the Convention on Biological Diversity 2014. *Global Biodiversity Outlook 4*. Montreal: Secretariat of the Convention on Biological Diversity.

Ceballos, G., García, A., and Ehrlich, P.R. 2010. The sixth extinction crisis loss of animal populations and species. *Journal of Cosmology*, 8, 1821–31.

Chape, S., Blyth, S., Fish, L., Fox, P., and Spalding, M. (eds) 2003. *2003 United Nations List of Protected Areas.* Gland and Cambridge: IUCN and UNEP-WCMC.

Chapin, F.S., III, *et al.* 2000. Consequences of changing biotic diversity. *Nature*, 405, 234–42.

Christ, C., Hilel, O., Matus, S., and Sweeting, J. 2003. *Tourism and Biodiversity: Mapping Tourism's Global Footprint.* Washington, DC: Conservation International.

Cox, G.W. 2004. *Alien Species and Evolution: The Evolutionary Ecology of Exotic Plants, Animals, Microbes and Interacting Native Species.* Washington, DC: Island Press.

Demeritt, D. 2001. The construction of global warming and the politics of science. *Annals of the Association of American Geographers*, 91(2), 307–37.

Dempsey, J. 2013. Biodiversity loss as material risk: Tracking the changing meanings and materialities of biodiversity conservation. *Geoforum*, 45, 41–51.

Dempsey, J., and Robertson, M. 2012. Ecosystem services: Tensions, impurities, and points of engagement within neoliberalism. *Progress in Human Geography*, 36, 758–79.

Devillers, R., Pressey, R., Grech, A., Kittinger, J., Edgar, G., Ward, T., and Watson, R. 2014. Reinventing residual reserves in the sea: Are we favouring ease of establishment over need for protection?. *Aquatic Conservation: Marine and Freshwater Ecosystems.*

Dietz, R.W., and Czech, B. 2005. Conservation deficits for the continental United States: An ecosystem gap analysis. *Conservation Biology*, 19, 1478–87.

Doody, J.P. 2012. *Sand Dune Conservation, Management and Restoration.* Dordrecht: Springer.

Drake, J.M., and Lodge, D.M. 2007. Hull fouling is a risk factor for intercontinental species exchange in aquatic ecosystems. *Aquatic Invasions*, 2, 121–31.

Duffy, R., and Moore, L. 2010. Neoliberalising nature? Elephant-back tourism in Thailand and Botswana. *Antipode*, 42, 742–66.

Dunham, J.B., Pilliod, D.S., and Young, M.K. 2004. Assessing the consequences of nonnative trout in headwater ecosystems in western North America. *Fisheries*, 29(6), 18–26.

Ellis, E.C., Goldewijk, K., Siebert, S., Lightman, D., and Ramankutty, N. 2010. Anthropogenic transformation of the biomes, 1700 to 2000. *Global Ecology and Biogeography*, 19(5), 589–606.

Fahrig, L. 2001. How much habitat is enough?. *Biological Conservation*, 100(1), 65–74.

Fennell, D. 1999. *Ecotourism: An Introduction.* London: Routledge.

Frost, W., and Hall, C.M. (eds) 2009. *Tourism and National Parks: International Perspectives on Development, Histories and Change.* London: Routledge.

Fuentes-George, K. 2013. Neoliberalism, environmental justice, and the Convention on Biological Diversity: How problematizing the commodification of nature affects regime effectiveness. *Global Environmental Politics*, 13(4), 144–63.

Garda, A.A., Da Silva, J., and Baião, P. 2010. Biodiversity conservation and sustainable development in the Amazon. *Systematics and Biodiversity*, 8(2), 169–75.

Gaston, K.J. 2003. *The Structure and Dynamics of Geographic Ranges.* Oxford: Oxford University Press.

Gibson, L., *et al.* 2013. Near-complete extinction of native small mammal fauna 25 years after forest fragmentation. *Science*, 341(6153), 1508–10.

Gillespie, G.R. 2001. The role of introduced trout in the decline of the spotted tree frog (*Litoria Spenceri*) in south- eastern Australia. *Biological Conservation*, 100, 187–98.

Goldewijk, K.K., Beusen, A., Van Drecht, G., and De Vos, M. 2011. The HYDE 3.1 spatially explicit database of human-induced global land-use change over the past 12,000 years. *Global Ecology and Biogeography*, 20(1), 73–86.

70   *C. Michael Hall*

Gössling, S., and Hall, C.M. (eds) 2006a. *Tourism and Global Environmental Change.* London: Routledge.

Gössling, S., and Hall, C.M. 2006b. An introduction to tourism and global environmenta! change. In S. Gössling and C.M. Hall (eds), *Tourism and Global Environmenta. Change: Ecological, Economic, Social and Political Interrelationships.* London Routledge, 1–33.

Gössling, S., Ceron, J.-P., Dubios, G., and Hall, C.M. 2009. Hypermobile travelers. In S. Gössling and P. Upham (eds), *Climate Change and Aviation.* London. Earthscan 131–49.

Gössling, S., Hall, C.M., Peeters, P., and Scott, D. 2010. The future of tourism: Can tourism growth and climate policy be reconciled? A climate change mitigation perspective *Tourism Recreation Research*, 35(2), 119–30.

Gössling, S., Hall, C.M., and Scott, D. 2015. *Tourism and Water.* Bristol: Channelview.

Gössling, S., Scott, D., and Hall, C.M. 2013. Challenges of tourism in a low-carbor economy. *WIRES Climate Change*, 4(6), 525–38.

Hall, C.M. 1989. The worthless lands hypothesis and Australia's national parks an(reserves. In K. Frawley and N. Semple (eds), *Australia's Ever Changing Forests* Canberra: Australian Defence Force Academy, 441–56.

Hall, C.M. 1992. *Wasteland to World Heritage: Preserving Australia's Wilderness.* Carlton Melbourne University Press.

Hall, C.M. 2006a. Tourism urbanization and global environmental change. In S. Gössling and C.M. Hall (eds), *Tourism and Global Environmental Change: Ecological Economic, Social and Political Interrelationships.* Abingdon: Routledge, 142–56.

Hall, C.M. 2006b. Tourism, biodiversity and global environmental change. In S. Gössling and C.M. Hall (eds), *Tourism and Global Environmental Change: Ecological, Economic Social and Political Interrelationships.* Abingdon, Oxon: Routledge, 211–26.

Hall, C.M. 2007. Biosecurity and ecotourism. In J. Higham (ed.), *Critical Issues in Ecotourism.* Oxford: Elsevier, 102–16.

Hall, C.M. 2009. Degrowing tourism: Décroissance, sustainable consumption and steady state tourism. *Anatolia: An International Journal of Tourism and Hospitality Research* 20(1), 46–61.

Hall, C.M. 2010a. Tourism and biodiversity: More significant than climate change? *Journal of Heritage Tourism*, 5(4), 253–66.

Hall, C.M. 2010b. Tourism and the implementation of the Convention on Biologica Diversity. *Journal of Heritage Tourism*, 5(4), 267–84.

Hall, C.M. 2010c. An island biogeographical approach to island tourism and biodiversity An exploratory study of the Caribbean and Pacific Islands. *Asia Pacific Journal o Tourism Research*, 15(3). 383–99.

Hall, C.M. 2011a. Biosecurity, tourism and mobility: Institutional arrangements fo managing biological invasions. *Journal of Policy Research in Tourism, Leisure an Events*, 3(3), 256–80.

Hall, C.M. 2011b. Policy learning and policy failure in sustainable tourism governance From first and second to third order change?. *Journal of Sustainable Tourism*, 19, 649 71.

Hall, C.M. 2013. The natural science ontology of environment. In A. Holden and D Fennell (eds), *The Routledge Handbook of Tourism and the Environment.* Abingdon Oxon: Routledge, 6–18.

Hall, C.M. 2014. You can check out any time you like but you can never leave: Ca ethical consumption in tourism ever be sustainable? In C. Weeden and K. Boluk (eds

Managing Ethical Consumption in Tourism: Compromise and Tension. Abingdon, Oxon: Routledge, 32–56.

Hall, C.M. 2015. Tourism and biological exchange and Invasions: A missing dimension in sustainable tourism? *Tourism Recreation Research*, 40(1), 81–94.

Hall, C.M., and Baird, T. 2013. Ecotourism, biological invasions and biosecurity. In R. Ballantyne and J. Packer (eds), *The International Handbook of Ecotourism.* Aldershot: Ashgate, 66–78.

Hall, C.M., and Boyd, S. 2005. Nature-based tourism and regional development in peripheral areas: Introduction. In C.M. Hall and S. Boyd (eds), *Tourism and Nature-Based Tourism in Peripheral Areas: Development or Disaster.* Clevedon: Channelview Publications, 3–17.

Hall, C.M., and Lew, A. 2009. *Understanding and Managing Tourism Impacts: An Integrated Approach.* London: Routledge.

Hall, C.M. and Saarinen, J. (eds) 2010. *Polar Tourism and Change: Climate, Environments and Experiences.* London: Routledge.

Hall, C.M., James, M., and Baird, T. 2011. Forests and trees as charismatic mega-flora: Implications for heritage tourism and conservation. *Journal of Heritage Tourism*, 6(4), 309–23.

Hall, C.M., James, M., and Wilson, S. 2010. Biodiversity, biosecurity, and cruising in the Arctic and sub-Arctic. *Journal of Heritage Tourism*, 5, 351–64.

Hall, C.M., Scott, D. and Gössling, S. 2011. Forests, climate change and tourism. *Journal of Heritage Tourism*, 6(4), 353–63.

Hannah, L., *et al.* 2002. Conservation and biodiversity in a changing climate. *Conservation Biology*, 16, 264–8.

Harvey, D. 2005. *A Brief History of Neoliberalism.* Oxford: Oxford University Press.

Head, L. 2008. Is the concept of human impacts past its use-by date? *The Holocene*, 18(3), 373–7.

Heikkilä, J. 2011. Economics of biosecurity across levels of decision-making: A review. *Agronomy and Sustainable Development*, 31, 119–38.

Hinds, W.E. 1979. The cesspool hypothesis versus natural areas for research in the United States. *Environmental Conservation*, 6(1), 13–20.

Hoekstra, J.M., Boucher, T., Ricketts, T., and Roberts, C. 2005. Confronting a biome crisis: Global disparities of habitat loss and protection. *Ecology Letters*, 8(1), 23–9.

Hughes, L. 2003. Climate change and Australia: Trends, projections and impacts. *Austral Ecology*, 28, 423–43.

Igoe, J. 2010. The spectacle of nature in the global economy of appearances: Anthropological engagements with the spectacular mediations of transnational conservation. *Critique of Anthropology*, 30, 375–97.

IUCN World Commission on Protected Areas 2012. *PARKS: The International Journal of Protected Areas and Conservation*, 18(2). Gland: IUCN.

Jeftic, L., *et al.* 1990. *State of the Marine Environment in the Mediterranean Region.* UNEP Regional Seas Reports and Studies, 132/1990, and MAP Technical Reports Series, 28/1989. Athens: UNEP.

Joppa, L.N., and Pfaff, A. 2009. High and far: Biases in the location of protected areas. *PLoS ONE*, 4(12), e8273.

Kullman, L. 2004. Tree-limit landscape evolution at the southern fringe of the Swedish Scandes (Dalarna province): Holocene and 20th century perspectives. *Fennia*, 182, 73–94.

Lande, R. 1998. Anthropogenic, ecological and genetic factors in extinction. In G.M. Mace, A. Balmford and J.R. Ginsberg (eds), *Conservation in a Changing World*. Cambridge: Cambridge University Press, 29–51.

Leader-Williams, N., and Dublin, H. 2000. Charismatic megafauna as 'flagship species'. In A. Entwistle and N. Dunstone (eds), *Priorities for the Conservation of Mammalian Diversity: Has the Panda Had its Day?* Cambridge: Cambridge University Press, 53–81.

Liu, J., *et al.* 2007. Complexity of coupled human and natural systems. *Science*, 317(5844), 1513–16.

Loureiro, M.L., Macagno, G., Nunes, P., and Tol, R. 2012. Assessing the impact of biodiversity on tourism flows: An econometric model for tourist behaviour with implications for conservation policy. *Journal of Environmental Economics and Policy*, 1, 174–94.

Mace, G., *et al.* 2005. Biodiversity. In R. Hassan, R. Scholes and N. Ash (eds), *Ecosystems and Human Well-Being: Current State and Trends. Findings of the Condition and Trends Working Group*. Washington, DC: Island Press, 77–122.

Martens, P., Rotmans, J., and Groot, D. de 2003. Biodiversity: Luxury or necessity?. *Global Environmental Change*, 13, 75–81.

Morgan, J.W., and Carnegie, V. 2009. Backcountry huts as introduction points for invasion by non-native species into subalpine vegetation. *Arctic, Antarctic, and Alpine Research*, 41(2), 238–45.

Pimentel, D., *et al.* 2001. Economic and environmental threats of alien plant, animal, and microbe invasions. *Agriculture, Ecosystems and Environment*, 84, 1–20.

Pimentel, D., Zuniga, R., and Morrison, D. 2005. Update on the environmental and economic costs associated with alien invasive species in the United States. *Ecological Economics*, 52, 273–88.

Pimm, S.L., *et al.* 2014. The biodiversity of species and their rates of extinction, distribution, and protection. *Science*, 344(6187), 1246752.

Pimm, S.L., Russell, G., Gittleman, J., and Brooks, T. 1995. The future of biodiversity. *Science*, 269, 347–50.

Rodrigues, A.S.L., and Gaston, K.J. 2001. How large do reserve networks need to be?. *Ecological Letters*, 4, 602–9.

Rodrigues, A.S.L., and Gaston, K.J. 2002. Rarity and conservation planning across geopolitical units. *Conservation Biology*, 16, 674–82.

Runte, A. 1973. 'Worthless' lands – Our national parks: The enigmatic past and uncertain future of America's scenic wonderlands. *American West*, 10 May, 4–11.

Runte, A. 1997. *National Parks: The American Experience*, 3rd edn. Lincoln, NE: University of Nebraska Press.

Scott, D., Hall, C.M., and Gössling, S. 2012. *Tourism and Climate Change: Impacts, Adaptation and Mitigation*. Abingdon, Oxon: Routledge.

Scott, D., Peeters, P., and Gössling, S. 2010. Can tourism deliver its 'aspirational' greenhouse gas emission reduction targets? *Journal of Sustainable Tourism*, 18, 393–408.

Soulé, M., and Sanjayan, M.A. 1998. Ecology-conservation targets: Do they help?. *Science*, 279, 2060–1.

Steffen, W., *et al.* 2009. *Australia's Biodiversity and Climate Change: A Strategic Assessment of the Vulnerability of Australia's Biodiversity to Climate Change*. Canberra: CSIRO Publishing.

Sullivan, S. 2006. Elephant in the room? Problematising 'new' (neoliberal) biodiversity conservation. *Forum for Development Studies*, 33, 105–35.

Tatem, A.J., Huang, Z., Das, A., Qi, Q., Roth, J., and Qiu, Y. 2012. Air travel and vector-borne disease movement. *Parasitology*, 139, 1816–30.

Teelucksingh, S.S., and Watson, P.K. 2013. Linking tourism flows and biological biodiversity in Small Island Developing States (SIDS): Evidence from panel data. *Environment and Development Economics*, 18, 392–404.

Travis, J. 2003. Climate change and habitat destruction: A deadly anthropogenic cocktail. *Proceedings of the British Royal Society B*, 270, 467–73.

United Nations World Tourism Organization, United Nations Environment Programme, and World Meterological Organization (UNWTO-UNEP-WMO) 2008. *Climate Change and Tourism: Responding to Global Challenges*. Madrid: UNWTO.

Vilà, M., *et al.* 2010. How well do we understand the impacts of alien species on ecosystem services? A pan-European, cross-taxa assessment. *Frontiers in Ecology and the Environment*, 8(3), 135–44.

Vilà, M., and Pujadas, J. 2001a. Socio-economic parameters influencing plant invasions in Europe and North Africa. In J.A. McNeely (ed.), *The Great Reshuffling: Human Dimensions of Invasive Alien Species*. Gland: IUCN Biodiversity Policy Coordination Division, 75–9.

Vilà, M., and Pujadas, J. 2001b. Land-use and socio-economic correlates of plant invasions in European and North African countries. *Biological Conservation*, 100, 397–401.

Wainwright, J. 2010. Climate change, capitalism, and the challenge of transdisciplinarity. *Annals of the Association of American Geographers*, 100(4), 983–91.

Walther, G.R., *et al.* 2009. Alien species in a warmer world: risks and opportunities. *Trends in Ecology and Evolution*, 24, 686–93.

Weyl, H. 2009. *Philosophy of Mathematics and Natural Science*, rev. and augmented English edn based on a translation of Olaf Helmer. Princeton, NJ: Princeton University Press.

Williams, S.E. 2009. Climate change in the rainforests of the North Queensland Wet Tropics. In W. Steffen *et al.*, *Australia's Biodiversity and Climate Change: A Strategic Assessment of the Vulnerability of Australia's Biodiversity to Climate Change*. Canberra: CSIRO Publishing.

World Economic Forum 2009. *Towards a Low Carbon Travel and Tourism Sector*. Davos: World Economic Forum.

Zalasiewicz, J., *et al.* 2008. Are we now living in the Anthropocene?. *GSA Today*, 18, 4–8.

Zalasiewicz, J., Williams, M., Steffen, W., and Crutzen, P. 2010. The new world of the Anthropocene. *Environmental Science and Technology*, 44, 2228–31.

Zoological Society of London (ZSL) and WWF 2014. *Living Planet Report*. London: ZSL and WWF.

Part II
Sustaining tourism in the Anthropocene

Figure II.1 Cap Thordsen, Svalbard, September 2011 – Being in the Anthropocene
©Tyrone Martinsson, published with permission

5 ANT, tourism and situated globality

Looking down in the Anthropocene

Gunnar Thór Jóhannesson, Carina Ren and René van der Duim

Introduction

The Anthropocene and tourism are often characterized as 'global' phenomena. As a consequence of their claimed globality, they are said to concern or at least to influence us all, in one way or the other. Perhaps we do not yet and directly grasp or sense their impacts, but so we will – we are increasingly becoming aware – sooner than later. Apart from both being 'global' phenomena, the Anthropocene and tourism are also very dissimilar kinds of phenomena. While the former is described as a looming reminder of our careless and growth-oriented past (and present), the latter is most often framed as a pleasurable and frivolous activity. As an industry it is moreover – at least partially – held responsible for our entering the geological epoch of the Anthropocene, which now reversely threatens the (frivolous) activities under its auspices. The relationship between the two can simplistically be summed up through binary accounts of how 'tourism activities ruin natural habitats/ecosystems/...' or how 'climate change/pollution/... threatens attractions/destinations...'

In the process of sorting out the connections between the two, the Anthropocene has so far been appointed to the ring side of Nature, while tourism was set in that of the Social. Increasingly however, scattered voices under the broad term of science and technology studies have begun to question this dualistic distinction which modernity makes between nature and society (Latour, 1993) Instead, they point to the intricate, co-constituting relationships between Anthropos and the Earth (see Gren, this volume). Amongst these voices is Actor-Network Theory (ANT) (Latour, 1993, 2005), an approach we focus on in this chapter. Drawing on ANT (Latour, 1993, 2005) and relational materialism (Law, 2002; 2004) more broadly, we wish to contribute to this ontological upending.

In the following, we take a different starting point than that of the global, or even planetary, which usually is the point of departure for discussions on the Anthropocene. Instead of 'looking up', we 'look down' by offering an account of a particular and situated globality (Law, 2004), that of tourism encounters and controversies of tourism in Lanzarote. We see this approach as an alternative to the growing inclination towards the global, towards thinking or acting global, towards taking on 'a global mindset'.

According to Jasanoff (2004), initial (and accelerating) attempts to identify and act upon the environment as global – or in our present case to appreciate both tourism and the Anthropocene as global phenomena and concerns – require a very particular global perspective involving the construction and alignment of what she terms 'the visual repertoire of environmentalism' (2004, 33). Space-based representations of the Earth, for instance the iconic Earth-rise photography from Apollo 17, are typical examples of this repertoire (Jasanoff, 2004). As she suggests, the adoption of the global view 'entails the overriding of local sensibilities and commitments, without necessarily acknowledging the political consequences at stake' (Martello and Jasanoff, 2004, 20). The urge to think and solve environmental problems globally engenders, according to Ingold, an understanding of the globe as a passive surface upon which a universal humanity has settled. This implies a gap between the (global) environment and humans. In his words:

> [O]nce the world is conceived as a globe, it can become an object of appropriation for a collective humanity. In this discourse, we do not belong to the world, neither partaking of its essence nor resonating to its cycles and rhythms. Rather, ... it is the world that belongs to us.
>
> (Ingold, 2000, 214)

Connecting tourism with global environmental change, and ultimately the Anthropocene, thus requires and is based on a particular 'global' outlook which sees the world 'as a globe, where a universal humanity is inflicting global environmental change' (Blok, 2010a, 900). While it might be possible to invest more complexity and entanglements, less causality and more stratification into our perception of the Earth as 'one', it undoubtedly leaves us with a conundrum. How to offer accounts of the Anthropocene without falling into the 'global trap' of externalizing or othering countless voices, issues and concerns? And second, how to avoid the Anthropocene taking over the (political etc.) role of the global as a universal cardinal co-ordinate in line with those of Nature and Society.

In the ensuing account, we follow Law (2004) and suggest replacing a *romantic* notion of the global which is not only assumed to be 'large' but also a 'complex' 'whole', with a *baroque* alternative. Where the first links to an (ideal-typical) holistic scientific vision, the baroque refers to 'an imagination that discovers complexity in detail or (better) specificity, rather than in the emergence of higher level order ... it is an imagination that looks down rather than up' (Law, 2004, 19).

Research has tended to rest on the romantic conception, associating 'grand' global phenomena, such as tourism and the Anthropocene with complexity and interconnectedness, or what Law terms 'the abstraction of an interrelated and emergent whole' (Law, 2004, 20). Whereas, the local is perceived as small and connected to things simple. Following the baroque, it is within the specific and concrete that complexity is located. Ultimately, everything is in everything else, there are no boundaries and 'no distinction between individual and environment' (Law, 2004, 22). However, this does not mean that everything is present and can be brought to the fore. 'There are limits to what can be made explicit' (Law, 2004, 23). We therefore must tend, in our inquiries, to how things manifest themselves, how they are made known or concealed, that is, our research practices.

For the view on the global, the shift from the romantic to the baroque has a number of methodological consequences, one of them being that we should not 'Look up. See things as a whole' (Law, 2004, 16) but rather think of the global as 'something that is broken, poorly formed, that comes into patches; as something that is very small, and pretty elusive' (Law, 2004, 18). As a way to bring forward the baroque complexity of tourism and the Anthropocene and to promote another way of imagining complexity as small, we offer here a modest account of *situated globality* (Law, 2004), the only kinds of globalities which are. It is a story of – among many other things – tourism development in Lanzarote, which pursues the encounters, the controversies and the ontological politics of co-configuring tourism, the Anthropos and the Earth. We ponder how tourism is part of creating and relating to the Anthropocene in particular ways in detaching and engaging itself to it. These connectivities, we argue, can be described with the help of ANT as enactments of diverse orderings taking topological shape.

The chapter proceeds in four parts. First, we introduce the case of Lanzarote as an example not only of contested tourism development, but also of how categories of Nature and Society, local and global, dissolve as tourism and earthly forces intertwine. We then present ANT and its relational materialism as potential devices in tourism research to bring forth the entanglements and encounters of humans and more-than-humans in tourism practices and to by-pass traditional dichotomies between Nature and Society and the local and the global, to name two usual divides in conceptualizing the Anthropocene. Next, we display different kinds of topologies, through which the spatialities of tourism encounters in the Anthropocene may be described. Our project explores the capacities of ANT and relational materialism at large to inspire alternative configurations of the Anthropos and the Earth and in this case more specifically between tourism and the Anthropocene. Lastly, we discuss how this is made possible by introducing improvisation, valuing and caring into tourism research and development alike, as they offer viable ways to work with tourism and its earthly connections. This, we argue, sits well with a methodology of small complexity, which looks down, searches for specificities and is aware of non-coherence (Law, 2004). So first, we 'look down'.

The Anthropocene, Lanzarote and the legacy of César Manrique

Those of us born of you [Lanzarote], those of us who know about your magic, your wisdom, the secrets of your volcanic structure, your revolutionary aesthetics; those who have fought to rescue from your enforced historical isolation and the poverty which you always suffered, begin to tremble with fear as we see how you are destroyed and submitted to massification. We realize just how futile our accusations and cries for help are to the ears of speculators in their hysterical avarice and the authorities' lack of decision that sometimes tolerates and even stimulates the irreversible destruction of an island which could be one of the most beautiful and privileged on this planet.

(César Manrique in Gómez Aquilera, 2001, 118–19)

Lanzarote is the most easterly of the Canary Islands, with its distinctive landscape shaped by volcanic eruptions between 1730 and 1736. In the early 1960s, a close friendship between the President of the Island Authority, José Ramírez Cerdá, and the artist César Manrique led to a tourism development on the island which retrospectively could be labelled as 'sustainable' (see also Jeukens, 1999; Van der Duim, 2005). In close cooperation with local communities, the island authorities created an airport, roads, an installation for the purification of water and the conditions for a limited number of hotels and apartments, as well as seven Centres for Art, Culture and Tourism. These seven creations of César Manrique assembled Nature and Society in tourism attractions like Jameos del Agua, a restaurant and concert-hall situated in a part of a cave seven kilometres long, a museum in Teguise where volcanic lava flows into the art exhibition, and the restaurant El Diablo in the midst of the Timanfaya National Park, with walls of grey-black lava blocks, round like the crater of a volcano, and with 'a floor covered with fireproof steel which encircles the well-like shaft, from which heat of around 400 degrees Celsius rises' (Maslonka and Wassiljewski, 1993). These three creations, as well as the other four (Monumento al Campesino, the Mirador del Rio, the Castillo San José and the Jardín de Cactus) reflect Society as well as the Earth of which Lanzarote as an island is made of.

The idea was based on what has later been described as the Manrique model; a philosophy of limited growth, respect for local architecture and tourist attractions in which tourism, nature and culture were architectonically integrated. José Ramírez Cerdá and César Manrique together with the Director of Public Works, formed the Group César Manrique. A local newspaper (*Antena*) played an important role in the public debate about the pros and cons of tourism development on the island. As César Manrique explains:

On Lanzarote we have worked with utter devotion, in close contact with its geology, understanding its composition and its volcanic essence, achieving the miracle of a new aesthetics, to create a greater capacity for art and to integrate all its facets into an all-embracing symbiosis, which I have described as: LIFE-MAN-ART.

(César Manrique in Gómez Aquilera, 2001, 114)

Until the 1980s, Lanzarote exemplified an 'environment-led' type of tourism development (Hunter, 1997). However, the Manrique model was increasingly challenged in 1980s (see also Bianchi, 2002; Brooks, 2010; Gómez Aquilera, 2001; Jeukens, 1999; Pezzi, 2013; Van der Duim, 2005, 2008). Investors from other Canary Islands, the Spanish mainland and other European countries, engaged and supported by local elites and authorities (see Bianchi, 2002), 'discovered'

Lanzarote, and shifts in the Island Authority, as well as conflicts between island and local authorities, created a rash of tourism constructions along the coast. The fishing village La Tinosa was renamed and became Puerto del Carmen and new resorts like Playa Blanca and Costa Teguise were developed, neglecting most of the ecological and socio-cultural values that so prominently dominated the pre-1980s development (Jeukens, 1999).

In the mid-1980s, Manrique's influence began to dwindle. Commercial interests gained the upper hand, increasingly influencing the decisions taken by the island's government and the various local governments and eventually the Group César Manrique broke up (Maslonka and Wassiljewski, 1993). In 1986, Manrique presented a manifesto in Madrid condemning the turn of events on his island.

> On this day [21 April 1986] I want to state in the most vehement terms my condemnation of this urban chaos and the architectural barbarities being committed; I want to make my attitude and my behaviour clear in relation to what Lanzarotians have done and all that I have created on this island, any possible negligence being out of the question.
>
> (César Manrique in Gómez Aquilera, 2001, 121)

Although the manifesto attracted a lot of attention, it was not enough to stop the building along the coastline. However, local protest demonstrations in 1988, combined with a crisis-driven drastic decrease in the number of visitors to the island in the following years, created a new awareness of the possible downsides of mass tourism development on the island. A few illustrations of an emerging consciousness include a territorial development plan for the island ('Plan Insular del Ordenacion del Territorio') and the 1993 declaration by UNESCO of Lanzarote as a Biosphere Reserve. As Brooks (2010, n.p.) recalls: 'Of the 564 biosphere sites around the world, Lanzarote is the only entire island to win the prestigious classification. The UNESCO website touts the island's ecological charms ... and it praises the way "priority was given to blend tourist infrastructure with the beautiful but inhospitable environment"'. Other examples are the 1995 World Conference on Sustainable Tourism (which attracted more than 1,000 participants from over 75 countries) and its subsequent Charter for Sustainable Tourism, and a 'Ley de Moratoria' (a moratorium on further construction on any of the Canary Islands (see Bianchi, 2002; Van der Duim, 2005, 2008).

These plans were contested. The Territorial Plan was opposed by local councils in whose areas tourism was concentrated, claiming that it violated 'municipal autonomy' (Bianchi, 2002). Thousands of planning applications (involving a total of 92,000 bed spaces) were approved by local councils literally days before the moratorium took effect, Nevertheless, in 2010 the Canary Island Supreme Court declared that 24 hotels had been illegally built in coastal resorts such as Playa Blanca (Brooks, 2010). Long before, in his 'SOS for Lanzarote' in 1978, César Manrique already foresaw these kind of developments and declared that 'if anything at all deteriorates the island [of Lanzarote], no matter what its source is, I shall never have anything to do with it' (in Gomez Aquilera, 2001, 108).

The case of Lanzarote is not only a captivating story of the controversies sparked by tourism development (Jóhannesson *et al.*, 2015). It also resonates with the main issues dealt with in this chapter. First, the example of Lanzarote demonstrates how the respective forces of tourism and the Earth are intertwined. On the one hand tourism at Lanzarote is sustained by Earth's potentialities for instance in the form of a volcanic landscape and lava. On the other hand, tourism impacts on Lanzarote's culture, nature and geophysical conditions, as passionately debated by Manrique. As we shall see, it also has a 'global' impact in the Anthropocene. 'In Anthropocene understanding, modern tourism is a geophysical force which has contributed to the reshaping of the Earth for human purposes and to climate change' (Gren and Huijbens, 2014, 9). From this follows the imperative for tourism studies to theoretically articulate the interconnectedness of tourism and the Anthropocene and thus to afford tourism and tourists an earthly connection (Gren and Huijbens, 2014; Huijbens and Gren, 2012).

Secondly, following recent connections between tourism studies and actor-network theory, we argue that tourism results from an assemblage of what we are used to define as separate spheres of nature and culture. Lanzarote as a tourism destination emerges as a particular effect of the 'processes of ordering' of human and non-human materials. As we have seen, this effect materializes over time, but is conditional and is never achieved once and for all (see also Van der Duim *et al.* 2013). More generally, tourism development is not only performed by humans but also transpires from 'more-than-human' things, like seas, mountains, flora and fauna, cultural artefacts and technologies. The world of tourism is materially heterogeneous (Haldrup and Larsen, 2006).

Thirdly, we see tourism as neither 'global', nor 'local'. In terms of the global-local nexus, which is commonly used to describe tourism dynamics, one could simplistically argue in the case of Lanzarote that 'local forces' created the Manrique model, and eventually 'global forces' (tour operators, hotel chains, investors with international speculative real estate capital) conquered local resistance (see Van der Duim, 2005). However, reality is more complex and becomes, following the idea of baroque as a method for imagining complexity, even more so as we look further down into specificities and details involved.

Although the story of César Manrique could be interpreted as the success and eventual failing of an entrepreneur of tourism, his influence during the 1960 and 1970s stemmed from his ability to position himself as an 'obligatory point of passage' between the 'local' and 'global' networks constituting tourism development on Lanzarote. His close friendship with José Ramírez Cerdá linked him to political and international economic networks; being both from Lanzarote and an international artist, he also connected 'the local' and 'the global'. As Jiméne (2012, 159) explains, Manrique, who has also lived in New York, 'rehearse integrating links for different geographies, cultures and aesthetic trends, through architecture, products and graphics, embracing regional and international features As an assiduous traveler he was very aware of the need to find common point lying within diversity' (see also Maslonka and Wassiljewski, 1993). By moving beyond the local–global distinction, Lanzarote was and is 'linked up, materially and discursively, with numerous other localities often – but by no means always – making more-or-less global scale connections' (Blok, 2010b, 514).

ANT, tourism and the Anthropocene

Originally ANT was devised to deal with processes of ordering. That is, the way in which societal order is composed and made (temporarily) durable (Latour, 2005; Law and Hassard, 1999). Since the 2000s, ANT has gradually come to be adopted in the field of tourism studies through studies, informed by a baroque sensibility (Law, 2004), which highlight the messy reality of tourism practices made up, among many other things, by materiality, social practices and technologies (Van der Duim *et al.*, 2012, 2013). They examine how destinations, tourism objects and spaces, entrepreneurship, and innovations work and make use of three notions central to ANT: ordering, materiality and multiplicity (Van der Duim *et al.*, 2012, 2013).

Ordering draws special attention to the processes underlying what appear to be more or less stable features of tourism. Materiality points to the inescapable entanglements of human and non-human worlds. Emblematic tourist performances are made possible and pleasurable by objects, machines, and technologies. Multiplicity reveals the numerous versions of tourism, destinations or objects that are enacted into existence. In terms of our example of Lanzarote, the Manrique model clearly afforded tourism an earthly connection by fusing people, things, technologies, volcanic lava, 'mountains of fire', discourses and values in his art and architecture. However this particular assemblage could only reach a temporary stabilization and hegemony. As Lanzarote was and still is entangled with other ordering attempts exemplified by thousands of planning applications approved days before the moratorium took effect (see also Brooks, 2010), various modes of ordering tourism and 'other things' co-constitute(d) each other. Related encounters between multiple ordering attempts led to some of the controversies earlier described.

Indeed, from an ANT perspective, tourism is seen as a relational achievement continuously entangled with other practices, things and ordering attempts (Van der Duim *et al.*, 2012). Through encounters with heterogeneous objects such as money, policies, earthly substances and discourse, it takes shape and also gains its energy as an ordering force in itself (Franklin, 2012). In a similar vein, and as illustrated by the Lanzarote example, tourism is part of producing localities and globalities (Blok, 2010a). As Blok (2010a) explains, ANT favours the symmetrical view that localities and globalities are equally unlikely end points of situated social processes. Tourism takes place in between these two extremes.

When looking down for the Anthropocene, we see how tourism practices taking place in Lanzarote are manifested along with the Earth, a global 'neoliberal' tourism production system, the (local) legacy of César Manrique and (public discourse of) global climate change. A relational-scalar understanding depicts the global neither as 'larger' nor more complex than the local. Only it is more durably connected. There is nothing which is global, only local summing ups (Latour, 1999). The mere fact that travelling to Lanzarote to see the seven creations of Manrique produces carbon emissions, an 'unsustainable' externality of the process of ordering a 'sustainable' tourism destination (see van der Duim, 2005), illustrates – as claimed by Latour (2005, 184) – that 'scale is the actor's own achievement'. Tourism as an actor and practice within the Anthropocene intertwines and produces humanity, globality and the Earth in particular ways. It does so, as proposed in this book, 'on a planetary scale'. The baroque complexity however urges us to ask: at the expense of what other scales, other manifestations? What we propose here, is an account which brings forward different kinds of knowledge, which in the words of Martello and Jasanoff (2004, 9) make room 'for more fragmented and multiple visions of what is wrong with the environment, what values are at stake, and above all what should be done about perceived harms and threats'. Hereby, expert knowledge, whether within tourism management or environmental sciences, is challenged as the *situatedness* (Haraway, 1991) of knowledge is given force in decision-making. As a non-humanist disposition (Gad and Jensen, 2010) ANT alters the view of the researcher and the focus of research to study tourism encounters in the Anthropocene. To come to grips with the Earth as 'an active, local, limited, sensitive, fragile, quaking, and easily tickled envelope' (Latour, 2014a, 4), ANT suggests to 'trudge like an ant, carrying the heavy gear in order to generate even the tiniest connection' (Latour, 2005, 25). Our tracing starts on Earth and remains there at every step. Instead of starting from a global perspective, thinking about the global environment as a closed object, we suggest tracing the making and manifestation of the global, or better, of the plurality of 'situated globalities' (Law, 2004). In order to trace questions of how tourism works on and with the Earth, a sensibility towards small, concrete and non-coherent complexities pushes us to start from scratch by focusing on practices through which tourism and other things, such as the Anthropocene, are intertwined, (re)assembled and valued. In the following section we will explore what such tracing might entail and what conceptual luggage we might usefully bring on the tour.

Tourism and earthly topologies in the Anthropocene

By looking down instead of looking up in situating the global manifestations of tourism and the Anthropocene we see how the global environment, as an associational form, comes in multiple topological shapes (Blok, 2010a), challenging 'traditional' spatial dimensions. In the Anthropocene we have more explicitly become participants in a becoming world, a world continuously in the making (Gibson-Graham, 2011). Society has become a topological society where 'we no longer live in or experience "movement" or transformation as the transmission of fixed forms in space and time but rather movement – as the ordering of continuity – composes the forms of social and cultural life themselves' (Lury *et al.*, 2012, 6). According to Harvey (2012, 78):

> The topological approach thus draws attention to the spatial figures where insides and outsides are continuous, where borders of inclusion and exclusion

do not coincide with the edges of a demarcated territory, and where it is the mutable quality of relations that determines distance and proximity, rather than a singular and absolute measure.

If inclusion or exclusion depends on mutable relations, it becomes crucial to describe diverse modes of relational ordering and how they matter in the process of assembling things like tourism or global climate change (Jóhannesson *et al.*, 2015). With reference to the enactment of Lanzarote as a place where tourism and the Anthropocene is manifested in a particular way, the question is what kind of topologies those connections create; what kind of topological forms does the Earth–tourism relation take? Mol and Law have suggested four types of social topologies to account for spatial configurations of relations (Law and Mol, 2001; Mol and Law, 1994). These are: the region, network, fluid and fire.

The region refers to Euclidean space, which depicts the world as a 'gridlike surface on which it is possible to draw durable lines of metric distances. The "network" refers to such lines that connect nodes, which may be situated in [this] geometric space' (Jóhannesson and Bærenholdt, 2008, 160). When the region and networks are connected they allow for the transfer of objects (immutable mobiles) across distances on the surface of Earth and simultaneously they underline the global perspective on Earth, where it is presented as a solid globe on which networks can be built. Tourism is made possible through these kinds of spatial ordering. It is imperative for successful travel that the physical presence of the island of Lanzarote stays put in regional space. At the same time it is critical that the dense network of technicians, meteorologists, computers, the plane and ground staff, just to mention a tiny part of the aviation network, works according to a plan if an airplane is going to carry any passengers to the destination. Similarly, we already argued in the above that Manrique's creations were 'regional' in the sense that they are entwined with the geological and spatial characteristics of the island. At the same time, his close friendship with José Ramírez Cerdá as well as his international reputation as an artist linked him to political and international economic networks of capital to finance tourism development on the island.

Fluid topology grasps the ways in which relational continuity is kept through change (Law and Mol, 2001; Mol and Law, 1994). Here, relations are durable because they are able to change; they bend, shift shape but do not break or tear. It is possible to transfer fluid objects through regional space due to their capacity to change, be it a bush pump (de Laet and Mol, 2000) or a tourism development project (Jóhannesson, 2005). Manrique postcards, T-shirts, crafts and souvenirs travel through the island and to the homes of visiting tourists and in some sense create a continuity of the legacy of Manrique's dream for Lanzarote. His own artwork, the seven creations, furthermore manifests a fluid topology as they afford continuous presence of the Earth's forces in the midst of a tourist product, best exemplified by Restaurant El Diablo where 'tricks performed with hissing steam, burning bushes and hot stones are not tricks at all – it's all real' (see Maslonka and Wassiljewski, 1993). Here, the Earth is not othered as a passive stage or spectacle but as an active component in the making of tourism experiences.

Fire topology differs from networks and fluids as it does not refer to movement through regional space. It refers to 'elements of passion, action, energy, spirit, will and anger, not to mention creative destruction and sexuality' (Law and Mol, 2001, 615). It furthermore draws attention to the interdependence of absences and presences. Present relational configurations are dependent on absences of other such configurations and thus, some things become othered or are kept absent when others come into being. Fire topology grasps how continuity can be an effect of discontinuity or frictional encounters and refers to what Diken (2011) terms *mutable immobiles*. Some of Manrique's creations change – at least conceptually – when different modes of ordering interfere and when some of the creations become part of the 'madding crowds' of tourism in the Canary Islands.

The passion, spirit, will and anger present in Manrique's manifesto and speeches all relate to fire topology and friction in one way or another. In his view, in order to preserve the continuity of Lanzarote, it is necessary to break away from the powerful discourse of mass tourism, while at the same time the need to connect to tourism mobilities for socio-economic development is also acknowledged. This would involve creative destruction, cultivating, tending to and caring for the island – framed in his words as a mother figure giving birth to life. Topology of fire is also evident in the tourism practices available on the island. Its volcanic landscape is a central attraction and it necessarily rests on the absent presence of eruptions. Here, the Earth itself is constantly present as a geological force, as a mutable immobile – it may burst into flames without much notice (Benediktsson *et al.*, 2011; Lund and Benediktsson, 2011).

Just as Manrique's creations enable us to tease out all four topologies, bringing about the diverse socio-spatial ordering of tourism development on the island in the Anthropocene, Blok points out how following the social trajectories of carbon emissions 'will enable us to draw persuasive maps of how the social life of carbon "translates" into sociospatial forms' (2010a, 902). According to him, 'the crucial point about these maps is that, depending on how we imagine sites and objects being connected across distances, they will end up looking topologically very different' (2010a, 902). The region, network, fluid and fire are useful metaphors for thinking through the multiple and earthly modes of ordering of tourism in the Anthropocene. That is, how tourism relates to the Earth and holds together in diverse ways. To some extent, the four kinds of topologies provide new discontinuities to the relational fabric of the world, different from the dichotomies of the modernistic episteme (Latour, 1993, 2014b). However, they first of all emphasize the abstract form and not the content, the experience or the practice through which they become. By pushing ANT to its limits, going beyond mere descriptions of topological forms and delving instead into the ways in which these forms take shape we might be able to distinguish some possible avenues for engagement with and interfering in tourism encounters in the epoch of the Anthropocene.

Improvising, valuing and caring: interfering with tourism research in the Anthropocene

Studies inspired by ANT have often stopped at the point where the 'black box' in question is opened up (Latour, 2005, 2007; Van der Duim *et al.*, 2012), as in the present case how the Anthropocene is not a global, human accomplishment, but rather an intricate intertwinement, construction and ordering of scales, topologies and actors. However, ANT and especially what has been termed post-ANT (Gad and Jensen, 2010), also offers possibilities to move beyond merely describing networks or modes of ordering by grappling with possible ways to stitch things together; things like tourism and the Anthropocene. Such possibilities reconfigure the position and roles of the researcher. Instead of focusing on identifying relations, we now engage in making relations and establish continuity (Latour, 2010). Actually, this is not a huge leap. The close description of ordering processes such as tourism topologies makes it possible to interfere in the making of tourism in the Anthropocene and thereby to engage in meaningful relations with places, people and the Earth. Lury *et al.* (2012, 4) argue that topologies emerge in practices

of sorting, naming, numbering, comparing, listing, and calculating. The effect of these practices is both to introduce new continuities into a discontinuous world by establishing equivalences or similitudes, and to make and mark discontinuities through repeated contrasts.

By anchoring tourism practices and global environmental change in relational and often mundane practices, a room for political engagement and ethical considerations is created for the researcher. By making visible the often controversy-ridden practices through which connections and discontinuities between climate change, mobility and tourism are created and sustained, it becomes possible to inspire what Gibson-Graham refers to as transformative connections, connections available to change the way we think and act in the world and to 'imbue our categories and practices with a "different mode of humanity"' (Gibson-Graham, 2011, 2). Along the lines of ANT this would involve the recognition of humans and more-than-humans as being 'socio-material configurations', meaning that the 'we' not only refers to human subjects as traditionally defined, making it crucial to tune 'into a dynamism that does not originate in human action' (Gibson-Graham, 2011, 3) when we engage in relational ordering including sorting, naming, numbering and comparing.

A strength of ANT is to allow for such tuning. It opens up ordering processes and makes visible the small but complex and most often non-coherent steps taken in accomplishing a thing like tourism – not only as a global phenomenon, but as an always concrete, earthly and situated practice. In terms of political engagement it also underlines how every single action is possibly politically charged. We do not know beforehand where the power to change or regulate the world resides or how it flows along lines of becoming (Deleuze and Guttari, 2004). We are faced with the possibility and responsibility to choose which realities to enact, i.e.

ontological politics (Law and Singleton, 2013; Law and Urry, 2004; Mol, 1999). However, the power of ANT does somewhat fade away when it comes to making decisions on which kind of reality we would like to enact (see e.g. Latour, 2014b). To do an ANT-inspired study does not automatically result in good connections, whatever that may mean. We do however argue that tracing tourism encounters with global environmental change, starting from local practices, must be the first step in 'making (transformative) connections; ... to "take in" the world in the act of learning' (Gibson-Graham, 2011, 4), which may create alternative paths towards tourism development in the Anthropocene. For this occasion and still with reference to Lanzarote, we suggest they can be framed by three intersecting (performative) concepts, namely: improvising, valuing and caring.

Improvising

Thinking about tourism and the global through 'baroque complexity'(Law, 2004) and topologies involves admitting that there is no whole, no outside or inside given in the order of things but a meshwork of interwoven lines or relations that demand acceptance of the non-coherent or the uncertain (Law and Singleton, 2013). The concept of improvisation stresses the relational aspects of creative processes and the way in which people 'construct culture as they go along and as they respond to life's contingencies' (Bruner, 1993, in Ingold and Hallam 2007, 2). Furthermore, '[t]o improvise is to follow the ways of the world, ... as Deleuze and Guattari write, "to join with the World, or to meld with it"' (Ingold 2010, 10). Life is scripting, it does not follow a script. Although there are many ways to make predictions about and imagine the future – the Anthropocene boasts countless of such predictions and scenarios – there is no way of knowing what is – or will be made into – something big or small. Improvisation also underlines the need of sensing as we move along and thus how information and knowledge is crucial at every step. Lanzarote also was made up as a tourism destination as it went along with encounters of, for example, the Manrique model with other political, economic and architectural ordering attempts.

Valuing

The 'unsettledness' of the ANT-inspired ontology, which lends itself so well to improvisation, is also well-suited for taking a new look at value and the practice of attributing value to things (Helgesson and Muniesa, 2013). In the words of Heuts and Mol (2013), 'valuing does not just have to do with the question of how to appreciate reality as it is, but also with the question what is appropriate to do to improve things' (p. 137). Since things are not already given or predictable, a lot remains to be done in tying together new relations, in attributing new kinds of value to entangled activities, things and places. Recent attempts to deconstruct mobility and to propose alternative mobility scenarios or futures (Urry, 2008) serve as examples of such endeavours of revaluing activities in which tourism and the Anthropocene interfere. In Lanzarote valuation for example centres around the controversy being on the one hand a UNESCO biosphere reserve and on the other hand a tourism destination which attracts tourists to Lanzarote for nothing more than 'a sunny beach and a pitcher of sangria with a cliff-top view' (Brooks, 2010). In fact, the César Manrique Foundation, created in 1992 and named after the late architect, blew the whistle on illegal hotels (see above). On the other hand, the coordinator for the Lanzarote government's Biosphere Reserve Observatory believes Lanzarote deserves its biosphere status despite the building abuses (see Brooks, 2010):

> It's true that corruption linked to development is a great problem on the island, but in many occasions, it has been we who have blown the whistle, and UNESCO knows that ... What people don't seem to realize is that this reserve is a pioneer in Spain regarding the fight against illegal hotels and taking away the title would be somewhat unfair.

But valuing refers also to the ordering attempts of Manrique himself, as his work has also been subject to critics that have accused them of trivializing and thematizing Lanzarote as well as domesticating and anaesthetizing the landscape, creating a sort of artificial place-object (see Pezzi, 2013; Gómes Aguilera, 2001).

Caring

ANT-inspired approaches call upon us as researchers to acknowledge the practices of valuing through its attentiveness to close description, controversial and improvised ordering attempts and in tending to the relational materialism of small complexity. As suggested in the above, this enables, we argue, a research practice which does not seek to reinforce or to merely debunk reality, but which rather engages into the field of research with *care*. According to Heuts and Mol (2013), the notion of care 'indicates efforts that are ongoing, adaptive, tinkering and open ended' (p. 130). In their words:

> The term 'care' suggests enduring work that seeks improvement but does not necessarily succeed. It also implies that the object of improvement should not be overpowered, but respected. Respect does not depend on leaving things and situations as they are. Instead it is a matter of calling on strengths and tinkering with weaknesses.
>
> (Heuts and Mol, 2013, 141)

As warned by Heuts and Mol (2013), the notion of care, like improvisation, does not offer full control, but 'involves sustained and respectful tinkering towards improvement' (p. 125). There is in other words, no final level ordering. Clearly Lanzarote did not find a grand solution to the challenges of the Anthropocene, if there ever was one (we believe not), but Manrique and colleagues at least tried by slowing down tourism development. Indeed, improvisation, valuing and caring most probably demand us to slow down (Ren *et al.*, 2015). This may be easier said than done in the case of tourism, as well as research. For tourism, the question may be if 'the dualism between (permanent, caring) dwelling and (temporary, carefree) tourist [is] writ in stone in tourism-related design and architecture' (Veijola and Falin, 2014, 8), not to forget businesses. The Manrique model as described above has been an interesting experiment to prototype new ways of relating the geophysical with tourism. Manrique's seven creations illustrate how we in the realm of tourism could fundamentally alter our relationship with the planet we inhabit in ways that would provoke care (see also Jiménez, 2012). However, the model also weaved, encountered and opposed other tourism and non-tourism related ordering attempts, leading to multiple versions of the tourism destination of Lanzarote. On 21 April 1986, César Manrique held a press conference in Madrid and stated that 'Lanzarote is dying'. He was astonished that, despite 'the catastrophic alteration of almost the entire Spanish coast, blurring the traits of each place with a complete lack of adaptation and the gratuitous introduction of a cold international standardization, we have failed to learn the lesson whereby we must stop and save what is left' (César Manrique in Gómez Aquilera, 2001, 108).

Concluding remarks

The rationale behind this chapter, as with the whole volume, is to explore potential ways to theorize and create novel insights into the relational configurations of tourism and the Anthropocene. We have suggested that ANT and relational materialism provide useful tools to inform our understanding of the relational construction of the Anthropos and the Earth and hereby also between tourism and the Anthropocene. Crucial in that regard is how it is possible to create moments of attentiveness to small complexities and topologies in the making, through which global tourism, the Earth and the Anthropocene is configured.

Instead of searching for a new way of grasping the interlocking of the Earth and the Anthropos, and the meaning or consequence of that connection for tourism, we have argued for a baroque approach to imagining complexity and the global which rejects a local–global divide and recasts tourism as concrete and specific practice and a becoming topological ordering. As we have seen, ANT's ontology refuses to postulate any deep, a priori rift between 'fragile localities' (as in the case of Lanzarote) and 'powerful global forces' (as in the case of climate change and systems of aviation); the locality of Lanzarote is just as far from self-evident as the globality of global environmental change. In this chapter we therefore argued that the debate on tourism development in Lanzarote or tourism and the Anthropocene are entwined, and ontologically and methodologically alike, since tourism-related (and other) actor-networks are neither local nor global (Latour, 1993).

The metaphors of network, fluid and fire worked as a way to by-pass the dualism of big and small, complex and simple, distant and close as well as absence and presence by offering descriptions of the collective condition of humans and more-than-humans in the Anthropocene through its flat, object-oriented ontology and methodology. The small complexities and the topologies of tourism underline that there is no final level ordering of the usual building blocks of society but rather 'movement – as the ordering of continuity – composes the forms of social and cultural life themselves' (Lury *et al.*, 2012, 6). Therefore we cannot escape the fate and responsibility to move along with the Earth and compose our daily existence the best we can. In fact, as proposed by the situated globality and baroque complexity, there is no shame in looking down, quite the opposite.

In our chapter, we proposed three approaches of engaging into the intricacies and entanglements of tourism and the Anthropocene; through improvisation, valuing and caring. These approaches underscore the need for alternative registers of valuing in terms of tourism development, the need to engage in enduring but open-ended and unsecure work of improvement that does not follow a script but depends on sensitivity towards life's contingencies. By opening up tourism as a topological ordering and bring forth its earthly connections, multiple spaces for political action are created, which also has implications for tourism development as well as for research practices. As tourism developers and researchers we need more than ever to attend to ontological repercussions of our own work and how it relates to tourism encounters in the Anthropocene.

References

Bianchi, R.V. 2002. Tourism restructuring and the political economy of sustainability – a critical view from the periphery (the Canary Islands). Paper presented to the ATLAS Annual Conference, Estoril.

Brooks, A. 2010. Building craze threatens to end Lanzarote's biosphere status. <http://www.independent.co.uk/environment/nature/building-craze-threatens-to-end-lanzarotes-biosphere-status-2020064.html#> [accessed Jan. 2015].

Benediktsson, K., Lund, K.A., and Huijbens, E. 2011. Inspired by eruptions? Eyjafjallajökull and Icelandic tourism. *Mobilities*, 6(1), 77–84.

Blok, A. 2010a. Topologies of climate change: Actor-network theory, relational-scalar analytics, and carbon-market overflows. *Environment and Planning D: Society and Space*, 28, 896–912.

Blok, A. 2010b. Mapping the super-whale: Towards a mobile ethnography of situated globalities. *Mobilities*, 5(4), 507–28.

de Laet, M. and Mol, A. 2000. The Zimbabwe bush pump: Mechanics of a fluid technology. *Social Studies of Science*, 30(2), 225–63.

Deleuze, G., and Guttari, F. 2004. *A Thousand Plateaus: Capitalism and Schizophrenia*. London: Continuum.

Diken, B. 2011. Fire as a metaphor of (im)mobility. *Mobilities*, 6(1), 95–102.

Franklin, A. 2012. The choreography of a mobile world: Tourism orderings. In R. Van der Duim, C. Ren and G.T. Jóhannesson (eds), *Actor-Network Theory and Tourism: Ordering, Materiality and Multiplicity*. London, New York: Routledge, 43–58.

Gad, C., and Jensen, C.B. 2010. On the consequences of post-ANT. *Science, Technology and Human Values*, 35(1), 55–80.

Gibson-Graham, J.K. 2011. A feminist project of belonging for the Anthropocene. *Gender, Place and Culture: A Journal of Feminist Geography*, 18(1), 1–21.

Gómez Aguilera, F. 2001. *César Manrique in his own Words*. Teguise: Fundacion César Manrique.

Gren, M., and Huijbens, E.H. 2014. Tourism and the Anthropocene. *Scandinavian Journal of Hospitality and Tourism*, 14(1), 6–22.

Haraway, D. 1991. A cyborg manifesto: Science, technology and socialist feminism in the late twentieth century. In D. Haraway (ed.), *Simians, Cyborgs and Women: The Reinvention of Nature*. London: Free Association Books, 149–81.

Harvey, P. 2012. The topological quality of infrastructural relation: An ethnographic approach. *Theory, Culture and Society*, 29(4/5), 76–92.

Haldrup, M., and Larsen, J. 2006. Material cultures of tourism. *Leisure Studies*, 25(3), 275–89.

Helgesson, C.F., and Muniesa, F. 2013. For what it's worth: An introduction to valuation studies. *Valuation Studies*, 1(1), 1–10.

Heuts, F., and Mol, A. 2013. What is a good tomato? A case of valuing in practice. *Valuation Studies*, 1(2), 125–46.

Huijbens, E., and Gren, M. 2012. Tourism, ANT and the Earth. In R. van der Duim, C. Ren and G.T. Jóhannesson (eds), *Actor-Network Theory and Tourism: Ordering, Materiality and Multiplicity*. London and New York: Routledge, 146–63.

Hunter, C.J. 1997. Sustainable tourism as an adaptive paradigm. *Annals of Tourism Research*, 24(4), 850–67.

Ingold, T. 2000. Globes and spheres: The topology of environmentalism. *The Perception of the Environment: Essays in Livelihood, Dwelling and Skill*. London: Routledge, 209–18.

Ingold, T. 2010. Bringing things to life: Creative entanglements in a world of materials. <http://eprints.ncrm.ac.uk/1306/1/0510_creative_entanglements.pdf> [accessed May 2015].

Ingold, T., and Hallam, E. 2007. Creativity and cultural improvisation: An introduction. In T. Ingold and E. Hallam (eds), *Creativity and Cultural Improvisation*. Oxford: Berg, 1–24.

Jasanoff, S. 2004. Heaven and Earth: The politics of environmental images. In S. Jasanoff and M.L. Martello (eds), *Earthly Politics: Local and Global Environmental Governance*. Cambridge, MA: MIT Press, 31–52.

Jeukens, L. 1999. *Lanzarote: Meerdere belangen onder de zon. Een analyse van de ontwikkeling en de invloeden van het toerisme in Lanzarote*. M.Sc.thesis, Wageningen University.

Jimenez, C. 2012. Paradise identity, between projection and protection: César Manrique's lessons for current challenges in territorial innovation. In P.L. Farias, A. Calvera, M. Braga and Z. Schincariol (eds), *Design Frontiers: Territories, Concepts, Technologies*. ICDHS 2012, 8th Conference of the International Committee for Design History and Design Studies. São Paulo: Blucher, 125–9.

Jóhannesson, G.T. 2005. Tourism translations: Actor-network theory and tourism research. *Tourist Studies*, 5(2), 133–50.

Jóhannesson, G.T., and Bærenholdt, J.O. 2008. Enacting places through connections of tourism. In B. Granås and J.O. Bærenholdt (eds), *Mobility and Place: Enacting European Peripheries*. Aldershot: Ashgate, 155–66.

Jóhannesson, G.T., Ren, C., and van der Duim, R. (eds) 2015. *Tourism Encounters and Controversies: Ontological Politics of Tourism Development*. Farnham: Ashgate.

Latour, B. 1993. *We Have Never Been Modern*, tr. C. Porter. Cambridge, MA: Harvard University Press.

Latour, B. 1999. On recalling ANT. *Sociological Review*, 47(S1), 15–25.

Latour, B. 2005. *Reassembling the Social: An Introduction to Actor-Network-Theory*. Oxford: Oxford University Press.

Latour, B. 2007. A plea for Earthly sciences. <http://www.bruno-latour.fr/sites/default/files/102-BSA-GB_0.pdf> [accessed May 2015].

Latour, B. 2010. An attempt at a 'composisionist manifesto'. *New Literary History*, 41, 471–90.

Latour, B. 2014a. Agency at the time of the Anthropocene. *New Literary History*, 45, 1–18.

Latour, B. 2014b. On selves, forms, and forces. *HAU: Journal of Ethnographic Theory*, 4(2), 261–6.

Law, J. 2002. Objects and spaces. *Theory, Culture and Society*, 19(5-6), 91–105.

Law, J. 2004. And if the global were small and noncoherent? Method, complexity, and the baroque. *Environment and Planning, D: Society and Space*, 22, 13–16.

Law, J., and Hassard, J. (eds) 1999. *Actor Network Theory and After*. Oxford: Blackwell.

Law, J., and Mol, A. 2001. Situating technoscience: An inquiry into spatialities. *Environment and Planning D: Society and Space*, 19(5), 609–21.

Law, J., and Singleton, V. 2013. ANT and politics: Working in and on the world. *Qualitative Sociology*, 36, 485–502.

Law, J., and Urry, J. 2004. Enacting the social. *Economy and Society*, 33(3), 390–410.

Lund, K.A., and Benediktsson, K. 2011. Inhabiting a risky Earth: The Eyjafjallajökull eruption in 2010 and its impacts. *Anthropology Today*, 27(1), 6–9.

Lury, C., Parisi, L., and Terranova, T. 2012. Introduction: The becoming topological of culture. *Theory, Culture and Society*, 29(4/5), 3–35.

Martello, M.L., and Jasanoff, S. 2004. Introduction: Globalization and environmental governance. In S. Jasanoff and M.L. Martello (eds), *Earthly Politics: Local and Global Environmental Governance*. Cambridge, MA: MIT Press, 1–30.

Maslonka, R., and Wassiljewski K. 1993. *Lanzarote: 7 Creaciones de César Manrique*. Lanzarote: Art-edition.

Mol, A. 1999. Ontological politics. A word and some questions. In J. Law and J. Hassard (eds), *Actor Network Theory and After*. Oxford: Blackwell, 74–89.

Mol, A., and Law, J. 1994. Regions, networks and fluids: Anaemia and social topology. *Social Studies of Science*, 24, 641–71.

Pezzi, M. G. 2013. We don't need to copy anyone. Cesar Manrique and the creation of a development model for Lanzarote. *Urbanities*, 3(2), 19–32.

Ren, C., van der Duim, R., and Jóhannesson, G.T. 2015. Postscript: Making headways, expanding the field and slowing down. In G.T. Jóhannesson, C. Ren and R. van der Duim (eds), *Tourism Encounters and Controversies: Ontological Politics of Tourism Development*. Farnham: Ashgate.

Urry, J. 2008. Climate change, travel and complex futures. *British Journal of Sociology*, 59(2), 261–79.

Van der Duim, V.R. 2005. *Tourismscapes*. Ph.D. thesis, Wageningen University.

Van der Duim, V.R. 2008. Tourism and innovation: An actor-network approach. In G. Richards and J. Wilson (eds), *From Cultural Tourism to Creative Tourism*. Proceedings of the ATLAS international conference Barcelona, 2005, part 2. Changing structures of collaboration. Arnhem: ATLAS, 11–26.

Van der Duim, R., Ren, C., and Jóhannesson, G.T. (eds) 2012. *Actor-Network Theory and Tourism: Ordering, Materiality and Multiplicity*. London and New York: Routledge.

Van der Duim, R., Ren, C., and Jóhannesson, G.T. 2013. Ordering, materiality and multiplicity: Enacting ANT in tourism. *Tourist Studies*, 13(1), 3–20.

Veijola, S., and Falin, P. 2014. Mobile neighbouring. *Mobilities*. doi: 10.1080/17450101.2014.936715.

6 Arctic whale watching and Anthropocene ethics

Berit Kristoffersen, Roger Norum and Britt Kramvig

Prologue: caring for whales

'Anger as fishing boat runs over humpback whale' (Pedersen, 2014). In November 2014, the front page of a local newspaper in Tromsø, in Arctic Norway, splashed a story about a whale being hit by a fishing boat. Social media channels were flooded with comments, accusing the fisherman of not caring about the whale and of lacking respect for its safety. The temperature in the heated debate rose to such an extent that the unfortunate fisherman invited the journalist who wrote the article to his house in an attempt to convince the public that he had not, in fact, touched the whale (Aaserud and Johnsen, 2014). One of Tromsø's most respected whale researchers was called in, and confirmed from footage that the fisherman had done his best to avoid hitting the whale, that it was a minor encounter, and that the whale was most probably not seriously injured. A local woman interviewed by the journalist about this specific encounter advocated care for the whale above all else: 'you have to consider the interests of the whales when you are out in the waters close to them. It's the whale that has to be in focus, not the photographer or the tourists.'

Around the same time, other whale stories hit the media. One covered a rescue operation in which Tromsø fire brigade divers were sent out to cut fishing nets in which a whale had become entangled. In this story, the fisherman was quick to acknowledge that his extremely valuable nets (worth thousands of dollars) had to be sacrificed to save the whale. Frequent other news articles included complaints about a wild, gold-rush growth in whale-related tourism, with too many boats getting too close to the whales. These items became hot news in the winter season 2014–15 as unprecedented numbers of whales began to appear in the inshore waters around Tromsø, giving rise to a rapid escalation of whale watching tourism there. What was striking about the tenor of the stories, in both traditional and social media, was an increasing concern articulated for the whales, a concern which to us suggests a possible ethical relationship with the cetaceans reflecting an attentive and hospitable ethos that can be aligned with current notions of the Anthropocene.

Introduction

These media debates and whale episodes raise questions about what, or who, the whale is that is emerging in the waters of the Arctic. The emotions aroused by the documented encounters and their articulation in public debates suggest that the whale is no longer perceived as prey, as distant other, or as a dangerous presence in the waters. Instead there is a 'new whale', one who seems to demand a duty of care from humans, and which has become even something of a companion species with territorial and existential rights. This transition to a new whale, and the onset of 'whale fever', triggered our curiosity during fieldwork in Tromsø in early 2014, prompting us to ask about the new position of the whale in the expanding network of relations associated with growing whale tourism in the Arctic. If a new kind of whale is emerging, through new relationships with humans, then what kind of ethics are emerging?

The Anthropocene also implies a reconnection of human activities with the ecologies they co-produce with other species, for example whale tourism in the Arctic. While fulfilling a long-standing touristic cliché, apparently promoting opportunities to see the imagined pristine nature of the region, tourism actually contributes to its demise through, for example, increasing carbon emissions. In a similar way, getting close to marine wildlife and episodes of physical encounters/ disturbance entail examples of propeller damage on the tail of the above-mentioned whale. Whale watching in itself embodies a modern notion of separation between 'man and nature', and tourist operators nurture a desire for tourists to encounter a nature that is beyond the human. Whale watching, too, is itself a product of modern environmental movements that helped to end whaling as the primary relation between humans and whales, simultaneously reifying an idea of nature as beyond the human realm, as Schmink notes (in Einarsson, 1993, 82).

Joanna Zylinska (2014) argues that a new set of ethics is required to enable humans to take responsibility for occurrences on Earth at different scales, and in order to rethink life after unhinging the man–nature dualism. From her perspective, ethics is a 'mode of human locatedness' on the Earth, and an Anthropocene ethics recognizes that humans are 'not the only beings that are capable of relating to and collaborating with others' (Zylinska, 2014, 91). Humans are engaged in being-with as well as being-in the world. Ethics, as the designation of goodness/rightness is the setting in which human relations to others are classified. Hence, if we define some beings as animals, they are always kept separate from our own morality which pertains to the domain of humans. As Zylinska (2014, 93) puts it; 'ethics is a historically contingent human mode of becoming in the world, of becoming different from the world, and of narrating and taking responsibility for the nature of this difference'. What she then defines as a minimal ethics for the Anthropocene entails a kind of openness, and a willingness to acknowledge that we are 'always already involved, obligated, entangled' (Zylinska, 2014, 95), in this case with cetaceans in the Arctic.

Indeed these are not ethics for all at all times and in all places. Approaches to the Anthropocene as a homogeneous occurrence involving all of humankind have been challenged, for instance by Haraway (2015) who argues that it is not the Anthropos that has caused the climate changes that threaten mass extinctions, and that we should instead consider the 'capitalocene' that started well before the industrial expansion of the 18th century. Haraway uses the idea of the Chthulucene to remind us that human responses to anthropogenic changes have largely taken the form of an anxiety inadequate to the scale of action required. According to Haraway, the Chthulucene and the Capitalocene layer onto the idea of the Anthropocene in ways that demand a deep rethinking of the stories we tell one another about our earthly existence, not merely thinking about business as usual – as Zylinska (2014) also argues. In the context of whale watching tourism, the emergence of human–whale relations that are involved, entangled and entail obligations, suggests that the being-with that is played out in this relatively new form of tourism can reveal a great deal about ethics of responsibility necessary for an Anthropocene understanding of the Arctic and its wildlife.

This chapter is part of a larger project for which seven weeks of fieldwork were conducted at various times over a period of 11 months in 2014 in both Iceland and Norway (Húsavík, Reykjavik, Tromsø and Andenes). Fieldwork utilized a range of ethnographic methods, including participant observation, informal conversation, semi-structured interviews and material gathered from local newspapers and relevant websites. Interviews, conducted in both English and Norwegian, were carried out with ten whale watching tourists, six tour operators, five guides, three boat captains and five other stakeholders in the industry, in total 29 interviews. In addition, a one-day workshop for whale watching tour operators in Norway was organized by Kramvig and Kristoffersen on 25 November 2014 in Tromsø. This event provided a number of insights presented throughout this chapter. First, though, we offer a general introduction to whale watching tourism, in the context of an Anthropocene Arctic.

The Anthropocene Arctic and whale watching tourism

Despite the continued (though probably decreasing) consumption of whales as meat, whales have become powerful eco-symbols not only in environmental and conservation movements, but also in global political discourse about territoriality and indigenous practices (Peace, 2010). Whales have come to be seen as 'charismatic mega-vertebrates' (Stoett, 1997), benevolent monarchs capturing the imagination of popular media as unique, intelligent and beautiful beings deserving of rights and protection, in what Einarsson describes as a 'profound shift in the perception of these animals' (Einarsson, 1993, 74). Their symbolic fixture in urban Western discourses represents both natural magnificence and human folly: these free, migratory mammals escape the confines of our own sovereignty, yet they appear to be doomed because of our own political and social projects to control the natural environment. With pseudo-human behaviours and mythical properties (Lawrence and Phillips, 2004), whales are thus no longer merely a local resource; they have acquired symbolic significance for millions of people, regardless of whether such people have ever seen a living whale. At the same time, the idea of encountering a whale has gradually become a popular touristic ambition, a staple on people's 'bucket lists' and tourist fantasies.

Commercial whale watching has developed into one the most important niche markets in tourism (Hoyt and Iñiguez, 2008), a US$2 billion global industry that is currently the largest economic activity reliant upon cetaceans (Parsons, 2012). The practice has capitalized on an iconic animal that is touted and perceived (not always accurately), as being under significant duress by looming threats, both human and non-human. The whale has thus become part of a global industry of cultural consumption, with the contemporary whale watching industry extending beyond the high seas. Whales and other cetaceans, living and dead, are displayed, exhibited and observed in a variety of places that include museums, aquariums, dolphinariums, on television and film, in the wild and on organized whale watching tours. At present, several European nations maintain active whale watching industries, including Norway, Iceland, the Canary Islands and the Azores, as do the United States and New Zealand. Although most countries now benefit from whale watching tourism having abandoned their whaling industries, both Norway and Iceland (as well as Japan) continue to pursue both at the same time (Cunningham *et al.*, 2012; Rasmussen, 2014). Neves-Graça (2004) has pointed out that whale watching is often reductively portrayed as the diametric opposite to whale hunting, but this tends to discount the existence of whale watching practices that may be detrimental both to the whale and its habitat. There are, however, linkages between the two. Both, for example, produce a fetishized commoditization of cetaceans, as well as encouraging rifts in human–cetacean relations (Neves-Graça, 2004, see also Kalland, 2009). And in both, nature, Neves-Graça argues, is 'produced first and foremost according to capitalist principles, which problematizes the pervasive assumption that whale watching correlates primarily and directly with conservation' (2010, 719). Whale watching as a practice thus at once exemplifies the growing conservationist potential of tourism while betraying its escalating consumerist threat.

Whale watching in the Arctic has a special significance in the context of the Anthropocene. Unprecedented oceanographic and meteorological changes in the Arctic over several decades (Larsen *et al.*, 2014) have been explored through ice and geological records from the polar regions, lending the region a special status as emblem of the Anthropocene. As a supposedly pure, wild, sometimes an indigenous space, the Arctic is now a global synonym for concern about anthropogenic change and the potentially destructive effects of human activities on the Earth. At the same time, it is widely promoted as a new tourism destination, imagined as one of the last great wilderness adventures available on the Earth. Today, a supposed 'scramble' for the Arctic has opened the region up to substantive global commercial and political interest (Craciun, 2009). The future of the Arctic is the focus of intense political action, attracting scientists and environmentalists as witnesses to its material evidence, and politicians to employ it symbolically as an environmental credential, while attempting to secure national rights in the exploitation of its potential resources (Kristoffersen, 2015; Steinberg *et al.*, 2015). Such conflicting imaginaries about the Arctic also imply questions about what kind of ethics are precipitated by the Anthropocene. The relations that humans engage in are both defining Arctic conditions and producing their consequences, as we will discuss below.

In recent years, environmental organizations, such as Greenpeace, have adopted the Arctic polar bear as the icon for their campaigns instead of the whale. Yet if the campaigners appear to have lost interest in the whale as a symbol of endangered environmental endurance, broader interest in whales has a deep and sustained history. Human encounters with whales have been recorded as far back as six thousand years. According to archaeologists, rock carvings in Alta (in Arctic Norway) show whales diving into perhaps sacred, underwater worlds. Humans have captured whales for a range of purposes, most notably for oil and food, and have mythologized them in a range of ways, the most recent being the campaigns against whaling in the late 20th century in which whales became shorthand for 'saving the planet' (Kalland, 1993; Epstein, 2008).

The beginnings of the industry of whale watching and the form of its subsequent development have both had palpable effects on the shifting ethics of the human–whale encounter, and the enactment of forms of regulation. Cetaceans, as Einarsson notes (2009), are a very particular kind of animal, and in whale watching tourism, one encounters people who desire to be with whales in companionable togetherness. At the same time whales have become an 'Arctic spectacle' for locals, researchers, photographers and tourists alike, and in this process the whale has been transformed from an object of searching and hunting to one for searching and observing. It can be argued that the whale in this process has been 're-mattered', that is to say its matter has been recast in different assemblages of techniques and practices that produce the whale as either a marketable meat product for consumption, or as a vehicle for the socio-technical networks of the tourism industry. Re-mattering the whale thus implicates a shift in ethical framing, so it becomes what Haraway (2003) calls a 'companion species' to humans: a co-species, to whom rights are ascribed, and to whom specific duties of care are due, and which plays out under the terms of the Capitalocene as much as an Anthropocene.

Encountering whales in Andenes, Húsavík and Tromsø

This re-mattering is particularly palpable in Andenes (Norway) and Húsavík (Iceland) with the rapid growth of their respective whale watching industries. Both places have experienced a steady transformation since the mid-to-late 1980s, from diminutive fishing villages with large-scale fishing industries into large-scale whale watching centres. In both Andenes and Húsavík, norms, rules and regulations for whale watching have been self-devised and are self-policed, and while they are still works in progress, they do serve to some extent to protect the whales from undue disruption. In Tromsø, whales have only recently found their way into the waters around the city, with hundreds of orca visiting the city's waterfront, feeding and giving birth during a short winter season, and humpback whales just a little further out in the fjords. This new appearance of numerous whales so close to the city has given rise to something of a gold rush of whale watching activity, with many under-regulated small boats rushing out to take tourists to see the action.

In total, about 20,000 tourists paid a ticket for whale watching in Norway in 2014, whilst in Iceland the number is about 250,000. In Húsavík, locals started up whale watching tourism based on a knowledge-based approach similar to that practised in Andenes. In Tromsø, in contrast, there have been other factors at play in the rapid growth of a whale watching industry. We present here a brief picture of these three whale watching worlds, highlighting similarities and differences between them, in order to shed light on the scene forming around whale-based tourism.

Andenes

Andenes is a small town of around 2,500 people on the northern tip of the island of Andøya in Vesterålen, a small archipelago that stretches out from the northern Norwegian coast, just north of the better-known Lofoten islands. Whale watching trips were initiated by anti-whaling activists who arrived in Andenes after the so-called 'whale wars' in Lofoten in the mid-1980s. They gradually raised awareness among local residents of the proximity of the whales and of the potential for a new kind of tourism. These early founders took a knowledge-based approach to whale watching, working with leading biologists to educate both locals and tourists about the whales, and in return they saw a steady growth in visitor numbers.

Being some way out into the North Atlantic Ocean, Andøya is a popular destination for tourists, at the northern tip of the picturesque Vesterålen islands. The continental shelf is at its narrowest here, and the cold waters rising to the warmer surface generate abundant food that attracts whales. More than 70 male sperm-whales have the Andenes area as their semi-permanent territory, only migrating south to African waters during the winter to breed, while other species move into these waters to feed in winter.

When Norway stopped whaling temporarily in 1988, some Lofoten based activists moved to Andenes. Locals described them as 'foreigners with long hair who came from Sweden, Finland or Denmark', denoting them as 'Greenpeacers'. A municipal representative recalled that, although they might initially have been seen as the enemy, 'many of them turned out to be trained biologists, and they became great guides for whale watching'. As he explained, 'they were chased out of Lofoten, but here we welcomed them'. Whaling thus gave way to a new kind of hunt: for the experience of being near an ocean-going whale, and of shooting it with a camera.

It was the municipality and the regional council who first sponsored and owned the single whale watching enterprise at Andenes harbour developed by these activists. After a few years, it was taken over by a local resident. A stream of scientists came to do research, including acoustic sampling experiments with hydrophones to record the communication between sperm whales and their hunting sounds (ticking sounds), which are now used to engage the whale watchers in the hunt.

While many tourists apparently take in a whale watching trip as one of a number of activities on their holidays, our interlocutors reported that many come specifically to encounter whales. One guide in Andenes explains that whale watching is for some 'a lifetime experience, a moment they have been waiting for'. For these visitors, he continued, 'it is so emotional, they are so excited, many times people cry ... it is like a life dream come true'. Tourists told us that they sought the experience 'of being so close to something so big'. One tourist who mentioned a whale watching trip to be on his bucket list explained his response to the whales as the antithesis of modernity, 'They are free: no internet, no decisions to make, always getting to eat and making love; in the wild; easy life.' According to the guide, bucket-list tourists saw the whales as 'the nice guy in the ocean', and sought companionship from the whales. As the guide put it, tourists 'see reality how they want to see reality', and interpreting the whales' lives in line with their existing concepts of the freedom of nature. According to the guide, many tourists saw whales as closely related to humans, having intelligence and feelings. 'They live in family bonds, they have a very social behaviour, and that all together – even if you see now that it looks like a reptile, still it creates so many emotions.'

Figure 6.1 The sperm-whale 'Helge' at Andenes, which breached the surface of the water twice during our July 2014 fieldwork. First spotted in 1995, Helge was one of the first whales to be mapped at Andenes and is easily recognizable from the white spot on his tale. The guides get excited every time Helge appears.

Photo: Britt Kramvig

Húsavík

Whale watching in Iceland began in the south-eastern village of Höfn in 1991 and was then taken up at other sites (Rasmussen, 2014). The village of Húsavík (population 2,338), at the Skjálfandi Bay on Iceland's north coast, is one of half a dozen communities in Iceland that currently maintain an active whale watching industry, but Húsavík and Reykjavík account for over 90 per cent of the country's whale watching tourism activities. Prior to the mid-1990s, Húsavík had long been a relatively large fishing settlement (Einarsson, 2011). In the 1960s, the fishing industry represented 90 per cent of the Iceland's exports, but dwindling fish stocks and changes in Icelandic fishing rights towards the end of the last century left the settlement open to other forms of commerce, and many of its residents sought new livelihoods.

In 2012, roughly 50,000 tourists visited Húsavík, nearly all of whom took part in whale watching activities. Activities in the town are provided by three individual enterprises, each of them 'locally family-owned and operated'. Most of the boats are converted fishing and whaling boats originally built in the middle of the last century, which have a capacity up to 85 passengers, plus newer inflatable Zodiac (RIB/SIB) boats, which can hold a maximum of 24 persons each. Interestingly, the converted boats were not restored by cunning businessmen wanting to confer

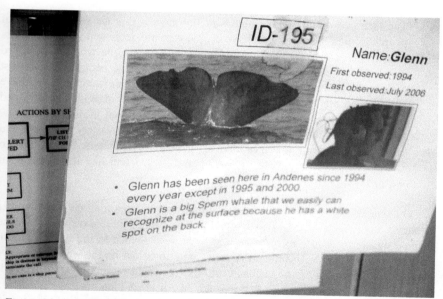

Figure 6.2 Glenn is perhaps an even bigger cetacean celebrity. He is named after the son of the Whalesafari Andenes manager. This sheet has hung in the bridge of the M/S Reine for many years. Glenn is still seen regularly in the waters off Andenes, and we encountered him many times during fieldwork trips with two operators.

Photo: Berit Kristoffersen

an authentic flavour on profitable whale watching activities, but by passionate boat owners who were keen to preserve the handsome, rugged boats, employing artisans skilled in wood restoration techniques. It is this juxtaposition between old and new (i.e. wooden trawlers and the new Zodiac inflatable boats) that is of particular value to Húsavík's lure as a contemporary whale watching destination, adding 'the authenticity of the stage for whale watching as part and parcel of genuine coastal culture' (Einarsson, 2011). The boats used for whale watching in Reykjavík, in contrast, are all modern, purpose-built vessels. Nevertheless, as in other parts of the Arctic, whaling and the products derived from the whale have long held symbolic value for Icelanders (Einarsson, 2011), even if Icelanders have never employed so-called traditional whaling practices for subsistence, unlike in Greenland.

The continuation or resumption of whaling has been a topic of debate about Icelandic tourism for some time, but there is no evidence that it deters some tourists from visiting Iceland. Yet the ethical dilemmas exist, neatly summed by a *Guardian* journalist as early as 2003, who asked 'Is it ethical to go whale watching in a country that still engages in whaling?' (Alderson, 2003). In Iceland, too, there are differences of opinion, and as a marketing director of Reykjavík-based whale watching tour operator, acknowledged, not everyone visiting Iceland is aware that whaling still takes place in the country. However, the director viewed this as an opportunity for the company to educate tourists:

> The interesting thing with whale watching here is that we have all kinds of people joining the tours: you have people who are dedicated whale watchers who come here to go whale watching; you have people who are into bird watching and nature watching in general ... you have people who are just looking for recreation and someone recommends whale watching; you have people who are on an organized group tour and their activities are decided before; you have people who want to just go on a boat in nice weather ... [This] gives us the opportunity to reach out to a wide variety of people and educate them about conservation, just general environmental work, and to inspire them, you know, to do the small things. I feel like it matters what we're saying.

On one of our visits, we met a Spanish couple spending their September honeymoon in Iceland, who had stopped in Húsavík for three days to experience whale watching. While there were said to be few whales in the bay so late in the season, the couple was nevertheless excited to be out on the water. 'I always wanted to see a whale,' the husband told us. 'We didn't come here [to Iceland] specifically for whale watching, but it felt like a great idea once we got here.' The couple did not appear to know much about the current status of whaling in Iceland, though they had noticed the 'Meet Us Don't Eat Us' signs (the slogan of an IFAW-Icewhale joint project launched in 2010) posted in the windows of several local restaurants in Reykjavík. The Spanish couple did not end up seeing any whales on that day (although several dolphins were spotted). This lack of a sighting seemed to be an anomaly for Húsavík that year, which had otherwise been extremely active. One foreign guide working for the company running the tour told of a fraught incident from earlier that year when the tour boats out in the bay had ended up crowding (and may have even hit) a whale:

> There was one really difficult whale, it was changing direction and moving very fast. And the boats were following it – it was a time when we had only one or two whales in the bay – and so all the boats went for the whale. We had, like, six boats out at the time. All the boats were going forward onto him [the whale] ... So one of them finally turned around and left the scene. The captain on this boat didn't see the whale even ... and the whale just popped up in front of him, because he [the whale] was diving underneath to get away from the boats ... And then the whale just swam straight out of the bay.

Yet after the captains had piloted the boats back into Húsavík's harbour, there was almost no formal discussion between the companies or the captains about what had happened. The guide explained that the incident was due to the lack of organized communication between the captains helming the boats:

> The [captains] talk on the radio [sometimes] but not too much. In that situation though, there was no real communication ... no one talked, no one said, like, 'Oh, let's move to the side.' ... It was not the first time [a whale] had changed direction while we were watching it. I think a regulation about the distance from boat to whale would be a good thing.

This incident is typical of tension between operators, captains and guides both at Húsavík and Andenes. Guides tend to want to guard the whales, while captains have the final say on what distance to keep from the whales. In February 2015, regulations (a voluntary code of conduct for whale watching companies) were agreed upon at the Icewhale meeting in Reykjavík between all of the major operators in Iceland. This will probably give the unfolding debates on regulations and norms a new frame of reference. In Tromsø on the other hand, this debate has just started and was the major topic during the aforementioned workshop on the growing whale watching industry.

Tromsø

A population of mostly humpback, killer and fin whales appeared in the waters around Tromsø in 2011, entering the fjords that surround the Arctic city. Although the reason for these (renewed) migratory routes has yet to be proven by marine biologists, the rising temperature of Arctic waters has been put forward as a possible explanation (ICES, 2011). The sea temperature directly affects the rates of metabolic processes in herring, which in turn affect their swimming activity, enzyme activity and the digestion rate of the fish. Warmer temperatures increase the rates, resulting in more deaths of larvae and young herring (Pacific Herring,

2014). Whatever the cause, these newly introduced whale populations attract a range of new actors and connections. In just three years, whale safaris have become one of the most popular tourist attractions in the Tromsø area. Numbers are rising fast. In the 2013–14 season over 800 tourists paid to go on a whale watching trip, distributed amongst the six companies that were offering whale safari that season. In the following season (2014–2015), the numbers were up to 1,900 whale watchers, distributed amongst nine companies, offering 12 different whale safaris. In addition to all the operators, many involved in the industry claim there are also unlicensed boats offering tours. In addition, locals also go out in their boats and kayaks for a closer encounter with the whales, leading occasionally to chaotic conditions at sea. According to news reports, verified in our own ethnographic experience, there have been similar conditions further out in the fjords beyond the city, with spectators driving out of Tromsø and into the fjords of the surrounding islands to see the whales from the shore.

Among the people travelling to experience encounters with whales, tourists from the UK comprised the biggest group in both seasons (about one-third of the bookings) whilst Norwegians overtook Germans in the 2014–15 season in second place, with Swiss and French tourists being next on the list, while the number of East Asian tourists is on the rise. Most of the tourists who travel from European countries tend be on shorter, 'city-break' winter-season holidays. New direct flights to Tromsø from London, Helsinki and Stockholm have contributed to the 21 per cent increase in annual airline arrivals to Tromsø between 2009 and 2013, and a much more significant increase in the winter season, with hotel nights in Tromsø up from nearly 15 per cent from 2013 to 2014 alone (Statistikknett Reiseliv, 2015). Some tourists come specifically for whale watching, with some coming specifically to photograph the whales (e.g. on photographic expeditions), while others come to go diving with whales and other marine species in the Arctic waters. Some companies are combining whale watching opportunities with dogsledding, snowmobiling and land and sea safaris to see the Northern Lights, as well as other winter activities. Whilst Visit Tromsø, the local Destination Management Organization, brands the city to tourists as being the best spot for 'hunting the Northern Lights', major tourism actors, such as Hurtigruten (the coastal steamer), is starting to question whether the whale may be 'our new Northern light' (Jacobsen, 2014). These are consequently putting significant effort into becoming leading purveyors of whale watching safaris.

Whales are not Northern Lights, however. The Northern Lights are in the sky irrespective of tourism activity, while the question of approaching whales throws into sharp relief the encounters between humans and wildlife. 'It's not like the northern lights, that's not nature,' one of the whale watching entrepreneurs told us. 'These are living species with their own rights, and when up to ten big ships gather around them, their interests are not really kept in the form that I consider correct, and because there are no regulations, we can only watch when ships … speed into a flock of whales.' He was very worried, he said, about what might happen in the following season.

For travellers coming to Tromsø, the experience is 'like entering a different reality', as one Italian visitor told us. For him, the lack of light and the intensity of the nature were difficult to deal with. In a conversation about sustainability, he wondered whether some brown areas that he had noticed on the mountains around Tromsø were indications of changes in nature, since the snow had disappeared. The group he was with began to discuss this. His girlfriend told us that on her visit to Polaria (a research-focused Arctic aquarium with knowledge-based exhibits branded as 'an Arctic experience'), she became aware for the first time of the melting of the Arctic ice sheet. When we asked whether they had talked about it amongst themselves after the experience, they said, 'No – we are tourists', suggesting that they weren't here to learn or 'stress' about global environmental change. Even so, they did observe that (environmental) changes were much more visible in Norway, whereas in their large Southern European city, anthropogenic change seems much less obvious to them, and thus they feel less immediately affected by it.

Companions that matter

People's accounts of their encounters with whales tend to confirm that whales are represented as conscious beings with emotions and individualities. People believe that the whales make their own choices in regard to which boat they approach, they decide how long they stay with the specific boats and thus whale watchers. The guides often tell these stories to the tourists, about specific whales knowing the boat and thereby becoming more likely to approach it. Their autonomy is captured in the words of one of the guides at Húsavík during a trip where it was difficult to spot whales: 'You cannot control nature.' Yet at the same time touristic practices contrast the holiday experience with everyday life, contributing to the reproduction of the modernist notion that nature is a separate realm. In this context the natural world provides a refuge, in much the same way that tourism is argued to provide relief from the everyday of modern life (Blok, 2007). Whale watching tourism endeavours to put people 'back in touch' with this nature. People boarding tourist vessels in Arctic water, enter turbulent and stormy waters where many learn that their bodies cannot withstand the waves as the boat rolls around. Seasickness both in Iceland and in Norway appears regularly, especially on the winter tours.

The whale watching tours frame the reconnecting to nature through the whale in a specific way. The whale is portrayed as an autonomous, sentient being, choosing which vessels to approach and stay with. This reflects anthropomorphism, in which people attribute human qualities to the whale. Yet as Blok (2007, 77) argues, interpreting human–whale relations solely through an idea of anthropomorphism implies that people only experience whales through species-specific categories, rather than through more general notions of human and non-human 'personhood'. The term anthropomorphism may thus underestimate our humanity by always seeing it as the attribution of human qualities *to* whales, thus working as a 'distancing device' to uphold

conceptual boundaries between humans and animals. As a consequence
humans deny themselves the opportunity to recognize personhood in whales
(Blok, 2007, 77). Through the cetaceans, we argue that the guides could be
said to be Anthropoceans, in that they make sense of climate change and the
other Anthropocene conditions as they encounter the whales. Mediating this
to the tourists, they seem to struggling with giving the tourists the 'authentic'
experience that the tourists expect and be true to their own personal motivation
and knowledge and thus ethically mediate Anthropocene conditions.

How the distancing device of anthropomorphism can be dampened through
notions of personhood is characterized by Kay Milton in her study of nature
protection (2002). She highlights the responsibilities that extend well beyond
other humans, and argues that by recognizing moral obligations towards non
humans or more-than-humans, these are accorded rights, 'thereby defining them
as the kinds of things that can have rights, in other words, as persons' (2002
28). This contrasts with those who value non-human things as resources for
human use (as food, or providing subsistence materials, for example), or for their
general value for ecological diversity. Accepting that whales and other animal
have forms of personhood that afford them rights helps to muddy the water
between the human and the non-human, in a way that complements rather than
reproduces the arguments associated with the Anthropocene. While the proposal
that we are in the geological epoch of the Anthropocene is supported by claims
that no area of the Earth is now unaffected by human activities, the notion of non
human persons forms part of a longer argument that has demonstrated that the
very idea of 'Nature' as a realm external to humans is itself a culturally specific
mode of thought (see Abram and Lien, 2011; Law and Lien, 2013). If implicit in
the notion of the Anthropocene is a recognition that humans and their cultures can
no longer be held apart from the nature of the Earth, that we must let go of human
exceptionalism, then we must take seriously the personhood of non-humans
Unlike Haraway's Capitalocene, which might offer an economic explanation of
the rapid expansion of human exploitation of fossil resources, the Anthropocene
tells us something more about the co-ecology of humans in the world (see also
Morton, 2007). Thinking about the Anthropocene can thus open up the concept of
non-human personhood, which in turn gives us new ways to think ethically about
our relationships with cetaceans and other animals.

A wave of scholarship has sought to re-entwine human culture into a collective
ecology, exploring the companionship between species and inspired, not least
by traditions of ecological writing that go back at least to Lewis Henry Morgan'
work in the 1860s (see Kirksey and Helmreich, 2010, 549). The emphasis in such
work has been to consider how humans live 'with' others, including humans and
non-humans. For Haraway (2008) this leaves the category of 'species' unstable
and less specific than imagined by, for example, the biological sciences. The
literature on multi-species ethnographies urges us to consider how relations
emerge, sometimes in the form of action, and sometimes in the form of species
themselves. This implies a shifting understanding of the status of species, and
helps us to rethink what is a whale, and what is a person. The term species

suggests discrete types, yet our worldly experience informs us that species are mingled and often co-dependent, and even that human nature is an interspecies relationship (Tsing, 2014).

Considering the whale through interspecies relations and personhood allows an understanding of charismatic oceanic mega-fauna as emerging beings, that are becoming *with* humans and accruing rights and relations of care, from the anti-whaling environmental movements of the 1970s to the new whale watching tourism of today. When whales are appreciated as sentient beings with personhood, they prompt human action, and as sentient beings themselves they respond to human action in turn. The whales rammed by the careless driving of boats in the Tromsø area were caught up in a scenario that entailed extensive networks of boats, tourists, guides, tour operators, different families of whales, international airlines, global media and so forth. In this maelstrom of actors, whales gained status and were afforded personhood and care (Meyer and Jepperson, 2000).

Implied in this attribution is a set of ethics that accords rights, and thus demands particular kinds of action, which establish the content of personhood and care. A public servant at the local authority at Andenes contrasted hunting and adventure, arguing that while many people 'have feelings for the big animal in the ocean, which is a good feeling that makes people oppose whaling', for him it was natural to eat whale meat. There are limits to acceptance, however. When someone at Andenes tried to establish a factory to make whale burgers, this was not explicitly resisted, but nor were they embraced. The sale of whale burgers was expected to put tourists off, so it would be inappropriate for Andenes to be associated with 'an industry where we would drag dead minke whales up the pebbles on Andøya to produce food of it, while conducting whale watching – the experience of the great spermaceti animal – at sea', the public servant told us during an interview. By contrast, in 2014, Iceland's Steðji brewery produced a beer made from the entrails of fin whales, the majority of which are otherwise exported to Japan. Despite concomitant controversy and protest, in 2015, the brewery produced a limited-edition Hvalur 2 beer, made from cured, salted and smoked whale testicles, in order to commemorate the mid-winter month of Thorri (BBC News, 2015).

Mediating the Anthropocene through tourism

These contradicting practices of care, concerning eating what you watch, chimes with our research which indicates that whale watching companies in Norway and Iceland incorporating global warming or ecological damage into the experience 'sold' to tourists are the exception rather than the rule. Our discussions with tourists have also made it clear that they are not there to observe changes in nature; for most people this is a leisure experience, not a pedagogical project. In other words, it is not *because of* environmental changes framed currently under the terms of the Anthropocene that they have come to spend their holiday in the Arctic – even if it is as a result of anthropogenic change that more of the region is accessible. However, the tour operators and guides who offer whale watching trips mediate tourists' whale watching experiences, and among these operators we have found many idealists. Many of the guides, as we have exemplified, are not only concerned with the preservation of whales, but are up to date with scientific discourse about climate and environmental change, and are often knowledgeable about how this affects the whales. Several guides working on whale watching boats in Húsavík mentioned the discussion of whether the return of some whales (e.g. the blue whale) to Iceland may be related to warming sea temperature, as is also one of the main theories explaining the 'return of the whales' in Tromsø. These guides thus strive to ensure that, through their experiences, tourists also adopt a knowledge-based approach to whales and ocean ecologies.

Tourists thus become new actors in the encounter with whales, and while they often articulate that whale watching enables them to feel close to nature, conjuring a notion of nature that corresponds with divisions between the human and the natural, they also encounter a new way to conceptualize their relations with a nature that draws ever closer to the human. In this, whale watching can be seen to straddle the ethical stipulations of the Anthropocene which, by definition, suggest that human action is not discrete from the Earth, and that nature is a constructed category that enables a category of non-nature-human to exist. In other words, encounters with whales in Artic waters enact a particular concept of nature that is conflicted and unstable. Tourism operators do not necessarily 'sell' an Anthropocene version of human–nature relationships in the Arctic, but the emergence of a companionable whale demonstrates human–nonhuman relations in practice. The ethical frame of whale watching as an Anthropocene tourism has thus been changed by the reimagination of the whale as an earthly companion species with characteristics of personhood, and with rights and territories that require humans to behave in a new way and engage in new relationships. This corresponds to Zylinska's minimal ethics entailing an acknowledgement of human entanglement, one that we see as the first step towards Haraway's call for a period of deep rethinking of the stories we tell about humans and nature. Thus far, we have seen whale tourism both prompting and fulfilling a vision of the companionable whale, but the deep rethinking for a new epoch is less evident.

Acknowledgement

The authors are grateful to Simone Abram for her work on earlier drafts of this article.

References

Aaserud, M., and Johnsen, L. 2014. Jeg var ikke borti hvalen. <http://www.itromso.no/nyheter/article10365733.ece> [accessed Feb. 2015].
Abram, S., and Lien, M.E. 2011. Performing nature at world's ends. *Ethnos*, 76(1), 3–18.
Alderson, A. 2003. Blowing it. *Guardian*, 23 Aug. <http://www.theguardian.com/travel/2003/aug/23/iceland.wildlifeholidays.guardiansaturdaytravelsection> [accessed Feb. 2015].

BBC News 2015. Iceland: Brewery makes 'whale testicle beer'. <http://www.bbc.co.uk/news/blogs-news-from-elsewhere-30777516> [accessed Apr. 2015].

Blok, A. 2007. Actor-networking ceta-sociality, or, what is sociological about contemporary whales? *Distinktion: Scandinavian Journal of Social Theory*, 8(2), 65–89.

Craciun, A. 2009. The scramble for the Arctic. *Interventions*, 11(1), 103–14.

Cunningham, P. Huijbens, E., and Wearing, S. 2012. Whaling or watching: Twisting the sustainability rhetoric and possible outcomes. *Journal of Sustainable Tourism*, 20(1), 143–61.

Einarsson, N. 1993. All animals are equal but some are cetaceans: Conservation and culture conflict. In K. Milton (ed.), *Environmentalism the view from anthropology*. London: Routledge, 71–82.

Einarsson, N. 2009. From good to eat to good to watch: Whale watching, adaptation and change in Icelandic fishing communities. *Polar Research*, 28, 129–38.

Einarsson, N. 2011. *Culture, Conflict and Crises in the Icelandic Fisheries: An Anthropological Study of People, Policy and Marine Resources in the North Atlantic Arctic*. Unpublished Ph.D. thesis, Uppsala University.

Epstein, C. 2008. *The Power of Words in International Relations: Birth of an Anti-Whaling Discourse*. Cambridge, MA: MIT Press.

Haraway, D. 2003. *The Companion Species Manifesto: Dogs, People and Significant Otherness*. Chicago, IL: University of Chicago Press.

Haraway, D. 2008. *When Species Meet*. London: University of Minnesota Press.

Haraway, D. 2014. Anthropocene, Capitalocene, Chthulucene: Staying with the trouble. Keynote speech to Arts of Living on a Damaged Planet. <http://anthropocene.au.dk/arts-of-living-on-a-damaged-planet> or <http://vimeo.com/97663518> [accessed Mar. 2015].

Haraway, D. 2015. Anthropocene, Capitalocene, Plantationocene, Chthulucene: Making Kin. *Environmental Humanities*, 6, 159–165.

Hoyt, E., and Iñiguez, M. 2008. *The State of Whale Watching in Latin America*. Chippenham: WDCS.

ICES 2011. Report of the Working Group on Widely Distributed Stocks (WGWIDE) 23–29 August 2011. <http://www.ices.dk/sites/pub/Publication%20Reports/Expert%20Group%20Report/acom/2011/WGWIDE/WGWIDE%20Report%202011.pdf> [accessed Mar. 2015].

Jacobsen, V.T. 2014. Talk given at whale watching workshop for operators, Tromsø, 27 Nov.

Kirksey, S.E., and Helmreich, S. 2010. The emergence of multispecies ethnography. *Cultural Anthropology*, 25(4), 545–76.

Kalland, A. 1993. Management by totemization: Whale symbolism and the anti-whaling campaign. *Arctic*, 46(2), 124–33.

Kalland, A. 2009. *Unveiling the Whale: Discourses on Whales and Whaling*. Oxford: Berghahn.

Kristoffersen, B. 2015. Opportunistic Adaptation: New discourses on oil, equity and environmental security. In K. O'Brien and E. Selboe (eds), *The Adaptive Challenge of Climate Change*. New York and London: Cambridge University Press, 140–59.

Larsen, J.N., *et al.* 2014. Polar regions. In V.R. Barros *et al.* (eds), *Climate Change 2014: Impacts, Adaptation, and Vulnerability. Part B: Regional Aspects. Contribution of Working Group II to the Fifth Assessment Report of the Intergovernmental Panel on Climate Change*. Cambridge: Cambridge University Press, 1567–1612.

Law, J., and Lien, M. 2013. Slippery: Field notes in empirical ontology. *Social Studies of Science*, 43, 363–78.

Lawrence, T.B., and Phillips, N. 2004. From Moby Dick to Free Willy: Macrocultural discourse and institutional entrepreneurship in emerging institutional fields. *Organization*, 11(5), 689–711.

Meyer, J.W., and Jepperson, R.L. 2000. The 'actors' of modern society: The cultural construction of social agency. *Sociological Theory*, 18(1), 100–20.

Milton, K. 2002. *Loving Nature: Towards an Ecology of Emotion*. London: Routledge.

Morton, T. 2007. *Ecology without Nature: Rethinking Environmental Aesthetics*. Cambridge, MA: Harvard University Press.

Pacific Herring 2014. Pacific Herring: Past, present and future. <http://www.pacificherring. org/climate-change> [accessed Mar. 2015].

Neves-Graça, K. 2004. Revisiting the tragedy of the commons: Ecological dilemmas of whale watching in the Azores. *Human Organization*, 63(3), 289–300.

Neves-Graça, K. 2010. Cashing in on cetourism: A critical ecological engagement with dominant E-NGO Discourses on whaling, cetacean conservation, and whale watching. *Antipode*, 42(3), 719–41.

Parsons, E.C.M. 2012. The negative impacts of whale watching. *Journal of Marine Biology*, 2012, 1–9.

Peace, A. 2010. The whaling war. *Anthropology Today*, 26(3), 5–9.

Pedersen, C. 2014. Reagerer kraftig på hvalpåseiling. <http://www.itromso.no/nyheter/ article10344020.ece> [accessed Feb. 2015].

Rasmussen, M. 2014. The whaling versus whale watching debate: The resumption of Icelandic whaling. In J. Higham, L. Bejder and R. Williams (eds), *Whale watching: Sustainable Tourism and Ecological Management*. Cambridge: Cambridge University Press, 81–94.

Statistikknett Reiseliv 2015. Norsk reiseliv i regionalt perspektiv. <http://www. statistikknett.no/nordnorge/Default.aspx> [accessed Jan. 2015].

Steinberg P.E., Tasch, J., and Gerhardt, H. 2015. *Contesting the Arctic: Politics and Imaginaries in the Circumpolar North*. London and New York: I.B. Tauris.

Stoett, P.J. 1997. *The International Politics of Whaling*. Vancouver: UBC Press.

Tsing, A. 2014. Unruly edges: Mushrooms as companion species. <http://tsingmushrooms. blogspot.co.uk> [accessed Mar. 2015].

Zylinska, J. 2014. *Minimal Ethics for the Anthropocene*. Ann Arbor, MI: Open Humanities Press.

7 Good versus bad tourism

Homo viator's responsibility in light of life-value onto-axiology

Giorgio Baruchello

Homo viator

A founding father of French existentialism, Gabriel Marcel (1889–1973) rediscovered the Augustinian notion of *homo viator*, whereby the human condition is understood as akin to a traveller whose true being is defined by the journeys that she chooses to pursue and, above all, by the relationships that she establishes along the way (Kuntz, 1980). Unless a person is condemned by early death or severely disabling conditions, choosing no journey at all and engaging in no relationships whatsoever are not options, for we are naturally bound to inhabit a specific place in time and space as well as a human community of sorts, as sedentary or even as suicidal as we may eventually decide to be. Whether we like it or not, we are cast in this world and will have made many choices, trodden many paths, endorsed many values and met many people, our own family relatives or guardians *in primis*, before we can even begin reflecting upon the possibility of taking a step into the nihilistic abyss of self-seclusion or self-destruction (Marcel, 1962, 1967).

Yet it is not the 'absolute despair' driving some individuals to isolation or suicide that Marcel (1967, 28) concentrates upon, unlike other famous French existentialists such as Sartre and Camus. Rather, it is the 'unconquerable hope' that, mysteriously, animates most human lives. Neither the nauseating awareness of inevitable mortality and seemingly absurd Sisyphean toil, nor the painful testimony of physical, mental and moral degeneration can disarm most people's ability to retrieve some value in their experiences, or the 'substance of *life*', as Marcel (1962, 43; emphasis added) dubs it. Fired by a hope-fuelled 'enthusiasm or ardor for *life*', we are generally capable of finding a modicum of fulfilment in our existence, as troublesome and as finite as we understand it to be (Marcel, 1962, 43; emphasis added).

According to Marcel (1962, 38–9), by informing our mental abilities with hopeful ardour for life, we set in motion a 'creative process' whereby we establish our 'I' through time (i.e. our individuality) and move beyond our immediate circumstances by conceiving of our own future constructively, recognizing value both around and within us, while at the same time opening ourselves to other persons like us, 'our neighbors'. In this manner, we may be able to overcome the 'temptation to despair' induced by the consciousness of our unavoidable transience, constitutional frailty and possible solitude (Marcel, 1962, 36). Echoing Augustine, Marcel (1962) depicts a human reality in which sin is always afoot; but so is the way to salvation. The latter requires acknowledging interpersonal relationships and how we are going to go about them, not least about the one that we may discover and accept to have with a divine person, as Marcel himself did in his adult life (he converted to Catholicism in the late 1920s, distinguishing himself once more from French existentialists like Sartre and Camus, who were professed atheists; Hernandez, 2011; Sweetman, 2008).

Given the inherent inescapability of our journeys on this Earth, the notion of *homo viator* is nothing but another philosophical definition of the human being, alongside Schiller's *homo ludens* and Bergson's *homo faber*. Whichever journeys we may be on, whichever relationships we may engage in, for as long as we live and act, we are travelling. Furthermore, we are not alone on our journeys, even if we may not like all or any of our fellow travellers, or choose not to believe that some do actually exist, such as present society, future generations, the Earth's local and global ecosystems, or these ecosystems unified totality as a living entity.

Consistent with Augustine's original emphasis, Marcel's (1962) notion of *homo viator* focuses eventually upon the immortal soul's journey from its earthly dwelling to *post-mortem* otherworldliness, and the significance of our earthly moral standing for this journey. Under this perspective, crucial is the relationship that we may or may not decide to establish with the supreme *fons vitae*, i.e. God. In daily experience, many journeys are undertaken in an apparently much more prosaic way, such as those of contemporary tourists. What we commonly associate with these journeys are evasion, relaxation, breaks from work routines, last-minute deals and a modicum of legal rights when things do not work as they should. The crushing power of mortality, frailty and solitude are not part of tourist brochures. God is hardly ever mentioned in connection with EasyJet or Ryanair, unless the traveller experiences much turbulence during a flight. The commonplace experience of tourism sounds not only anti-climactic *vis-à-vis* Marcel's *homo viator*; it seems totally unrelated.

This unrelatedness is obvious only *prima facie*. No matter how profound or exceptional the key questions of existentialism may sound, ordinary tourism is also affected by how we give shape to our own identity, how we think about our future, what type of values we opt for and what kind of interpersonal relationships we cherish. As banal as people's summer holidays may seem at first, these too are journeys that impinge upon matters of life and death; they too define our identity and the authenticity of our existence. For one, albeit catered as an alternative among many in conventional tourist marketing, pilgrimages in Christian, Muslim and Buddhist cultures are a patent example of journeys that aim at more than sheer entertainment. Supposedly, the fate of one's own soul may depend on them. For another, choosing to travel in order to hunt down or eat animals listed among an ecosystem's endangered species, or to seek sexual gratification with adults or minors in poverty-stricken communities, says a lot about the person that we are, that we become, and how we associate ourselves with other persons.

As to less faith-inspired and morally extreme examples, the way in which we decide to travel (e.g. by more or less polluting means of transportation), the way in which we look – at, upon or after – the persons that we meet (e.g. waiters or travel guides) and the way in which we select our souvenirs and memorabilia (e.g. by purchasing archaeological artefacts of dubious origin) can tell us something about the ilk of persons that we are, become and associate with. The same can be said of whether one travels to discover oneself, be oneself or amuse oneself into oblivion of her circumstances. The very fact that we may or may not think about some of the moral implications of our not-so-extraordinary journeys reveals much about ourselves.

Tourism, like any other dimension of human agency, is no stranger to ethical and axiological assessment. As the pivotal World Tourism Organization's (WTO) (1999) Global Code of Ethics for Tourism (GCET) asserts, if ethically conducted, 'tourism' is capable of 'contributing to economic development, international understanding, peace, prosperity and universal respect for, and observance of, human rights and fundamental freedoms'. By implication, if tourism is not ethically conducted, some of the above goods may be diminished. In essence, depending on who gives shape to it and how, tourism can be good; or it can be bad.

Who is to say what is good and bad, though? On what ground can this kind of judgement be passed? How can assertions like those contained in GCET, which was adopted in 2001 by the United Nations (UN), be assessed and, if challenged, defended? Questions of this variety have kept philosophers busy for centuries and a number of answers have been provided over the long history of the discipline – far too much for a sheer book chapter like the present one. Rather, in what follows, whilst keeping the ground-breaking GCET in the background, I endorse, outline and apply John McMurtry's life-value onto-axiology, which is in all probability the most articulate theory of value developed by any philosopher in the 21st century. By doing so, given that the reader of this book is more likely to be a scholar in tourism studies than an academic philosopher, I offer first a detailed yet succinct presentation of a significant development in contemporary philosophical thought. Secondly, I offer a set of criteria whereby the reader can think about, and discriminate between, good and bad tourism, grounding GCET and any analogous normative approach to tourism in as deep a source of value as philosophical thought can retrieve. Moreover, as the paragraphs below show, the criteria offered by life-value onto-axiology are pertinent to the science and politics of tourism in the Anthropocene, neoliberalism and the global age, theorizing the Earth and humanity, carbon-fuelled capitalism and the end of nature and society – all of these being central themes of the present volume. I conclude this chapter by reflecting upon our being *homines viatores* in light of the implications of life-value onto-axiology for human agency, tourism included.

Life-value onto-axiology

McMurtry's entire endeavour is based upon the reasoned belief that, *pace* fashionable relativism and subjectivism, it is possible to identify a universal and objective ground of value. There may exist a 'marketplace of ideas' about what is good and what is not, but some preferences are actually better than others. According to McMurtry (2009–10a, para. 1.16; emphasis added), we can 'recover step by step the missing *life-ground* of values and the ultimate meaning of how we are to live'. The definition of the life-ground is not overly complicated: 'Concretely, all that is required to take the next breath; axiologically, all the life support systems required for human life to reproduce or develop' (McMurtry, 2009–10b). Without enough bread, clean water, breathable air, open spaces in which to move, regular sleep, acceptable education and meaningful socialization, no value whatsoever that we cherish will ever be expressed in reality. No value whatsoever, whether ethical, political, legal, economic, epistemic, spiritual or aesthetic, can be given independently of this vital platform. Life is the fundamental precondition for any and every other value that there can be (hence the prefix 'onto-' i.e. 'concerning being') and, *a fortiori*, it is itself valuable and inescapable whenever reflecting upon evaluations (hence 'axiology', i.e. 'value theory'). There can be no life as such, not to mention any good life, outside the life-ground. As McMurtry (2009–10a, para. 6.2.1) states:

> Life support systems – any natural or human-made system without which human beings cannot live or live well – may or may not have value in themselves, but have ultimate value so far as they are that without which human or other life cannot exist or flourish.

If Earth qua totality of its biodiversity-sustaining ecosystems is akin to a living individual, which one may wish to dub 'Gaia' (Lovelock, 1972), then the planet's life-support systems are akin to the functioning metabolic, psychological and socio-cultural apparatuses allowing a living individual to lead a life as such, and possibly a good life. To all effects, they are vital functions allowing concrete individuals to be alive as animals and active as human beings. Therefore, to deny the life-ground's import constitutes a token of performative contradiction, for she who denies it has been meeting her vital needs for the very long time entailed in developing the faculties required to deny its import. Even pessimists, suicides and gnostics affirm it, albeit *via negativa*, for they take their departure from a better life that is no more, that is dreamt or conceived of, or that is to be gained *post-mortem* (Baruchello, 2007). Logically, it is possible to distinguish between life's intrinsic value and the life-ground's instrumental value. Ontologically, it is not: 'All that is of worth consists in and enables life value to the extent of its experienced fields of thought, felt being and action (intrinsic value), and what underlies and enables these fields of life themselves, life support systems' (McMurtry 2009–10a, para. 6.1.4).

As revealed in the preceding quotation, McMurtry (2009–10a) maintains that life manifests itself in three modes of being: 'action' (also 'biological movement' or 'motility'), 'felt being' (also 'experience' or 'feeling') and 'thought' (para. 6.1). In the religious sphere, these modes of being are exemplified in the believer's gratitude for one's being alive, the comforting or even exhilarating presence of the divine within one's heart, and the thought-provoking subtleties of theological argumentation. In the secular sphere, health professionals come across these ontological modes under the guises of physical, psychological and mental well-/ill-being. Tourists encounter them too, for instance as healthy, pleasant, meaningful ethnic food in its original historic setting. Also, as shown by Baruchello and Johnstone (2011), human rights legislators and lawyers run into them qua constitutional provisions regarding, *inter alia*, 'rest, leisure and reasonable limitation of working hours and periodic holidays with pay', 'age limits below which the paid employment of child labor should be prohibited and punishable by law', and 'the diffusion of science and culture' (ICESCR, 1966, arts 7(d), 10 and 15).

All that is intuitively saluted as genius, justice, happiness or health is – if truly good – a constructive and comprehensive expression of life-value, in one or more of these modes of being: action (e.g. fitness), felt being (e.g. wonder at nature's intricate complexity) and thought (e.g. proportionality in judiciary adjudication). No sharp ontological tri- or dualism is implied by McMurtry's tripartite distinction:

> Although we can distinguish the cognitive and feeling capacities of any person, this does not mean dividing them into separate worlds as has occurred in the traditional divisions between mind and body, reason and the emotions. Life-value onto-axiology begins from their unity as the nature of the human organism.
>
> (McMurtry, 2009–10a, para. 6.3; emphasis removed)

Thus, the fundamental axioms in McMurtry's 'life-value onto-axiology' read as follows:

> *X is value if and only if, and to the extent that, x consists in or enables a more coherently inclusive range of thought/feeling/action than without it*
> *X is disvalue if and only if, and to the extent that, x reduces/disables any range of thought/experience/action.*
>
> (McMurtry, 2009–10a, para.6.1; emphasis in the original)

These axioms apply to all types of human agency. For instance, as far as contemporary environmentalism is concerned, McMurtry (2013, 42) distinguishes between 'zero growth' and 'zero bad growth', claiming the former to be negative and the latter to be positive, since 'growth of production that serves universal human life-needs is necessary and good the more there is deprivation'.

To all intents and purposes, McMurtry's life-value onto-axiology achieves a traditional goal of philosophical inquiry, since it allows for the determination in principle of good and evil, cutting across received dualisms, e.g. nature vs. culture, geoengineering vs. sustainable retreat, *res extensa* vs. *res cogitans*, utilitarianism vs. deontology, free choice vs. paternalism, free trade vs. protectionism, individualism vs. collectivism, liberalism vs. conservatism, cooperation vs. competition, theism vs. atheism, description vs. prescription, present vs. future, economic value vs. environmental value, etc. In theory, the definitive axiological criterion is sharp: *life-enablement is good; life-disablement is bad.*

In practice, there are going to be simpler and more complex evaluations to be made. Thorny cases and dilemmas are part of the fabric of the human world. Not even the most perceptive philosophy can save us from having to face them. Nevertheless, if life-value onto-axiology is correct, then the better option is bound to be always the result of comparisons of coherent life-value, since no good can be given outside the life-ground, the composition and scope of which McMurtry clarifies by means of two key concepts: 'need' and 'civil commons'.

On the former key concept, McMurtry (1998, 164) observes that not anything that we may claim to 'need' is, after closer scrutiny, a need: '"n" is a need if and only if, and to the extent that, deprivation of n always leads to a reduction of organic capacity'. Only that 'without which life-capacities are always reduced' counts as need (McMurtry, 2013, 19). We can live, and even prosper, without travel cheques or credit default swaps, but we cannot live, not to mention prosper, without 'sufficient nutriment, clean water, sewage facilities, learning of society's symbol systems, home and love, and expert care when ill' (McMurtry, 2013, 1). To strengthen the point, McMurtry scholar Noonan (2006, pp. xiv and 57) neatly separates needs from economic preferences ('wants'): (A) 'deprivation of needs always leads to harm whereas deprivation of wants is only harmful in light of revisable self-interpretation'; (B) 'needs are satiable whereas wants are not'. No much-desired expensive consumer goodies will ever be vital like water and bread.

McMurtry (2002, 156; emphasis removed) identifies humanity's fundamental 'means of life' or 'vital need[s] ... for none can be deprived without reduction of vital life capability'. In his formulation for the *Encyclopedia of Life Support Systems* (EOLSS), established in 2002 by the UN's Educational Scientific and Cultural Organization (UNESCO), McMurtry (2009–10a, para. 10.10.4) lists seven vital goods that refer to as many vital needs:

1   the atmospheric goods of breathable air, open space and light;
2   the bodily goods of clean water, nourishing goods and waste disposal;
3   the home and habitat goods of shelter from the elements;
4   the environmental good of natural and constructed elements all contributing to the whole;
5   the good of care through time by love, safety and health infrastructures;
6   the good of human culture in music, language, art, play and sport; and
7   the good of human vocation and social justice – that which enables and obliges all people to contribute to the provision of these life goods consistent with each's enjoyment of them.

If these goods are not provided, then vital needs are not met; and if these needs are not met, then human capabilities disintegrate, to the eventual point of individual and/or social annihilation. If these needs are met, instead, then human capabilities do not merely endure: they can 'flourish' into the good life, individual as well as social (McMurtry, 2002, 156).

On the latter key concept, McMurtry (2009–10b) defines 'civil commons' as '[a] unifying concept to designate social constructs which enable universal access to life goods'. McMurtry (2013, 240) lists an array of concepts, arrangements and artefacts aimed at fulfilling life-enabling ends under diverse socio-historical contexts (I italicize those that seem particularly relevant as regards tourism):

> The nature of language, *the air we breathe*, the common fire, *food recipes*, universal health plans, *the world wide web*, common sewers, international campaigns against US war crimes, *sidewalks and forest paths, sports and sports fields*, the open science movement, the Chinese concept of jen, the Jubilee of Leviticus, *public streetscapes*, effective pollution controls, *birdwatching, city squares and sidewalks*, Buddha's principle of interdependent origination, old-age pensions, the rule of life-protective law, universal education, universal hygiene practices, *footpaths and bicycle trails*, fair elections, unemployment insurance, *the global atmosphere, maximum work hours and minimum wages, public parks*, clean water, the Tao, community fish-habitats, public broadcasting, the ancient village commons before enclosures, the unnamed goal of the Occupy Movement.

Albeit usually devoid of an explicit overarching theory of value as their intellectual foundation, societies have been valuing, protecting, respecting and fulfilling life-requirements and life-support systems for millennia. Possibly built upon the cooperative inclinations that have helped the survival of many animal species, including ours, these many concepts, arrangements and artefacts have established 'commons' that are characterized by the predicate 'civil'. This predicate reveals the socially constructed and socially aimed dimensions of the institutions nurturing 'real capital', i.e. 'life-capital – the natural and human-made wealth that produces more through time without loss' (McMurtry, 2013, 199; emphasis removed).

McMurtry is not talking, say, of pastures available to all without supervision and sanctions for misuse, but of pastures that the community consciously or pre-consciously (i.e. akin to linguistic syntax) recognizes in its symbolic systems and manages in order to yield life-supporting fruits through time for all its members, thus reducing a prime cause of internecine competition. McMurtry's 'civil commons' should not be confused with Hardin's (1968) unregulated natural 'commons', whose tragic doom justifies their appropriation for private ends (McMurtry, 2013, 239). McMurtry's works are consistently critical of such an appropriation, since it has regularly taken place for class or elite benefit (e.g. 19th-century Highlands clearances), and/or converted the existing civil commons into means of non-universal (e.g. costly for-profit academic indexes) and/or life-disabling ends (e.g. employing higher human knowledge for the production of speculative 'financial weapons of mass destruction' [Buffett, 2003, 15]).

As to what constitutes 'real' or 'life capital', McMurtry (2013) treats it consistently as the evolving onto-axiological base for measurable life loss and gain through generational time. It is the totality of the biological species, their life-support systems, human cultures and technologies as they produce, reproduce and enable more life capacities. The Anthropocene implies *per se* no destructive agency on humankind's part. However, it has witnessed an exponential increase in the significance of human agency for this life-capital accumulation, which the human economy directs by its own corresponding order – and disorder – of production, reproduction and growth (cf. Johnson and Morehouse, 2014). How to steer human agency on Earth, and therefore the economy itself, constitutes the ultimate context for the exercise of freedom, as anxiety-laden and burdensome as such a responsibility may be.

Good and bad tourism

Given McMurtry's two fundamental axioms of life-value onto-axiology, tourism can be deemed good or bad depending on whether it enables life-means provision and enjoyment or not. Also, given the composition and scope of the life-ground, we can better grasp GCET's intended positive function for 'responsible tourism'. In essence, GCET is a token of civil commons, insofar as it is a social construct attempting to steer human activities nationally and internationally so that life-enabling goods, in this case those related to tourism, may be provided universally. As article 7(1) of GCET (WTO, 1999, 5; emphasis added) reads: 'The prospect of direct and personal access to the discovery and enjoyment of the planet's resources constitutes a right equally open to *all* the world's inhabitants.'

But there is more. Life-value onto-axiology can help the discerning mind not to take even GCET's declared aims of 'economic development, international understanding, peace, prosperity and universal respect for, and observance of human rights and fundamental freedoms' at face value, but to discriminate in principle between good and bad forms of each. This principled discrimination may sound counter-intuitive, yet it is most relevant in connection with 'economic development', to which I confine the present discussion, for not all activities that fall under this notion are genuinely life-enabling.

Consider for instance the effects that GDP-engrossing tourism can have *vis-à-vis* the 'environmental crisis' denounced by the international scientific community at its highest levels (McMurtry, 2013, 170). Depletion of freshwater sources and pollution of the atmosphere by fossil fuel consumption are not the exclusive province of more commonly vilified industries, such as agribusiness and mining. They can apply to the tourist industry too (e.g. high water consumption in tropical resorts; increased aerial traffic). These negative contributions to the environmental crisis of the Anthropocene are not the result of any inherent malevolence or callousness in the business sector, even though such cases do exist (e.g. hydro-intensive golf courses built in desert regions). Rather, they are the result of the inherent incapacity of private enterprise at large to act in accordance with ultimate endogenous, life-grounded criteria.

Somewhat convolutedly, the preamble of the GCET (WTO, 1999, 2) itself admits this inherent incapacity by stating that 'the world tourism industry as a whole has much to gain by operating in an environment that favors the market economy, private enterprise and free trade' for the sake of 'the creation of wealth', which is not life-grounded *per se*. On the contrary, in order to bring forth life-enablement, such a wealth-driven 'tourism industry' must bow to 'a number of principles and a certain number of rules' (ibid.). Without such exogenous constraints, 'responsible and sustainable tourism' would be '*incompatible* with the growing liberalization of the conditions governing trade in services and under whose aegis the enterprises of this sector operate' (ibid.; emphasis added). Left to their own devices, business agents in the tourist sector would concern themselves chiefly if not solely with making money, not with protecting and enabling life at large; the former is their paramount *telos*, the latter is not. It is only by means of criteria external to prevailing economic logic 'that it is possible to reconcile in this sector economy and ecology, environment and development' (ibid.).

The conflict between standard business logic and what is actually needed for life-enablement lies at the heart of McMurtry's life-value onto-axiology in its application to world affairs, tourism included. Spanning across, and delving into, an immense amount of scientific literature, McMurtry's research since the 1980s constitutes an empirically solid demonstration of how 'common interest' and 'money-demand growth' are not one and the same thing (McMurtry, 2013, 256–7), as so often claimed under the superstitious assumption of an all-optimizing invisible hand (Baruchello, 2013). Quite the opposite, in spite of the theodicy hidden within mainstream economics' assumed *equilibria* and much-repeated notions of 'positive spill-overs' and 'trickle-down' boons, common interest and money-demand growth have been increasingly at war with each other:

> The air, soil and water cumulatively degrade; the climates and oceans destabilize; species become extinct at a spasm rate across continents; pollution cycles and volumes increase to endanger life-systems at all levels in cascade effects; a rising half of the world is destitute as inequality multiplies; the global food system produces more and more disabling and contaminated junk food without nutritional value; non-contagious diseases multiply to the world's biggest killer with only symptom cures; the vocational future of the next generation collapses across the world while their bank debts rise; the global financial system has ceased to function for productive investment in life-goods; collective-interest agencies of governments and unions are stripped while for-profit state subsidies multiply; police state laws and methods advance while belligerent wars for corporate resources increase; the media are corporate ad vehicles and the academy is increasingly reduced to corporate functions; public sectors and services are non-stop defunded and privatized as tax evasion and transnational corporate funding and service by governments rise at the same time at every level.
>
> (McMurtry, 2013, 6; emphasis removed)

This picture of contemporary reality may sound hyperbolic to some, yet a search for even one exception to these empirical generalizations reveals how exact and precise they are (IPCC, 2012; Jonas, 1984, 1993; UNESCO, 2002–13; Weston and Bollier, 2013). An engaged intellectual, former journalist and *maître à penser* of Peter Joseph's (2007–13) *Zeitgeist* movement, McMurtry does not shy away from forceful, effective language. Yet the picture offered above is not a matter of rhetoric. So bleak are the bio-environmental and socio-economic trends of the past decades that McMurtry (1995; 1999; 2002; 2013) diagnoses the Anthropocene's malaise to be a cancer.

The first, crucial step in McMurtry's oncological diagnosis is the determination and assessment of the defining *modus operandi* of the world's leading economic agents, i.e. national and transnational corporate businesses, of which tourism ones are but a small fraction. Whether cast as 'money-sequences', 'money-making', 'profits', 'return on equity', 'quarterly earning reports', 'shareholder value' or other accounting formulae, and taking account of the actual behaviour of private bureaucracies, the one and essential characteristic or 'ruling value code' (McMurtry, 2013, 9) that best describes what paramount goal these agents pursue is: 'to maximize by any vehicle, method, or channel open to its entry the ratio of its owners' money-demand increases to money-demand inputs' (McMurtry, 2013, 179; emphasis removed). In the words of Chicago economist Milton Friedman: 'The one and only responsibility of business is to make as much money for stockholders as possible' (cited in McMurtry, 2013, 115; emphasis removed)

This 'responsibility of business' is very far from GCET's pursuit of 'responsible tourism', i.e. a 'tourism development' that 'safeguard[s] the natural environment with a view to achieving sound, continuous and sustainable economic growth geared to satisfying equitably the *needs* and aspirations of present and future generations' (WTO, 1999, 3, art. 3(1); emphasis added). In Friedman's iconic formulation, no vital needs are mentioned, whether present or future, only making money. Consistent with this understanding, common economic practice refers to carcinogenic pesticides, junk food, cigarettes, armaments, pollution quotas and many pathogenic types of labour as economic 'goods', for they generate profits to businessmen and investors, even if bad for life. As McMurtry (2013, 11; emphasis in the original) concludes: 'The ruling paradigm is *in principle life-blind*.' Such an economic logic pursues relentless self-expansion and yet can draw 'no distinction between what serves organic, social and ecological life-hosts and what poisons, dismantles and loots them' (McMurtry, 2013, 188; emphasis removed). In oncology, that is precisely what cancerous cells perform: *a theoretically endless process of self-replication within a host body, whose health or eventual survival is not and cannot be perceived by the self-replicating cells as an effective control response.*

The second step in the diagnosis consists in the recognition that the effects of this theoretically endless self-replication are also analogous in practice. As any oncological record can show, *the uncontrolled sprawling of cancerous cells leads eventually to loss of organic capacity*, down to the very point of killing the cancer's living host. As McMurtry (2013, 169) writes: 'As global capitalist exploitation of the environment has advanced and advances across global life-conditions and elements, all of these global life-conditions and elements – the atmosphere, freshwaters and oceans, top soils, trees, animal habitats and species and mineral resources – degenerate in direct proportion in their life-carrying capacities and biodiversity.' Life-blindness may not signify hostility to life in theory, but it does so in practice.

The third step in the diagnosis relates to the fact that, in cancerous pathologies, *the immune defences of a living organism fail to identify the cancerous cells as harbingers of death and keep facilitating their self-replication.* Analogously, societies' civil-commons institutions have been largely unresponsive to the ongoing assault upon local and/or global life-conditions. Instead of providing and enforcing life-grounded distinctions in the business sphere, these institutions have actually cooperated with the process of life-blind and life-destructive sprawling by facilitating, *inter alia*:

> [R]uin of government programmes, workers' jobs and small business with the cranking up of interest rates to over 20 per cent prime in the 1980s ... [,] the repeal of Depression-installed regulations like Glass-Steagall ... the race to the bottom of wages, benefits and social legislation by global competition with no life-standards ... cannibalist interest rates and debt charges ... 'market reforms', trade-treaty edicts prohibiting legislation reducing 'profit opportunities', and wars on resource rich regions with social control ... supranational treaties in vast all-or-nothing tranches of 'investor' rights ... according all rights only to transnational corporations ... [and] binding regulations ... [overriding] *all human and natural life-requirements through generational time* ... private bank displacement of sovereign control over currency and credit
>
> (McMurtry, 2013, 3–4 and 14; emphasis in the original)

Some genuine civil-commons responses have been attempted, undoubtedly, as exemplified by GCET in the tourism sector. They have been very timid, though. The measure of their timidity is easy to gauge: have they stopped or reverted the life losses that McMurtry (2013) compiles *vis-à-vis* the Earth's atmospheric degradation, arable-topsoil desertification, water-aquifer impoverishment, biodiversity reduction, rising income inequality, food contamination, production and consumption of addictive pathogenic commodities, non-contagious disease multiplication, growing private debt levels, public-sector investment cuts or proliferating tax evasion schemes? Apart from occasional local progress, which indicates how alternative courses of action are possible, the answer is globally negative (e.g. Cecchetti *et al.*, 2011; CHRP, 2013; European Commission, 2013; IPCC, 2012; House of Commons, 2013; House of Lords, 2013; IFS, 2013; ILO, 2013; OECD, 2011, 2013a–b; TFAH, 2011; UN, 2012; WHO, 2011).

Concluding remarks

Thus far, as McMurtry's publications adamantly record and explain, the depletion of life-support systems in the Anthropocene has been so severe that the international scientific community has repeatedly denounced the threat posed by human agency to the present well-being and the long-term survival of our species. Over the past four decades, we have been told over and over again that if the governments of the world do not act in a concerted, life-enabling way, major suffering will unfold inevitably and many of humankind's achievements will be lost, if not humankind itself (UNESCO, 2002–13). And with humanity being lost, who will ever have consciousness of what we have done, and failed to do?

The threat of species-wide suffering, extinction and oblivion can have a terrifying, paralysing effect. They are certainly dreadful thoughts to entertain, unless we are engulfed by a nihilistic death wish. Indeed, the threat at issue mirrors in collective form the terrifying, paralysing awareness of mortality, frailty and solitude that Marcel observed in the sphere of individual existence. Yet, reasoning by analogy, the temptation to despair can be overcome by means of hope. If anything, Marcel's *homo viator* reminds us of the mysterious resilience that we display before that which makes us fear and tremble. There is hope. Perhaps it is a fool's hope, but it is hope nonetheless.

McMurtry (2013, 288), despite the dismal facts and trends that he conveys in his oeuvre, states that 'recovery from the Great Sickness' is possible, though by no means undemanding. His research does not aim solely at regaining sight of the common root of both the environmental and the economic crises, but also at finding ways to let the human economy be life-enabling rather than life-disabling. Collective choice might opt eventually for the former path; or it may not. Freedom's burden, which existentialists like Marcel explored thoroughly, contemplates the possibility of self-destruction. As tourism is concerned, GCET itself can either remain a mere list of good intentions or become a well-established set of binding guidelines.

The first step towards a cure is McMurtry's (2013, 20ff.) set of definitions of 'human', 'natural', 'knowledge' and 'social' capital as well as 'globalization' and 'development' in terms of 'real capital', i.e. 'life capital'. After defining these key concepts along life-grounded lines of interpretation, he proceeds to outlining three 'universal parameters of diagnosis' of the 'general determinants of social health and disease' that should guide any ensuing social actions and, *a fortiori*, modern tourism too: [I] 'Continuity of life-necessities and means to members of society', [II] 'Functioning contribution of citizens to society's life-requirements', and [III] 'Sustaining the life-carrying capacities of the environmental life-host' (McMurtry, 2013, 62–3). Whatever viable community we may choose to conceive of, its members must have their vital needs met, which can be done by letting all able members participate in life-sustaining economic activities, which in turn must not be harmful to the natural and human-made preconditions for need-satisfaction, i.e. natural and human life-support systems or civil commons.

It should be noted that nature's life-support systems, insofar as they are thought of and/or managed for life-enablement, are *ipso facto* civil commons. As soon as any natural or human activity is conceived of as having an import upon life and is managed so as to let this import be comprehensively and coherently positive, then that activity becomes a token of civil commons. The great challenge of the Anthropocene is for humanity to acknowledge to itself that nature's life-support systems themselves, such as the Earth's water and nitrogen cycles, are now well within the province of human understanding and steering, however varying the latter may be in degree, and can turn all too easily into life-disabling systems when poorly managed. The deep and extensive intermingling of natural and human factors in the Anthropocene can then be deemed good or bad depending on its life-valued implications. No realm where human agency is involved can be excluded. Tourism itself, by fulfilling parameters [I]–[III], would become a true token of civil commons.

The second step towards a cure is a set of four shifts in prevailing economic policy that would turn money-making into a means of life-enablement, instead of continuing to treat life-hosts as a means of money-making: [1] 'higher taxes and disincentives for the very rich' (McMurtry, 2013, 262–5), [2] 'aggressive national recovery of control over public owned resources' (McMurtry, 2013, 268–72), [3] 'public banking and investment' (McMurtry, 2013, 286–94), and [4] 'policy-led elimination of structural depredation of the poor and the environment' (McMurtry, 2013, 295–9). All four shifts are articulated for the sake of nurturing 'real capital', not for the sake of predatory 'State power' (McMurtry, 2013, 258–60) or even 'equality' as such (McMurtry, 2013, 300). Still, in today's world, McMurtry (2013) argues that only state power qua civil commons is likely to achieve such ambitious shifts. To make the point clear, who or what else, if not state power, could ever let Ray Anderson's (1998 and 2009) much-praised case of 100 per cent sustainable industrial production become the effective norm for *all* businesses on Earth? Who or what else, if not state power, could actually streamline the tourist industry along the parameters [I]–[III] defined above by means of consistently enforced GCET's 'principles' and 'rules' (WTO, 1999, 2)?

Besides, none of the advised policies is unknown to modern humankind. They are not trite utopias, but policies that have been tested practically and successfully in the recent past on several occasions, showing how 'the right of states, charged with vigilance for the common good' (Pope Francis, 2013) can be employed to a vastly life-enabling effect. McMurtry (2013) recounts *inter alia* the 1940s–2010s Scandinavian fiscal regimes, 1990s–2010s Latin America's renationalization of strategic resources, 1920s–2010s North Dakota's public bank, the 1987 Montreal Ozone Protocol and the 1966 UN's ICESCR.

In the case of tourism, the principles and regulations invoked by GCET fit squarely within the fourth policy shift discussed by McMurtry (2013), given above all the explicit connection made therein between 'responsible tourism' and existing human-rights legal 'instruments', especially the ICESCR (1966, 2, 5, art. 7(2)). Furthermore, without watchful monitoring and concrete enforcement of life-grounded principles and regulations, there would be little chance for any truly responsible tourism, the economic 'competitiveness' of which would be easily undermined by business practices cutting corners *vis-à-vis* environmental standards or 'the fundamental rights of salaried and self-employed workers in the tourism industry' (WTO, 1999, 6, arts 8(4), 9(1) and 10(2)). The first and third policy shifts are relevant with regard to the costs associated with monitoring and enforcement by societies' civil commons agencies, since more substantial and more readily available public funds could support these agencies, the ambitious aims of which the WTO's code extends to 'saving rare and precious resources', 'avoiding ... waste production' (WTO, 1999, 3, art. 3(2)) and 'preserving and upgrading monuments, shrines and museums as well as archaeological and historic sites' (4, art. 4(2)).

McMurtry's focus, unlike Marcel's, is set upon collective dimensions of agency. However, life-value onto-axiology applies equally to the individual dimension, particularly with respect to existential choices and moral behaviour. The fundamental axioms of life-value onto-axiology tell us what is good and what is bad. Therefore, they offer ultimate criteria for each person's existential and moral evaluations. Thus, we can make sense of McMurtry's (2009–10a) claim that through life-value onto-axiology we can 'recover step by step the missing life-ground of values *and the ultimate meaning of how we are to live*' (emphasis added): it is also on a personal level that life-enablement constitutes the good and life-disablement its opposite. The good life is a life in which life-capacity is nurtured as extensively as possible, as exemplified emblematically by the life-nurturing healing and caring acts of religious prophets and saints.

Given the social and natural milieus in which individuals live and act, the individual's good life means for her to operate as a life-capacity multiplier 'The more human beings subsume the requirements of their fellows' and their environment's life-capital capacities into their organizational regulation, the better they are' (McMurtry, 2013, 310; emphasis removed). In the pursuit of the good life, we cannot limit ourselves to fostering our own life-capacity in isolation We must equally nurture other persons', living creatures' and ecosystems' life-capacity qua extensions of our own, as instantiated daily in the subjectively and inter-subjectively rewarding experiences of parenthood, education, nursing, care genuine friendship, empowering leadership and service, constructive cooperation compassion to people and animals, humane animal husbandry and environmentally sound behaviour. Responsible tourism qua individual agency falls under this line of understanding.

Although McMurtry (2009–10a) acknowledges extensively the commonalities between the recognition of life's supreme value to be found in many spiritual traditions and the one articulated in his own philosophy, neither the bulk of his work nor life-value onto-axiology is focused primarily on the meaningful relationship that individuals may establish with a personal God. In this, Marcel's discussion of *homo viator* emphasizes quintessentially religious themes that are not central within McMurtry's philosophy. Nevertheless, the recognition of life's supreme value is sufficient to clarify how the awe and existential import *vis-à-vis* life's majesty characterizing many spiritual traditions persist within life-value onto-axiology, which extrapolates 'the ultimate meaning of how we are to live' from the life-ground. On this point, illustrative are the words of 20th-century environmentalist, bio-ethicist and historian of religion Hans Jonas (1993, 48–9), who explains the implicit continuity between the spiritual traditions' existential and moral focus points – at least the Judaeo-Christian ones – and the secular concern with the environmental crisis threatening life's continuation on Earth:

> [T]he 'human condition' has been transforming ... In the old days religion told us that we were all sinners because of the original sin. Today it is our planet's ecology that accuses all of us of being sinners because of the overexploitation of human ingenuity. Back in the old days, religion terrified us with the Last Judgment at the end of times. Today our tortured planet predicts the coming of that day without any divine intervention. The final revelation ... is the silent scream emerging from things themselves, those things that we must endeavour to resolve to rein in our powers over the world, or we shall die on this desolate earth which used to be the creation.

The ruling economic paradigm is not only blind to life-needs, it is also deaf to the peculiar scream that the 'tortured' Earth emits. Worshipping Mammon rather than Gaia, many human beings seem oblivious to the sacred primacy of life. This peculiar scream is therefore a call to renewed personal responsibility *vis-à-vis* creation itself. It is a secular path to salvation or, if failing, damnation.

Responding constructively to the threat to life caused by the 'Great Sickness' is not merely a social task, but one that involves, and gives ultimate meaning to, individual agency as well, just like the pursuit of redemption has done traditionally for countless believers. First of all, no social task would ever be accomplished without widespread individual agency. Secondly and more distinctively, to be conscious of, and positively responsive to, the ecological crisis of the Anthropocene is part of what the individual's good life requires, since the properly directed expression of an individual's life-capacity cannot but enable to some extent the surrounding individuals, living beings and life-conditions. In order for a specific individual's life to be truly good, her contribution to life in general must be truly good, now and in the future.

As odd as such a notion may have sounded at the beginning of this chapter, it should be clear by now that the same ethical and existential considerations apply to individual choices within the realm of tourism, whether entrepreneurial, recreational or occupational. Tourism is no vacation from personal responsibility. We have no guarantee that the individual should opt always, primarily or even frequently for the good life. Freedom's burden entails having the concrete prospect of opting for its opposite too. Ignorance, greed, stupidity, ennui and capriciousness are but a few of the failures conspiring to draw the worst out of humankind. Uncompromisingly, the sprawling cancer diagnosed by McMurtry (2013) shows how systematically humankind has been capable of taking a path that is not good. Yet, humankind's long-evolved civil commons, GCET included, remind us also of our potential for taking a positive one. Following Marcel, we can *hope* that this latter path may be the decisive one for most of us in the face of the Anthropocene's greatest challenge: our own survival as a species.

References

Anderson, R. 1998. *Mid-Course Correction: Toward a Sustainable Enterprise: The Interface Model*. White River Junction, VA: Chelsea Green Publishing.

Anderson, R. 2009. *Confessions of a Radical Industrialist: Profits, People, Purpose. Doing Business by Respecting the Earth*. New York: St Martin's Press.

Baruchello, G. 2007. Western philosophy and the life-ground. *Encyclopedia of Life Support Systems*. Paris and Oxford: Eolss. <http://www.eolss.net> [accessed Apr. 2014].

Baruchello, G. 2013. The hopeful liberal: Reflections on free markets, science and ethics. *Nordicum-Mediterraneum* 8(2). <http://nome.unak.is/nm-marzo-2012/vol-8-no-2-2013/58-conference-paper/395-the-hopeful-liberal-reflections-on-free-markets-science-and-ethics> [accessed Apr. 2014].

Baruchello, G., and Johnstone, R.L. 2011. Rights and value. Construing the International Covenant on Economic, Social and Cultural Rights as civil commons. *Studies in Social Justice*, 5(1), 91–126.

Buffett, W. 2003. *Berkshire Hathaway Inc. 2002 Annual Report*. <http://www.berkshirehathaway.com/2002ar/2002ar.pdf> [accessed 28 Apr. 2014].

Cecchetti, S.G., Mohanty, M.S., and Zampolli, F. 2011. *The Real Effects of Debt*. BIS Working Papers, 352. <http://www.bis.org/publ/work352.htm> [accessed 28 Apr. 2014].

Center for Human Rights in Practice (CHRP) 2013. *Reports on the Impact of Public Spending Cuts on Different Disadvantaged Groups within the UK*. <http://www2.warwick.ac.uk/fac/soc/law/chrp/projects/spendingcuts/resources/database/reportsgroups> [accessed Apr. 2014].

European Commission 2013. *EUROPA – Food Safety – Chemical Safety of Food – Food Contaminants*. <http://ec.europa.eu/food/food/chemicalsafety/contaminants/index_en.htm> [accessed Apr. 2014].

Hardin, G. 1968. The tragedy of the commons. *Science*, 162, 1243–8.

Hernandez, J.G. 2011. *Gabriel Marcel's Ethics of Hope: Evil, God and Virtue*. London: Continuum.

House of Commons 2013. Environment, Food and Rural Affairs Committee (HC 141), *Food Contamination*, vol. 1. Fifth report of session 2013–14, incorporating HC 1035-i-ii, session 2012–13. London: The Stationery Office.

House of Lords 2013. Select Committee on Economic Affairs (HL 48), *Tackling Corporate Tax Avoidance in a Global Economy: Is a New Approach Needed?* 1st Report of Session 2013–14. London: The Stationery Office.

ICESCR 1966. International Covenant on Economic, Social and Cultural Rights, adopted 16 Dec. 1966, G.A. Res. 2200A, U.N. GAOR, 21st sess., Su No. 16, at 49, U.N. Doc. A/6316 (1966), entered into force 3 Jan. 1976. <http://www.ohchr.org/EN/ProfessionalInterest/Pages/CESCR.aspx> [accessed Apr. 2014].

Institute for Fiscal Studies (IFS) 2013. *Food Expenditure and Nutritional Quality over the Great Recession*. IFS Briefing Note BN143. <www.ifs.org.uk/bns/bn143.pdf>. [accessed Apr. 2014].

Intergovernmental Panel on Climate Change (IPCC) 2012. Managing the risks of extreme events and disasters to advance climate change adaptation. <http://www.ipcc-wg2.gov/SREX> [accessed Apr. 2014].

International Labour Organization (ILO) 2013. *Public Sector Shock: The Impact of Policy Retrenchment in Europe.* Geneva: ILO.

Johnson, E., and Morehouse, H. (eds) 2014. After the Anthropocene: Politics and geographic inquiry for a new epoch. *Progress in Human Geography,* 38(3), 439–56.

Jonas, H. 1984. *The Imperative of Responsibility: In Search of an Ethics for the Technological Age.* Chicago, IL: University of Chicago Press.

Jonas, H. 1993. *Il concetto di Dio dopo Auscwitz: Una voce ebraica.* Genoa: Il melangolo.

Joseph, P. 2007–13. The Zeitgeist Film Series. Official Website for Peter Joseph's Award Winning Documentary Trilogy. <http://www.zeitgeistmovie.com/> [accessed Apr. 2014].

Kuntz, P.G. 1980. Augustine: From *Homo Erro* to *Homo Viator. Augustinian Studies,* 11, 79–89.

Lovelock, J.E. 1972. Gaia as seen through the atmosphere. *Atmospheric Environment,* 6(8), 579–80.

Marcel, G. 1962. *Homo Viator.* New York: Harper Torchbooks.

Marcel, G. 1967. *The Philosophy of Existentialism.* New York: The Citadel.

McMurtry, J. 1995. The social immune system and the cancer stage of capitalism. *Social Justice,* 22(4), 1–25.

McMurtry, J. 1998. *Unequal Freedoms: The Global Market as an Ethical System.* Toronto: Garamond.

McMurtry, J. 1999. *The Cancer Stage of Capitalism,* 1st edn. London: Pluto.

McMurtry, J. 2002. *Value Wars.* London: Pluto.

McMurtry, J. 2009–2010a. What is good? What is bad? The value of all values across time, place and theories. *Encyclopedia of Life Support Systems.* Paris and Oxford: Eolss: <http://www.eolss.net> [accessed Apr. 2014].

McMurtry, J. 2009–2010b. Glossary. *Encyclopedia of Life Support Systems.* Paris and Oxford: Eolss: <http://www.eolss.net> [accessed Apr. 2014].

McMurtry, J. 2013. *The Cancer Stage of Capitalism: From Crisis to Cure,* 2nd edn. London: Pluto.

Noonan, J. 2006. *Democratic Society and Human Needs.* Montreal and Kingston: McGill-Queen's University Press.

OECD 2011. Divided we stand: Why inequality keeps rising. <http://www.oecd-ilibrary. org/social-issues-migration-health/the-causes-of-growing-inequalities-in-oecd-countries_9789264119536-en> [accessed Apr. 2014].

OECD 2013a. *Addressing Base Erosion and Profit Shifting.* <http://www.oecd-ilibrary.org/taxation/addressing-base-erosion-and-profit-shifting_9789264192744-en> [accessed Apr. 2014].

OECD 2013b. Crisis squeezes income and puts pressure on inequality and poverty. <http://www.oecd.org/els/soc/OECD2013-Inequality-and-Poverty-8p.pdf> [accessed Apr. 2014].

Pope Francis 2013. Evangelii Gaudium. <http://w2.vatican.va/content/francesco/en/apost_exhortations/documents/papa-francesco_esortazione-ap_20131124_evangelii-gaudium.html> [accessed May 2015].

Sweetman, B. 2008. *The Vision of Gabriel Marcel: Epistemology, Human Person, the Transcendent.* Amsterdam: Rodopi.

Trust for America's Health (TFAH) 2011. *F as in Fat: How Obesity Threatens America's Future.* <http://healthyamericans.org/reports/obesity2011/Obesity2011Report.pdf> [accessed Apr. 2014].

UN 2012. Political Declaration of the High-Level Meeting of the General Assembly on the Prevention and Control of Non-Communicable Diseases. Adopted 24 Jan. 2012, G.A. Res. 66/2, U.N. GAOR, 66th Sess., Agenda item 117, U.N. Doc. A/RES/66/2 (2012).

UNESCO 2002–13. *Encyclopedia of Life Support Systems.* Paris and Oxford: Eolss. <http://www.eolss.net> [accessed Apr. 2014].

Weston, B., and Bollier, D. 2013. *Green Governance: Ecological Survival, Human Rights, and the Law of the Commons.* Cambridge: Cambridge University Press.

World Health Organization (WHO) 2011. *Noncommunicable Diseases: Country Profiles 2011.* <www.who.int/nmh/publications/ncd_profiles_report.pdf> [accessed Apr. 2014].

WTO 1999. *Global Code of Ethics for Tourism.* UN references A/RES/406(XIII) and A/RES/56/212. <http://www.unwto.org/ethics/full_text/en/pdf/Codigo_Etico_Ing.pdf> [accessed Apr. 2014].

Part III
Tourism becomings in the Anthropocene

Figure III.1 Hecla Cove, Sorgfjorden (Bay of Sorrow), Svalbard, September 2011 – Departures

©Tyrone Martinsson, published with permission

8 The movement heritage

Scale, place and pathscapes in Anthropocene tourism

Daniel Svensson, Sverker Sörlin and Nina Wormbs

Introduction – differentiating the understanding of the Anthropocene

What would sustainability and tourism be in the Anthropocene? It has been argued for a long time that not only is 'sustainability' an oxymoron, but sustainable tourism an even more bizarre one (e.g. Hardy *et al.*, 2002; Liu, 2003; Sharpley, 2000; Hunter, 1995). Tourism, or perhaps better, tourists, in and of themselves bring more mobility, more pollution, more stress on landscapes and resources and more greenhouse gas emissions through air, sea and car travel (Redclift, 1987, 2005; Eijgelaar, Amelung and Peeters, this volume). Tourists have also been singled out as a major threat to biodiversity, as a destroyer of traditional cultures and livelihoods; tourism itself even is a particularly unsustainable business, as measured for example by its ecological footprint (Williams, 2004; Gössling *et al.*, 2002; Hunter and Shaw, 2007; Scott, 2011; Gössling and Peeters, 2015; Hall, this volume). Making your travel and mobility more low impact doesn't seem to help much, even if sustainable tourism has sometimes been linked with small, rural destinations (e.g. Lane, 1994). Even the hiker in the mountain range 'needs' equipment and has often travelled by a fossil-fuel-driven mode of transportation in order to get there in the first place. A very small percentage of the world's population fly, and an even smaller percentage do it frequently as tourists. It is in fact this fraction of humanity who, on their own, create the oxymoronic nature of 'sustainable tourism'.

Does this change if we move the language to that of Anthropocene? The Anthropocene argument is all about impacts and 'signals'. The chief criterion set up by the Royal Geological Society for whether there is an Anthropocene is if the Earth signals of human activities will be strong enough to remain perceptible in the future. In their search for evidence geoscientists look for enough lasting and significant traits left in the 'strata' of the Anthropocene to designate it an individual geological period, or epoch (Zalasiewicz *et al.*, 2011). This is less a philosophical or judgemental than an empirical issue. Are the assembled impacts and remnants of human activities in the lithosphere, biosphere, atmosphere, pedosphere (the layer of soils) and cryosphere (the layer of ice) so overwhelming that we can be certain that the distant future will still be able to register the strata of humanity embedded into earth itself?

If the Earth signals from human presence are strong enough we live in the Anthropocene, if they are not we don't. This empirical condition does not, however, say anything about whether the human imprint on the planet is good or bad. When it is commonly assumed that the arrival of the Anthropocene is evidence of the destructive powers of humanity it is because many of the resulting impacts threaten Earth's life-sustaining capacities. In the end, we must accept that the strata that make up the Anthropocene represent human deeds that have been both good and bad and that the values placed on various features of the Anthropocene will be different between individuals, societies, and, perhaps most importantly, time periods. In a future period much distant from the present, when humans may have found effective ways of storing carbon, the signal from that human product may perhaps be regarded very differently from what we get from atmospheric CO_2 today which brings undesired climate change. Such value shifts have occurred in the past, not least with CO_2 which used to be seen, as late as in the middle of the twentieth century, as bringing much appreciated 'climate embetterment' to the cold countries in northern Europe (Sörlin, 2009).

Sustainable tourism in the Anthropocene, we would argue, needs to take its cue from such a differentiated understanding of the proclaimed new epoch. Certain traits left behind will be compatible with a 'good' Anthropocene, which we understand as a sustainable Anthropocene. Almost by definition, weak signals from the past and subtle traits in landscapes will belong in this category. The tourism that sustains and preserves these signals and traits will be asked for, especially if it at the same time minimizes other kinds of impacts, or to put it in terms of the Anthropocene discourse: if it contributes to the effort to stay within 'planetary boundaries' (Rockström *et al.*, 2009; Steffen *et al.*, 2015). So, could tourism be rethought to demonstrate Anthropocene and its dilemmas while at the same time accommodating some of the virtues that useful and sustainable human traces represent? Could tourism be conceived as an activity that doesn't transgress planetary boundaries?

For the sake of the argument of this chapter we will make these very complex and challenging questions operational by separating the wider impact framework of tourists – primarily their long-distance travel and transportation – from their *local* impacts. This chapter focuses on the latter. We will argue that there is a relationship between the local impacts and the Anthropocene and that there are choices to be made in tourism planning and management that can make tourists more or less compatible with a 'good Anthropocene', where human impacts may be significant but still congruent with an Anthropocene that stays within planetary boundaries, while distancing ourselves from the more simplistic eco-modernist interpretations of the phrase 'good Anthropocene'. In fact, much of the current debates on Anthropocene can be read as variations of the old discourse on whether human civilizations can manage nature and its resources responsibly and efficiently. Some are optimists and argue for the possibility of a good Anthropocene based on eco-efficient business as usual (Hajer, 1995; De Fries, 2014). We would instead like to propose that the properties of it are linked to issues of place, landscape and the possibilities of scaling, with ethics as a key dimension. The Anthropocene is, predominantly, about the planetary scale. The *movement heritage* is a local phenomenon. Local is commonly antithetically linked to global. Here, however, we propose local-planetary as related through scaling.

The ethics of place is an established tradition of philosophy, with Norwegian philosopher Arne Næss, himself a climber and avid traveller and tourist, as a key thinker (Naess, 1972; Næss and Rothenberg, 1990). Here we will connect to this tradition and use it as a way to organize a thinking around tourists and the Anthropocene. Listening to the place, tuning in on its scales, nuances, rhythms and traces, represents a kind of ethical practice and may be seen as case of *what we at least must do if we are serious about a sustainable tourism*, along the lines of what Joanna Zylinska, drawing on Adorno's *Minima moralia* (1951), has called a 'minimal ethics for the Anthropocene' (Zylinska, 2014). It is also a way of putting the oxymoron of sustainability to the test.

Pathscapes of mobility

We will hone in on a kind of tourism which may qualify as a potentially sustainable tourism in the Anthropocene, thus defined: minimizing impacts and staying within planetary boundaries, using place, ethics, and local tradition as guiding concepts. The focus of our attention is landscape mobility as it is and has been performed in the Scandinavian mountain range through indigenous and local livelihoods and practices, sport, outdoor life, tourism and other outdoor activities. How do these different kinds of mobility impact on landscapes? What roles can they, and the 'pathscapes' that are derived from them, perform, as seen through the lens of the Anthropocene?

The Scandinavian mountain landscape has great significance, culturally, ecologically and economically. It is also a major cultural and natural heritage. This chapter will underline the importance of movement in understanding the mountain landscape. The Scandinavian mountain range is a landscape of movement. It has been shaped by Sami herding practices for centuries, but also through hunting, fishing, outdoor life, tourism, sports and science. The movement heritage, in terms of paths, skiing tracks, hiking trails, etc. has shaped the understanding of the mountain landscape. We will investigate how these landscapes of movement can contribute to sustainable tourism development in the mountain landscape. Creating a balance between tourism and sustainable solutions is one of the great challenges to capture a potential for innovations that can strengthen local communities and tourism without destroying the natural resources and landscapes that are attractive to visitors in the first place.

The movement heritage is not only the remaining physical traits and the collective memory of low-impact landscape use in the past. It also encourages continued building on knowledge of the rich history that visitors follow when they move around in these landscapes. To remain a resource for tourism the movement heritage must be wisely and actively managed, preferably in cooperation with other sectors and forms of landscape use. There are numerous examples of trail development on the basis of history, whether for hiking (such as the King's

Trail, *Kungsleden*, in northern Sweden) or for pilgrimage (like *St Olavsleden* in Norway). The Scandinavian mountains are in this respect no different from the tourist landscape of the European Alps, for which the 'slow' movement – slow food, cities, mountains, etc. – has argued that there is an 'enormous potential ... not yet matched by a political strategy. In many contexts, activities have been gradually interrupted, breaking ties with the local contexts, losing the transmission of knowledge and leading to the decline of services' (Slowfood.com, 2014).

There has been, until now, a significant theoretical under-articulation of the often subtle landscape heritage that is left by bodily movement. Bodily movement in general, as a landscape practice, is better theorized. There is a cultural history of walking, with famous names such as Petrarch, Rousseau, Austen, Thoreau, and including the ideas about the virtues of motion as expressed by alpinists, moralists, political ideologues and health prophets (i.e. Solnit, 2002). The theoretical understanding of landscapes as monuments is commonly associated with nationalism and focuses mainly on buildings, infrastructures, historical events (battles, worship) or so-called national landscapes (Lowenthal, 1998, 2008; Nye, 1996; Sörlin, 1998; Ehn and Frykman, 2007). At the same time movement as a practice for landscape understanding and for the shaping of 'life worlds' has been underscored, building on the idea of 'tacit knowledge', but also on the spatial and temporal perceptions and scales connected to physical experience (Ingold, 2000, 2011; Hastrup, 2009; Ingold and Vergunst, 2008; Polanyi, 1958; Lund and Jóhannesson, 2014; Lund, 2012).

Although there is an emerging theoretical understanding of bodily movement based on anthropology and cultural history, it is rarely combined with theory that tries to grasp the mobility landscape related to recent trends in mountain tourism, focusing on for example recreational walking, trekking or cross-country skiing (Medway and Varley, 2011; Anderson, 2012; Ek and Hultman, 2007). These activities now provide their own additions to the movement heritage through paths, tracks, signs, light poles and other manifest or tacit infrastructure. Some of the promotional ideas behind this kind of endurance tourism came from work in physiology in the middle decades of the twentieth century which helped turn recreational mobility into a massive popular activity and, later, commodification and innovation (Åstrand, 1958; Svensson, 2013). But not much reflection has been directed towards the landscapes which these activities have generated. Some of these, connected in particular to fitness running, have been called 'portable landscapes', characterized by their replicability, i.e. to be built according to a similar concept in many places (Qviström, 2013). This more commodifying approach is not what we have in mind when we think of movement heritage in the Anthropocene. On the contrary, we would underscore the uniqueness of the pathscapes and their irreproducibility. This may in fact sit more comfortably with a tourist industry that is prepared to change and use 'social articulation', visualization and, ultimately, another kind of commodification of landscapes through meaning-making tools and narratives such as maps, signs, texts, images, events, rituals, instruction, etc. based on situated knowledge and lived experience (Sörlin, 1998; Green, 1990). This in turn is related to the by now sizeable literature on place making and cultural resource management (CRM), with its emphasis on the economic benefit from articulated places with iconic heritage (King, 2003). This has recently been complemented with a literature on the enhancement of place-based values for sustainable development and on sustainable tourism at large (Kent, 2012; Buckley, 2012; Lee, 2013; Welford and Ytterhus, 1998). Very few, if any, of these sources has so far addressed issues of heritage and bodily movement, let alone probed their relevance for tourism in the Anthropocene.

We will approach this topic through three case studies from the Swedish part of the Scandinavian mountains, each illustrating different facets and potentials of movement heritage as exemplars of tourism in the Anthropocene.

Vålådalen – a divine training ground?

Our first example is Vålådalen, a valley in the Swedish mountain range west of Östersund. Traditionally a landscape used by Sami reindeer herders for many centuries, and by settlers since at least the 1830s, it has also been shaped by its more recent history as a landscape for training. The combination of several interest groups and their small-impact landscape use leads to the question: could this area be a model for how different interests can be sustainably combined in the Anthropocene?

Founded in 1923, the Vålådalen Alpine Station soon became a favoured location for training camps among elite athletes (and other cultural and political elites). The traditional paths shaped by reindeers, herders and hunters formed the base of a network of paths, complemented by new trails for running, skiing and hiking.

It was the training ideologist, alpinist and film-maker Gösta Olander (1893–1972) who, together with his wife Olga made Vålådalen a centre for skiers and other athletes in the mid-20th century. Olander had high status in the athletic community and was responsible for the training advice given to the Swedish cross-country skiing team. Swedish and international sports stars (like runners Gunder Hägg, Michel Jazy and Michel Bernard, boxers Ingemar Johansson and Floyd Patterson, skiers Nils Karlsson and Nils Täpp) all visited Vålådalen for training (Krüger, 2006, 322; Olander, 1950, 2; Nygaard, 1996, 39–40). The training methods that Olander argued for were in close connection with the surroundings. During summer the idea was to run on mountain paths and on muddy ground. In the winter, long skiing sessions and running in deep snow were the main ingredients. A training session should be performed without stress, with time to take in the views and the beauty of the landscape. Olander (1950, 4) warned athletes of the danger of becoming 'a training machine'.

Olander's ideas about training and nature included moral, spiritual and ideal aspects. In his training handbook he wrote: 'Our Lord has through a grand and varied nature given us the best training ground' (Olander, 1950, 4). This is the core of what Olander tried to frame Vålådalen as: a divine training landscape, unique and not reproducible anywhere else. And implicitly, because of its uniqueness and divine origin, Olander wanted to preserve it for future generations while at the same time allowing athletes and others to use the landscape for training and recreation (Svensson, 2014). This training ground, discretely but undeniably altered by decades of training in Vålådalen, is now the base of tourism here. Let us now look at some of the attempts in Vålådalen to make this history of training useful as a cultural heritage of movement, a movement heritage.

When arriving in Vålådalen, one of the first things you'll see is a small sign in a bog by the road. The sign reads 'Gunders mosse' (Gunder's mire) and marks one of the places in Vålådalen where Gunder Hägg conducted his training. This sign is one of many in Vålådalen, and they all contribute to the articulation of the rich history of training here. Vålådalen also has a museum that further strengthens the claims for authenticity. In the museum, memorabilia from famous athletes are displayed side by side with autographs from other famous visitors (writers, actors, politicians and others). Signs, monuments, museums, maps and other visualizations of history and tradition underline the authentic and genuine aspects of training in Vålådalen, and can be used to strengthen claims of being a cultural heritage (Lowenthal, 2008). Vålådalen's cultural heritage as a site for training has given this valley an elevated status among tourists that come to train here.

The running paths in Vålådalen (that are transformed into skiing tracks in the winter) are named mostly by references to the landscape. But pieced together with the pictures and writings in the museum and on the website, these paths are given status due to the history of training there. Running on a random trail in the mountains is all well and good, but to conduct 'natural training' in Vålådalen, on the paths where Olander once guided some of the best athletes in the world, adds another layer of authenticity. It is a landscape perceived through personal effort, like Nordic landscapes traditionally have been (Kayser Nielssen, 1997, 87–9; Olwig and Jones, 2008; Sandell and Sörlin, 2008). This fits very well with the increasing interest in training-oriented tourism.

Vålådalen is also a large nature reserve, and as such is protected from major exploitation by forestry, mining or large-scale alpine tourism like in nearby Åre. By articulating and marketing this as a movement heritage, and opening it up for simultaneous use for environmental protection, small-impact tourism and herding, the dichotomy of nature/culture is slowly undermined. Discrete but visible imprints of historical and current movement in the nature reserve underline the potential for a combination of nature protection (the reserve), living local identity and activity (the reindeer herding) and tourism (the exercisers coming here to train). Small-impact landscape use, like in Vålådalen, has made massive imprints on the ideas and understandings of landscape. But the physical alterations remain small and, at least compared to other forms of more invasive landscape use, sustainable. As there is a possibility to travel here by train, both the local and the global environmental effects can be kept to a minimum.

Following the tradition of Olander's natural training, the website of Vålådalen stresses the importance of the beautiful landscape in making Vålådalen an 'inspirational place for hard training' (Vålådalens fjällstation, 2014). The focus here is not on mass tourism on the scale of neighbouring Åre. Instead, Vålådalen wants to attract tourists that come for hard training and nature experience. The station in Vålådalen has been and is still part of the Swedish Tourist Association (STF), founded in 1885. The focus on physical activity and nature experience fits quite nicely with historical ideas about qualitative tourism and fear of tasteless exploitation (Schama, 1996, 501–2). Ideas like these were at the core of the STF, and were expressed by STF board member and Secretary General of the UN, Dag Hammarskjöld, who also visited Vålådalen (Hammarskjöld, 1962, 43). The need for physical effort in order to experience the landscape unites the STF, Vålådalen and Olander. The combination of physical exercise and nature experience is important in order to understand the history of this place. It is also a key ingredient in Nordic tradition of landscape use, as well as in other traditions (Solnit, 2002; Ingold and Vergunst, 2008).

The perceived authenticity of Vålådalen as a place for training is the base of its tourist marketing. That makes for a clear contrast to other landscapes used for training, such as jogging tracks. Other examples of similar, reproducible and portable landscapes are skiing tracks with artificial snow or the Torsby Ski Tunnel where indoor skiing is possible all year, no matter the conditions outside. In these places, history does not carry the meaning it does in Vålådalen. These landscapes have been labelled as portable in the sense that they can be (and have been) reproduced in many different areas. They are based on function, not on heritage. In contrast to this portability, the landscapes of movement we focus on are not portable (Qviström, 2013). Their status, attraction and in some cases protection are based on their cultural history and emotional value. The identity of Vålådalen is based on its status as a landscape of movement (in this case mainly training). But the fact that Vålådalen is also a nature reserve gives it a dual status that sets it apart from other, more expansive tourist locations. So, even if cultural heritage can be understood as a product in the market of tourism, large-scale expansion is not an option here (Strömberg, 2007, 160–1). This is a form of place-making that is not mainly commercial, but rather a potential basis for environmentalism (Kent, 2012).

Hikers and exercisers come to walk, run or ski in the area. They leave no major marks on the landscape, partly because this is not a mass tourism site, and partly due to the scale of the activities they undertake and the infrastructure needed. The narrative of Vålådalen is one where stillness, solitude and natural training are at the core. By using history as a resource for current tourist marketing, Vålådalen adds story-telling to attract visitors (Mossberg and Nissen Johansen, 2006). As Thom van Dooren (2014, 18) has pointed out, 'responsible inheritance is necessarily grounded in a recognition of ... multiple voices'. A treasured outdoor recreational area is most often not just a recreational landscape, but also a home, a workplace and much more (e.g. Lykke Syse, 2000). The way in which we identify, articulate and visualize history in a landscape is crucial for current and future understandings of that place. Vålådalen, like other examples of movement/ mobility heritage sites, is often characterized precisely by this multitude of voices (tourists, athletes, Sami reindeer herders, settlers, animals and others) who have at least one thing in common – they move through and affect the landscape, but are dependent on and affected by it in return.

So, is sustainable tourism possible here? So far, it seems to be. The modest imprints in this landscape (by several groups of users) indicate that if you look only at this particular place (and not so much at how the tourists got here), Vålådalen is a sustainable destination. But then again, hiking, strolling and cross-country skiing are among the most popular recreation activities in the region (Fredman *et al.*, 2014) and are expected to increase even more in the near future. As Vålådalen is also a nature reserve and the herding ground of two Sami villages (Handölsdalen and Tåssåsen), how would increasing numbers of visitors affect this landscape and the qualities that currently attract tourists here (Vålådalens naturreservat, 2003, 29)? Is there a need for an ethic (further developed in the conclusions of this chapter) that clearly urges tourists and locals to use and travel through the landscape in sustainable, small-scale and low-impact ways? If the number of tourists increases, then sustainable tourism would have to see the individual imprint of each tourist decrease. In this process, places of relatively harmonious coexistence between locals, tourists and nature preservation like Vålådalen deserve further attention, as a potential example of how low-impact tourism locally can address problems on the much larger scale of the Anthropocene. This need not result in a total abandonment of preservation of 'wild' nature, a critique voiced against the whole Anthropocene nomenclature (Crist, 2013), but rather complement the much-needed preservation efforts with sustainable, low-impact landscape use.

Nikkaluokta – the density of traces

Our second example is Nikkaluokta, a village at the foot of Sweden's highest mountain massif, Kebnekaise. The nearest town is Kiruna, 60 km to the east. Nikkaluokta has served as a vantage point for tourism into the Scandinavian alpine landscape since the beginning of the 20th century when a few Norwegian Sami families settled there and found that they could partially sustain their livelihoods through providing services to visitors. Modern infrastructure was then non-existent. Tourism on any scale could only begin when the railway connecting Gällivare with Kiruna and Norway was built around 1900, almost 100 km away from the Kebnekaise mountains. The Swedish Tourist Association, STF, erected a cabin, or 'mountain station', in 1908, right below the highest summit.

More than a century later Nikkaluokta is the hub of a dense and multi-layered, although sparsely documented, mobility landscape combining traces and heritage from tourists, alpinists, field scientists, artists, photographers, ethnographers and of course the Sami, using a wide range of traditional and modern technologies of travel, from skis to helicopters.

Sami heritage is something to keep alive as a local knowledge tradition, 'a bank of knowledge', argues Anna Sarri, third-generation inhabitant and director of the visitor centre with restaurant and accommodation. She also tries to interest visitors and has recently been standing in front of 2,300 people in the Fjällräven Classic where trekkers are dispatched in cohorts of 400 each to Abisko some 100 km to the north. 'I stand there telling stories about our landscape and our past.

The participants ought to understand, this is not just the final stop of the bus and a toilet, it is a cultural landscape.' Her mission is linked to both economic well-being and cultural continuity. 'Small Sami villages are friction points (*bromsklossar*). It is a matter of understanding the values.'

At the same time there is a risk in going too far in making the mobility and knowledge landscapes available. She talks about the ethics of knowledge, some of which should be the preserve of the Sami. Her company has arranged small walking paths with information posts on stones, plants and history. There is a rich heritage out there that if it isn't observed risks falling into oblivion. That is a dilemma. 'We are losing knowledge with each generation.' Art, landscape, connections in time and space are necessary to read and understand the environment. If not, you run the risk of flattening it, thinning the experience, denouncing the ancestors.

The wider background to what is now this dense landscape of mobility was the surging interest in the Lapland mountains in the late 19th century, what has been called a 'borealism' with strong repercussions in cultural and public life (Ísleifson, 2011; Sörlin, 1988; Bravo and Sörlin, 2002; Byrne, 2013; Broberg, 1982). One of its most vocal propagandists was Fredrik Svenonius, a geologist, born and bred in Norrbotten in the north of Sweden and an early instigator of scientific research in the mountains, especially on glaciers, and heading work in the Stockholm Natural Science Association to promote research on 'nature within the Arctic region of the Fatherland' (Svenonius, 1905, 3–5). Glaciers, which he preferred to call by their Saami name, *jiekna*, had once been one major ice sheet during the Ice Age and formed the Swedish soil, a common theme of nationalist economic geography in the period. They provided 'our fields, meadows, and forests – the condition for our country's livability and present high cultivation' (Svenonius, 1890, 127). To him the glaciers were beautiful, majestic and of international standing as tourist attractions. He also argued for the rights and qualities of the Sami, whom he knew well from many years of close collaboration in the field.

Tourism would not have been possible had it not been for the solid anchoring in yet another layer of local infrastructure, which was provided by the Sami. When the tourist station was completed the first caretaker was Nils Sarri, of one of the Sami families; the others were Haugli, Inga, Niia, and Rikko, who had moved to the inner Ladtjovagge valley to settle around 1911 on a site where they had previously had summer homes. Nils Sarri and Petter Haugli were authorized by the STF as mountain guides, soon followed by other men in the village. Their reindeer herding, hunting and fishing was complemented by mountaineering services as part of the local economy. They also started running a boat service for tourists from the end of the road in Holmajärvi 20 km to the east, and they acquired considerable skills in glacier walks and mountaineering to the highest peaks in the area, skills that were also learned by their sons (Henrik Sarri interview; Hellström-Boström, 1997, 75).

There was a strong mountaineering interest in the region as well. Emmerich Rossipal, of Austrian origin, introduced climbing courses in Kebnekaise during the inter-war years (Hellström-Boström, 1997). In 1931 a small cabin was built in Nikkaluokta as the local home of the Swedish Lapland Mountain Men's Club

(*De Lappländska fjällkarlarnas klubb*). The club had been founded in Stockholm in 1920 by 13 men. Membership was increased to 20 and among the four criteria for membership were 'danger to life', or 'first ascent to a peak of 1,200 meters or more', or 'any performance of similar magnitude'. The club had a scientific-military-aristocratic composition, and it is hard not to see the creation of it as a classic case of sociological distinction as tourism grew more common. The club supported scientific investigations in Lapland, and in 1929 started issuing a yearbook, *Ultima Thule*. They also advocated skiing as a national sport and one of the founding members, General Gösta Lilliehöök, became a leader of military ski sports (Sörlin, 1995).

Another infrastructure aiding the ascendance of Nikkaluokta to its position as a tourist site was the establishment, beginning in 1945, of a glaciological research station at Tarfala at 1,100 m above sea level some 8 km north of the STF mountain station and surrounded by glaciers right below the Kebnekaise summit. Again, mobility work by the local Sami proved essential for the enterprise. Already for two generations they had learned to master multi-faceted cooperation with alpine tourists and scientifically leaning elites. They could also boast crucial infrastructure and, perhaps most importantly, they were experts in technologies of travel and transportation, with horses and skis. Relations between the different parties were generally cordial and friendly.

This trajectory of Nikkaluokta, from a commonplace reindeer herding summer camp to a year-round base station of mountain tourism, made the Sami into personalities through the pages of the *Yearbook of the Swedish Tourist Association*. Already in its very first issue (1886), Fredrik Svenonius commented that Sami should not be regarded as 'below us standing half-people' – in intelligence and other 'natural properties' they are 'equal with the Swede' – a comment necessary given conventional racism at the time (Svenonius, 1886, 10; on scientific racism towards Swedish Sami, see Lundborg and Wahlund, 1932).

It could not have been taken for granted that the Sarris, Hauglis, and Niias in Nikkaluokta would provide such superb and comprehensive services. The reliability of the Sami was an issue of constant debate, not surprisingly since they had been the object of racist anthropology for almost a century. As late as 1947 ethnographer Ernst Manker at the Nordiska Museet in Stockholm reiterated the old notion in his book *De svenska fjällapparna* (Swedish Mountain Saami) that the 'Laps' were shortheaded (*bracylocefalic*) and therefore by implication a lower race (Manker, 1947). A systematic anthropological study, guided by racist presumptions, was undertaken in the 1920s and 1930s by the Institute for Race Hygiene in Uppsala (Lundborg and Wahlund, 1932). The Nikkaluokta Sami proved, of course, such assumptions completely false. The Sarris had considerable help from their traditional knowledge of snow, seasons, travel and equipment. They knew how to manufacture sleds, how to use reindeer and horses for traction, and how to look for the good weather and avoid storms. At an age of 79, Henrik Sarri, who had worked in transportation for Tarfala for several decades, said that he had never ever had to seek shelter from a storm. 'I have always turned around when the weather was too bad' (interview, 2007).

The Sami of the Kebnekaise area and the glaciologists at the Tarfala station both had their micro-geographies of mobility but they only partly overlapped. The glaciologists' 'observation landscape' is small, covering only the Tarfala valley, 'ending as the downhill starts' (Ninis Rosqvist, interview, 2007), dominated by glaciers and moraines and dotted with measuring and monitoring instruments geared towards translating local observations into universal facts (Latour, 1987; Sörlin, 2009). The Sami landscape is much more multi-dimensional, with features of hunting, fishing, reindeer paths, and it is also much larger. It includes the glaciers which all have names, but their relations to glaciers are precisely the opposite of that of the glaciologists. Glaciers are to be avoided. They are dangerous for the reindeer, which can easily fall into crevasses. Only the best dogs could be sent out on the glaciers to drive the reindeer since even the dogs may not always be aware of the danger (Henrik Sarri, 2007).

An important dimension of the mobility landscape is gender. Reindeer husbandry involved everyone in long seasonal treks across the Scandinavian peninsula from the forests near the Gulf of Bothnia to the summer grazing near the Atlantic. The Nikkaluokta Sami, as tourism entrepreneurs, did not do that. Instead their mobility landscape was shaped around their mixed economy of tourism services combined with hunting, fishing and gathering and the keeping of goats and domesticized reindeer for milk, cheese and meat. Some of the mobility involved everyone, like berry picking. 'Every family had their own bogs for cloudberries. It was a tacit order', says Olof Sarri, third generation inhabitant like his sister Anna (interview, 2014). The same unwritten law applied to the grasses on the marshes which provided hay for the winter: every family had their own area and entire families were engaged in the harvesting. Resources were knitted together through networks of walking paths or by boat (Ostrom, 1990). Some of the hunting was done by both girls and boys, like the snaring of rock ptarmigan (*Lagopus muta*; *ripa* in Swedish). But most of the mobility was distinctly gendered. 'The boys came further, like the men, on foot, on horseback, or with snowcats (named after *Mustela nivalis*; *vessla* in Swedish)' (Olof Sarri, 2014). Long-distance transportation work, boating and mountain guiding was invariably performed by the men and boys. Knowledge itself was passed on in a gendered fashion. Olof Sarri learned hunting techniques from his father, for example how to snare hares in winter skiing, carefully avoiding any duplication of tracks.

Climate change is being observed. Olof Sarri notes that the *johka* (creeks) and *ätno* (rivers) are getting smaller as the glaciers are shrinking. Vegetation is getting ever more dense. When he was a child the grass in the valleys was low. 'Now it is so high you can't see.' Winter seasons are shrinking, just like the periods of seasonal ice in the Arctic. It is particularly ironic that the research station at Tarfala can provide the world's longest systematic record of monitoring glacial retreat: primary evidence of the Anthropocene is literally produced in the area.

This speaks to what Anthropocene tourism might mean for Nikkaluokta and Kebnekaise: to maintain and make wise use of their mobility landscape. The 'micro-geographies of authority' could be understood to include the authority of knowing how to live close to a place and preserve it, despite mobility and moving around in the landscape and knowing it. Scientific knowledge of glaciers would play a role just as much as Sami knowledge of reindeer and their pathways. As we have seen this involves difficult ethical decisions. How much of the subtle traces in the landscape should be made into common knowledge? How can, alternatively, the landscape be turned into narratives and visuals and be made accessible in a managed way so that the Anthropocene dilemmas and virtues appear without compromising the innate qualities of the area?

Grövelsjön – uses of history

The Grövelsjön area is our third example. It is the southern part of the mountain range, located in the county of Dalarna, on the border to Norway, approximately 500 km from Stockholm and 600 km from Gothenburg. These distances are of importance in understanding the development of the area in later years and the subsequent commodification that is salient to the establishment. To be close and at the same time distant is a unique offer that speaks to the dilemma of sustainable travel. To some extent Grövelsjön is just the mountain range-extension of the Sälen and Idre installations where the expansion of primarily downhill skiing in the last three decades has been particularly prominent (Fredman and Heberlein, 2003, 485–488). Grövelsjön also offers downhill skiing possibilities, but on a very limited scale; the focus here is different.

Grövelsjön example will discuss the main building in the complex, STF Fjällstation, but it should be pointed out that there are a number of lodges, hotels and huts for rent in the area, offering a wide variety of housing. Grövelsjön uses history to establish itself and its position. History speaks in three different ways. One is the expansion of the mountain station and the ways and times in which it has grown to its present and mature size. The other is the presence of Linnaeus, the Swedish naturalist and founder of the species classification system, who travelled in the area in 1734. Thirdly, the history of the STF is displayed in an old-fashioned exhibit, but tangible and quite prominent in a passageway to the second floor. Together these three uses of history situate the mountain station in a longer time frame than that of shorter trends and mountain fads.

The use of Linnaeus is especially functional in this respect. Linnaeus documented Grövelsjön on his Dalekarlia journey in 1734. Some of his findings are prominently displayed in the 'Linnaeus room', with images, texts and items displayed on boards and in glass cabinets. Peculiarities of the surroundings are brought forward but his ideas are also discussed and, when proven wrong, corrected. One of the main hiking trails is named *Linnéstigen*, the Linnaeus path, and his name is frequently invoked both in brochures, advertisements and in the landscape on signs and posters. Even though it might not have been regarded by himself as the most important discovery, for the mountain station, the freshwater spring, a ten-minute walk from the station is an important site. Through beautiful sand in a smallish pond with outlets into the bogs, cold water bubbles up to the surface. 'That water is the best, which does not taste' Linné wrote in his Dalecarlia diary and the sentence is hanging framed in the restaurant, used as an argument supporting the overall profile of organic food and sustainability by reaching back in time.

This connects to a prominent feature of the formation of a specific identity in the Anthropocene, namely the organic and the sustainable features of the mountain station. The station boasts to be the most environmentally friendly mountain station in Sweden (and the webpage adds that it is 'maybe' the best in the world in this respect, knowing that a 'maybe' is indeed necessary in making such a claim), with certified eco-tourism, a Swan-marking of the entire station and KRAV certified restaurant. The guests are not only encouraged to sort their leftovers but expected to do so; abstaining is actually rather difficult.

Finally the commodification of the experience is salient. This is not, like Vålådalen, a place for star athletes and high-profile training. Instead this is marketed as accessible and friendly, with a focus on families and children, groups of friends or people with converging interests. It is easy to reach and can offer something for everyone. Activities listed for the summer season include introduction courses for families, with one or two parents; qigong, yoga or meditation in a mountain setting; a running camp with instructor; walks for older women – *tantvandring*; bring your dog; children with Down's; or courses in nature photography. The winter season offers dance lessons, flying kites, yoga, and of course skiing instruction, among other things (STF Grövelsjön, 2014a, b).

As mentioned above, Grövelsjön is in the southern part of the Scandinavian mountain range and therefore also closest to the big cities like Stockholm or Gothenburg. However, the mountains are also modest and cannot offer steep climbing or high falls like Kebnekaise and Nikkaluokta. The stretched out, eroded hills around Lake Grövelsjön instead offer friendly walks for elderly and young, a soft mobility. The commodification might be seen as a way of finding a niche in relation to the downhill skiing areas, also within reach from the bigger cities, and the more dramatic scenery of the northern mountains. This is more cosy, close and easy. At the same time it offers sufficient drama. The lake, over which a boat takes hikers back and forth, is deep and beautiful and harbours a wreck from a German Second World War airplane. The Silver fall with icy water allows for heroic bathing, and if you walk up the Storvätteshågna, 1,204 m above sea level, you have been on the highest point in Svealand, the mid part of Sweden.

The efforts in Grövelsjön to bridge the gap between sustainability and luxury might be argued to have two parts. One is to offer an experience that is close to nature but still not too cumbersome. The other is to ensure that this experience is sustainable but at the same time part of a growth economy and thereby viewed also as a means of maintaining the area as an economic sector of some value. The restaurant offers three-course dinners with an organic wine list of some length. The station has a spa section where one can get a massage or facial treatments and the shop does not just offer a basic line of foods for the cabins, but a whole range of clothes and items of high quality and with a sustainable profile. You are expected to move in the landscape in garments produced in harmony with the environment, preferably with the latest design. The commodification could also, however, simply be a way of mitigating the expected decreasing income in winter due to climate change and declining snow (Moen and Fredman, 2007). Also here primary evidence of the significant climate and environmental changes of the Anthropocene are visible, in the form of altered seasonality and temporalities.

What ideas of mobility and sustainability are performed in Grövelsjön? As the above suggests, the ideology is close to the ground, or one can perhaps say grounded in an everyday practice of movement, which is mostly horizontal. However, the mobility in itself is not a defining feature of the sustainability ideology of Grövelsjön. Rather it is when you are not mobile, at the station, that you can perform sustainability through sorting waste, energy use and ecological consumption. Grövelsjön is at the end of the road, but still displays features that are closer to those of a sustainable town than a remote area. Sustainability is centralized, as is the ethics of performing it. It is relatively easy to be 'good' in Grövelsjön. The question is whether the visit, the exception, can educate the visitor to behave wiser in other places or if the eco-friendly sojourn in its friendly pathscapes remains as a situated performance?

Conclusions – pathscapes for a new land ethic?

In the opening section of this chapter we suggested that it would be useful to imagine a practical ethics of tourism that is congruent with the demands of (a certain understanding of) a 'good Anthropocene' where planetary boundaries are not transgressed and where the material impacts of tourism are taken as the criteria of success. We also indicated that such an undertaking will have to include the local and be nuanced and attentive to the scales on which material impacts are less severe, and be observant of the distinction between tourism, as conflating singularity, and tourists, which so far have defined tourism as unsustainable. In the three cases we have proposed how pathscapes of bodily experience can play a concrete role in the evolution of tourism in a responsible direction. This, we believe, is a possible and even realistic ambition, although far from easily compatible with current business-as-usual tourism practices. Could it, rather, be a part of an emerging new ethic of tourism in the Anthropocene, a 'subversive critical unmasking of the ideology of tourism' (Gren and Huijbens, 2014, 12) as one embracing a libertarian, subjective idea of freedom for tourists?

As the three case studies demonstrate, the movement heritage, in terms of skiing tracks, hiking trails, herding paths and other traces of historical and current mobility is an essential, indeed defining, feature of mountain tourism in these instances. This heritage has also shaped the understanding of the landscape, although much of the heritage is also quickly falling into oblivion. The tourism industry is selective in the commodification process.

The case studies further suggest that there is a relatively harmonious coexistence between locals, tourists and nature preservation which in its simplicity deserves attention. So, the question arises whether the landscape can be turned into narratives and visuals and be made accessible in a managed way so that the Anthropocene dilemmas and virtues appear without compromising the innate qualities of the place? And, also, can the visit, the exception, travel in the sense that it can serve as an education for behaviour in other places or will it remain as a situated performance? In that sense we could indeed talk of 'portable pathscapes', but of a totally different kind than the endurance sport landscapes that are portable because they are standardized and designed to provide a commodified sameness of experience. This is also why the movement heritage that we offer as the alternative is not about ready-made content through story-telling, as so much place-making has been in the last couple of decades. On the contrary, the dense mobility landscape of the Kebnekaise area, for example, is the result of a complicated pattern of local practices, technologies of mobility, and remembering and forgetting across the generations of inhabitants in Nikkaluokta but also generations of tourists, scientists and other visitors.

The importance of movement as a practice for understanding landscape and the forming of 'life worlds' has been underlined in previous research (Ingold, 2000, 2011; Hastrup, 2009). Seen from an Anthropocene perspective the traces and signals of the human presence in Vålådalen, Kebnekaise and Grövelsjön may seem almost antithetical. These are traces which rather demonstrate how it is perfectly possible for human mobility and resource use and appreciation of spectacular landscapes pursuing health-fostering mobility to be conducted over many generations without contributing at all to strata on the geological scale, nor to the transgressions of planetary boundaries. On the other hand, these areas too have their evidence of Anthropocene phenomena. Even if there are few traces that will show on the geological strata, evidence of climate change is everywhere. As in an open-air laboratory the vegetation seen from the trails and the mountain station in Grövelsjön grows higher and denser year by year, a fact that has yet to be turned into one of its uses of history. The potential is great and the evidence itself an integrated part of the narrative; the scientific station in Abisko on the northern edge of the Kebnekaise mountains has a wide range of climate data since 1913 that shows a significant warming in the region, especially in the winter (Abisko Scientific Research Station, 2014).

We started out with a question: what would sustainability and tourism be like in the Anthropocene? Sustainability in the strict sense is hard to achieve, primarily given the long-distance travel that is necessary to access the mountains, but compared to other forms of tourism, and other economic activities like mining, it is probably *more* sustainable, not least because the primary resource, the landscape and its silent infrastructures, can fairly easily be sustainably managed. Making tourism sustainable poses several difficult challenges. Looking at a local level, tourism as described in our three cases is more sustainable than other forms, such as large-scale hotel complexes, alpine skiing resorts or heli-skiing. But then there is the issue of travelling to and from these landscapes of movement and the possibly sustainable activity conducted there. Can international tourism be sustainable at all, when modern tourism has been identified as a geophysical force that contributes to climate change (Eijgelaar, Amelung and Peeters, this volume)? At least, tourists of our time and day cannot. The nature/culture dichotomy is an obstacle when discussing effects of tourists in the Anthropocene. Landscapes of mobility are an example of landscapes that evade classic, Western divisions and categories. They are 'gaps' (as described by Anna Tsing, 2005, 174–6), i.e. landscapes that do not fit into traditional nature/culture dichotomies. These gaps show a potential way out of how places are being portrayed as either cultural or natural. Landscapes of mobility are both, simultaneously, and it is not a matter of whether humans are present or not, but rather how they act and to what extent their actions affect the landscape.

The threat of the recreation paradox is evident in all the landscapes discussed above. The more successful tourism becomes in a specific location, the less sustainable it is. Ecological, economic and social sustainability is threatened (Klijn and Vos, 2006; Antrop, 2006). Even the most emblematic landscape writers have risked turning their favoured landscapes into tourist sites, as Thoreau's *Walden* eventually transformed Walden pond (Schama, 1996, 576). But today, becoming a tourist site might actually help secure protection from other, more invasive forms of exploitation. At least, there is a possibility to work in that direction (e.g. Hall and Richards, 2003; Spenceley 2008). There are many more examples of this, but Vålådalen and the Vasalopps Arena are two places that have gained status and been declared reserves partly due to their movement heritage. By attracting tourists who enter in a relation with the landscape, the status of a landscape can be elevated. As Arne Næss pointed out in the 1970s, local communities often lack the power to resist exploitation of their surrounding landscapes (Næss, 1981 [1973], 212; Næss and Rothenberg, 1990). But when allied with at least certain kinds of tourists, they might have a better chance. For example, a mining company who see prospects in Vålådalen will have to face resistance from far more people than the few permanent dwellers, some of whom may also have a personal self-interest in the development. In a Swedish context, members of tourist organizations like the Swedish Tourist Association or the Swedish Alpine Club have often argued for nature protection and resisted large-scale exploitation. So did the Lapland tourism propagandist Fredrik Svenonius in the fierce and emblematic debate over the Stora Sjöfallet hydro-electric dam in the 1910s (Sörlin, 1988; Lundgren, 2009). He faced a large majority that accepted the sacrifice of the majestic waterfall for electric energy, but over the years the anti-development and preservationist attitudes of tourism organizations have solidified (Vedung and Brandel, 2001).

The cases of Vålådalen, Nikkaluokta and Grövelsjön show a multitude of possible understandings of these places. Different actors have different interests and therefore describe these places in different terms. But the overall image is still kept together – there are limits to what could be fitted into what Edward Said called an 'imaginative geography' of a place. This is certainly true for places that are perceived as ecological, small-scale and genuine (Said, 1977, 167 *et passim*; Said, 2003 [1979]). On the tourist market, our three examples all fit the general discourse of the Swedish mountain range. They are part of larger narrative of dreamt refuge from everyday life, but are at the same time (like other iconic landscapes such as the Stockholm archipelago) places where people live, work and move around in different ways (Saltzman, 2007, 220–1). The mountain landscapes we have studied are in a sense refuges for those weary of civilization, and they have a long history in that tradition. But they could also be seen as examples of sustainable landscape use. The traveller visiting Vålådalen does not only affect the place but is also affected in return. In that sense, small-scale, slow, ecological tourism on a local or national scale could also have far-reaching effects on anthropogenic change globally.

Such a 'place ethic', in analogy with the 'land ethic' of Aldo Leopold (1949), implies that tourists are responsible not only for their impact on the destination but also for bringing something back – to let the destination have an impact on their everyday life. The famous land ethic quote by Leopold reads: 'A thing is right when it tends to preserve the integrity, stability, and beauty of the biotic community. It is wrong when it tends otherwise' (Leopold, 1949, 224–5). An Anthropocene tourism land ethic could be phrased thus: 'A tourist is right when s/he tends to preserve the integrity, stability, and beauty of the landscape as a whole and its human and biotic communities. S/he is wrong when s/he tends otherwise.'

The Anthropocene scale is global and geological, but in order to manage this new reality we should also pay attention to local examples, and indeed extend the scales to our inner worlds of bodily experience. After all, the world is a patchwork of landscapes, some more sustainably managed than others. Landscapes of mobility show that landscape use over long periods of time does not necessarily change the physical geography to any larger extent (but certainly the imaginative). If these landscapes can become an inspiration for how to interact with the world, tourism could be part of dealing constructively with the dilemmas at hand, rather than accelerating the problems.

Acknowledgements

This chapter was funded by research grants from MISTRA Foundation for Environmental Research, the Swedish National Heritage Board, and the Swedish Environmental Protection Agency.

References

Abisko Scientific Research Station 2014. <http://polar.se/abisko-naturvetenskapliga-station/abiskoogat-med-fokus-pa-klimat/temperaturen-stiger> [accessed Oct. 2014].

Adorno, T.W. 1951. *Minima moralia: Reflexionen aus dem beschädigten Leben*. Berlin and Frankfurt: M.

Anderson, B. 2012. The construction of an alpine landscape: Building, representing and affecting the Eastern Alps, c. 1885–1914. *Journal of Cultural Geography*, 29(2), 155–83.

Antrop, M. 2006. Sustainable landscapes: Contradiction, fiction or utopia? *Landscape and Urban Planning*, 75, 187–97.

Åstrand, P.O. 1958. *Hur man skall få bättre kondition*. Stockholm: Forum.

Bravo. M.T., and Sörlin, S. (eds) 2002. *Narrating the Arctic: A Cultural History of Nordic Scientific Practices*. Canton, MA: Science History Publications.

Broberg, G. 1982. Lappkaravaner på villovägar: antropologin och synen på samerna fram mot sekelskiftet 1900. *Lychnos*, 1981/2, 27–86.

Buckley, R. 2012. Sustainable tourism: Research and reality. *Annals of Tourism Research*, 39(2), 528–46.

Byrne, A. 2013. *Geographies of the Romantic North: Science, Antiquarianism, and Travel, 1790–1830*. New York: Palgrave Macmillan.

Crist, E. 2013. On the poverty of our nomenclature. *Environmental Humanities*, 2013(3), 129–47.

de Fries, R. 2014. *The Big Ratchet: How Humans Thrive in Face of Natural Disasters*. New York: Basic Books.

Ehn, B., and Frykman, J. (eds) 2007. *Minnesmärken: Att tolka det förflutna och besvärja framtiden*. Stockholm: Carlsson Bokförlag.

Ek, R., and Hultman, J. (eds) 2007. *Plats som produkt. Kommersialisering och paketering*. Lund: Studentlitteratur.

Fredman, P., and Heberlein, T. 2003. Changes in skiing and snowmobiling in Swedish mountains. *Annals of Tourism Research*, 30(2), 485–8.

Fredman, P., *et al.* 2014. *Besök och besökare i fjällen: Resultat från en undersökning avseende svenskarnas fritidsaktiviteter i fjällen, besök i olika fjällområden, landskapsrelationer, fjällen i sociala medier, upplevelser av vindkraft och attityder till skyddad natur*. Östersund: Mid-Sweden University, ETOUR, Report 2014:3.

Green, N. 1990. *Landscape and Bourgeois Culture in Nineteenth-Century France*. New York: St Martin's Press.

Gren, M., and Huijbens, E. 2014. Tourism in the Anthropocene. *Scandinavian Journal of Hospitality and Tourism*, 14(1), 6–22.

Gössling, S., and Peeters, P. 2015. Assessing tourism's global environmental impact 1900–2050. *Journal of Sustainable Tourism*, 23(5), 639–59.

Gössling, S., Hansson, C.B., Horstmeier, O., and Saggel, S. 2002. Ecological footprint analysis as a tool to assess tourism sustainability. *Ecological Economics*, 43(2002), 199–211.

Hajer, M.A. 1995. *The politics of Environmental Discourse: Ecological Modernization and the Policy Process*. Oxford: Clarendon Press.

Hall, D., and Richards, G. 2003. *Tourism and Sustainable Community Development*. London: Routledge.

Hammarskjöld, D. 1962. Att flyga i Sarek. *Från Sarek till Haväng*. Stockholm: Swedish Tourist Association.

Hardy, A., Beeton R.J.S., and Pearson, L. 2002. Sustainable tourism: An overview of the concept and its position in relation to conceptualisations of tourism. *Journal of Sustainable Tourism*, 10(6), 475–96.

Hastrup, K. 2009. Taking the life world seriously in environmental history. In S. Sörlin and P. Warde (eds), *Nature's End: History and the Environment*. London: Palgrave Macmillan, 325–342.

Hellström-Boström, E. 1997. *Svensk klättring: Pionjärerna*. Stockholm: Alpina Förlaget.

Hunter, C. 1995. On the need to re-conceptualise sustainable tourism development. *Journal of Sustainable Tourism*, 3(3), 155–65.

Hunter, C., and Shaw, J. 2007. The ecological footprint as a key indicator of sustainable tourism. *Tourism Management*, 28, 46–57.

Ingold, T. 2000. *The Perception of the Environment: Essays on Livelihood, Dwelling and Skill*. London: Routledge.

Ingold, T. 2011. *Being Alive: Essays on Movement, Knowledge and Description*. Abingdon Oxon: Routledge.

Ingold, T., and Vergunst, J.L. (eds) 2008. *Ways of Walking: Ethnography and Practice on Foot*. Aldershot: Ashgate.

Ísleifsson, S.L. (ed.) 2011. *Iceland and Images of the North*. Quebec: Presses de l'Université du Québec.

Kayser Nielsen, N. 1997. Movement, landscape and sport: Comparative aspects of Nordic nationalism between the wars. *Ethnologia Scandinavica*, 27(1997), 84–98.

Kent, E. 2012. Placemaking as a new environmentalism: Reinvigorating the environmental movement in the 21st century. <http://www.pps.org/reference/placemaking-as-a-new-environmentalism> [accessed Sept. 2014].

King, T. 2003. *Places that Count: Traditional Cultural Properties in Cultural Resource Management*. New York: Altamira Press.

Klijn, J., and Vos, W. (eds) 2006. *From Landscape Ecology to Landscape Science*. Wageningen: Kluwer Academic Publishers.

Krüger, A. 2006. Training theory and why Roger Bannister was the first four-minute miler. *Sport in History*, 26(2), 305–24.

Lane, B. 1994. Sustainable rural tourism strategies: A tool for development and conservation. *Journal of Sustainable Tourism*, 2(1–2), 102–11.

Latour, B. 1987. *Science in Action: How to Follow Scientists and Engineers through Society*. Cambridge, MA: Harvard University Press.

Lee, T.H. 2013. Influence analysis of community resident support for sustainable tourism development. *Tourism Management*, 34(10), 37–46.

Leopold, A. 1949. *A Sand County Almanac: And Sketches Here and There*. New York: Oxford University Press.

Liu, Z. 2003. Sustainable tourism development: A critique. *Journal of Sustainable Tourism*, 11(6), 459–75.

Lowenthal, D. 1998. *The Heritage Crusade and the Spoils of History*. Cambridge: Cambridge University Press.

Lowenthal, D. 2008. Authenticities past and present. *Journal of Heritage Stewardship*, 5(1), 6–17.

Lund, K.A. 2012. Landscapes and narratives: Compositions and the walking body. *Landscape Research*, 37(2), 1–14.

Lund, K.A., and Jóhannesson, G.T. 2014. Moving places: Multiple temporalities of a peripheral tourism destination. *Scandinavian Journal of Hospitality and Tourism*, 14(4), 441–59.

Lundborg, H., and Wahlund, S. (eds) 1932. *The Race Biology of the Swedish Lapps*, part 1. Stockholm: Almqvist & Wiksell.

Lundgren, L.J. 2009. *Staten och naturen: Naturskyddspolitik i Sverige 1869–1935*, vol. 1 (of 2). Brottby: Kassandra.

Lykke Syse, K.V. 2000. *Lende og landskap: En analyse av skogens fysiske landskap og landskapspersepsjon i Nordmarka fra 1900 til 1999*. Oslo: Institutt for kulturstudier, Universitet i Oslo.

Manker, E. 1947. *De svenska fjällapparna*. Stockholm: Swedish Tourist Association.

Medway, D., and Varley, P. 2011. Ecosophy and tourism: Rethinking a mountain resort. *Tourism Management*, 32(4), 902–11.

Moen, J., and Fredman, P. 2007. Effects of climate change on alpine winter tourism in Sweden. *Journal of Sustainable Tourism*, 15(4), 418–37.

Mossberg, L., and Nissen Johansen, E. 2006. *Storytelling: Marknadsföring i upplevelseindustrin*. Lund: Studentlitteratur.

Næss, A. 1981 [1973]. *Ekologi, samhälle och livsstil*. Stockholm: LTs förlag.

Næss, A., and Rothenberg, D. 1990. *Ecology, Community and Lifestyle: Outline of an Ecosophy*. Cambridge: Cambridge University Press.

Nye, D. 1996. *The American Technological Sublime*. Cambridge, MA: MIT Press.

Nygaard, A. 1996. *Vålådalen: en pärla bland turiststationer*. Östersund: Jamtli.

Olander, G. 1950. *Träningsråd för skidåkare*. Stockholm: Svenska skidförbundet.

Olwig, K.R., and Jones, M. (eds) 2008. *Nordic Landscapes: Region and Belonging on the Northern Edge of Europe*. Minneapolis, MN: University of Minnesota Press.

Ostrom, E. 1990. *Governing the Commons: The Evolution of Institutions for Collective Action*. Cambridge: Cambridge University Press.

Polanyi, M. 1958. *Personal Knowledge: Towards a Post-Critical Philosophy*. Chicago, IL: University of Chicago Press.

Qviström, M. 2013. Landscapes with a heartbeat: Tracing a portable landscape for jogging in Sweden (1958–1971). *Environment and Planning A*, 2013(45), 312–28.

Redclift, M.R. 1987. *Sustainable Development: Exploring the Contradictions*. London: Routledge.

Redclift, M.R. 2005. Sustainable development (1987–2005): An oxymoron comes of age. *Sustainable Development*, 13, 212–27.

Rockström, J., Steffen, W., Noone, K., *et al.* 2009. Planetary boundaries: Exploring the safe operating space for humanity. *Nature*, 461, 472–5.

Said, E.W. 1977. Orientalism. *Georgia Review*, 31(1), 162–206.

Said, E.W. 2003 [1979]. *Orientalism*. London: Penguin.

Saltzman, K. 2007. Skärgård till salu: Öar på drömmarnas marknad. In R. Ek and J. Hultman (eds), *Plats som produkt: Kommersialisering och paketering*. Lund: Studentlitteratur.

Sandell, K., and Sörlin, S. (eds) 2008. *Friluftshistoria: Från 'härdande friluftslif' till ekoturism och miljöpedagogik: Teman i det svenska friluftslivets historia*. 2nd edn. Stockholm: Carlsson Bokförlag.

Scott, D. 2011. Why sustainable tourism must address climate change. *Journal of Sustainable Tourism*, 19(1), 17–34.

Schama, S. 1996. *Landscape and Memory*. New York: Vintage Books.

Sharpley, R. 2000. Tourism and sustainable development: Exploring the theoretical divide. *Journal of Sustainable Tourism*, 8(1), 1–19.

Slowfood.com 2014. <http://www.slowfood.com> [accessed Oct. 2014].

Solnit, R. 2002. *Wanderlust: A History of Walking*. London: Verso.

Sörlin, S. 1988. *Framtidslandet: Debatten om Norrland och naturresurserna under det industriella genombrottet*. Kungl. Skytteanska Samfundets Handlingar, 33. Stockholm: Carlsson bokförlag.

Sörlin, S. 1995. Nature, skiing and Swedish nationalism. In J.A. Mangan (ed.), *Tribal Identities: Nationalism, Europe and Sport*, theme issue of *International Journal of the History of Sport*, 12(2), 147–63.

Sörlin, S. 1998. Monument and memory. *Worldviews: Global Religions, Culture, and Ecology*, 2(3), 269–79.

Sörlin, S. 2009. Narratives and counter narratives of climate change: North Atlantic glaciology and meteorology, ca 1930–1955. *Journal of Historical Geography*, 35(2), 237–55.

Spenceley, A. (ed.) 2008. *Responsible Tourism: Critical Issues for Conservation and Development*. London: Earthscan.

Steffen, W. *et al.* 2015. Planetary boundaries: Guiding human development on a changing planet. *Science*, 347, 6223.

STF Grövelsjön Fjällstation 2014a. *Sommar 2014*, printed folder. Stockholm: Swedish Tourist Association.

STF Grövelsjön Fjällstation 2014b. *Vinter 2014–2015*, printed folder. Stockholm: Swedish Tourist Association.

Strömberg, P. 2007. *Upplevelseindustrins turistmiljöer: Visuella berättarstrategier i svenska turistanläggningar 1985–2005*. Uppsala: Fronton.

Svenonius, F. 1886. Några vinkar för resande i Lule lappmark. *STF Yearbook*.

Svenonius, F. 1890. Ett besök vid Kårsojökeln. *STF Yearbook*.

Svenonius, F. 1905. Den naturvetenskapliga stationen vid Vassijaure i Torne Lappmark. *Teknisk tidskrift*. Citation from Carl Gustaf Bernhard, *Abisko Scientific Station* (Stockholm: Royal Swedish Academy of Sciences, 1985), 3–5.

Svensson, D. 2013. I fäders spår? Längdskidåkningens landskap som kulturarv. *RIG – kulturhistorisk tidskrift*, 96(4), 193–212.

Svensson, D. 2014. Changing tracks? The battle between natural and scientific training in Swedish cross-country skiing, 1948–1972. *Idrott, historia och samhälle*, 33(1), 12–41.

Tsing, A.L. 2005. A history of weediness. *Friction: An Ethnography of Global Connection*. Princeton, NJ, and Oxford: Princeton University Press.

Vålådalens Fjällstation 2014. <http://valadalen.se/idrott-a-friskvard> [accessed Oct. 2014].

Vålådalens naturreservat 2003. Östersund: Länsstyrelsen Jämtlands län.

van Dooren, T. 2014. Life at the edge of extinction: Spectral crows, haunted landscapes and the environmental humanities. *Humanities Australia*, 5, 8–22.

Vedung, E., and Brandel, M. 2001. *Vattenkraften, staten och de politiska partierna under 1900-talet*. Nora: Nya Doxa.

Welford, R., and Ytterhus, B. 1998. Conditions for the transformation of eco-tourism into sustainable tourism. *European Environment* 8(6), 193–201.

Williams, S. 2004. *Tourism: Tourism, Development and Sustainability*. London: Routledge.

Zalasiewicz, J., *et al.* 2011. Stratigraphy of the Anthropocene. *Philosophical Transactions of the Royal Society A*, 369(1938), 1036–55.

Zylinska, J. 2014. *A Minimal Ethics for the Anthropocene*. Ann Arbor, MI: Open University Press.

Interviews

Anna Sarri, interview, Nikkaluokta, 14 Aug. 2014, by Sverker Sörlin and Daniel Svensson.

Henrik Sarri, interview, Nikkaluokta, 20–21 Apr. 2007, by Sverker Sörlin.

Olof Sarri, interview, Nikkaluokta, 14 Aug. 2014, by Sverker Sörlin and Daniel Svensson.

Ninis Rosqvist, telephone interview, 30 Apr. 2007, by Sverker Sörlin.

Erica Schytt, Margareta Sarri, Anna Sarri, and Kristina Sarri, interview, Nikkaluokta, 21 Apr. 2007, by Sverker Sörlin.

Kristina Sarri, interview, Nikkaluokta, 21 Apr. 2007, by Sverker Sörlin.

9 Anthropocene ambiguities

Upscale golf, analytical abstractions, and the particularities of environmental transformation

Erik Jönsson

Introduction

When the first course, in 2007, opened in full at Bro Hof Slott Golf Club, this was the result of massive environmental transformations. Soil was transplanted, rocks were blasted and 24,000 m² of crushed white marble was laid out to ensure that bunkers looked picture-perfect regardless of weather. These transformations signalled a deliberate attempt to 'globalize' (cf. McCarthy, 2008; Woods, 2007) a rural landscape, making this shoreline site in Upplands-Bro 32 km north-west of Sweden's capital Stockholm the potential destination for golf enthusiasts from all over the world. Club-owner Björn Örås's vision was that this course (the Stadium course) should 'become the highest ranked course in Sweden, the highest ranked course in Europe, and ... the best spectator course in the world' (interview, November 2011).

Likewise, when Trump International Golf Links Scotland (TIGLS), located 14 km north of Aberdeen along the Scottish North Sea coast, opened its first (and to date only) course in 2012 also this was the result of immense environmental transformations. Turning mobile sand dunes to golfing grounds required both the movement of 'biblical volumes of sand' (DPEA, 2008, 129), and extensive, ongoing, stabilization efforts. Also here, reimagining a previously relatively unknown site as global attraction was central. The developer has repeatedly referred to TIGLS as the 'world's greatest golf course', while pro-development politicians hoped that TIGLS would lure top-tier tourists to Aberdeenshire (Jönsson and Baeten, 2014).

In this chapter I utilize these two developments to explore tourism and the Anthropocene in light of what I perceive as an important ambiguity concerning what is expressed as the Anthropocene's drivers. To the extent that the Anthropocene premiers 'humanity' (Steffen *et al.*, 2007), 'human activity' (Zalasiewicz *et al.*, 2008, 2010) or 'mankind' (Crutzen, 2002; Crutzen and Stoermer, 2000) as focal point for understanding current and future planetary-scale environmental transformation, non-reflexively importing it into tourism studies could be problematic. Such accounts offer a broad-brush conceptualization where humans, and groups of humans, become bundled together as one rather abstract mass. To grasp tourism's, or upscale golf's, entanglements in planetary environmental transformation, centring on this abstract mass as driver of environmental change lends little.

But while the Anthropocene read literally (*anthropos*, Greek for man or human being) might direct our attention thus, there are today many versions – emphasizing a range of driving forces – of what the Anthropocene would be. Engaging with influential accounts of the Anthropocene (Crutzen, 2002; Steffen *et al.*, 2007, 2011a, 2011b; Zalasiewicz, 2010), and with recent critiques of the notion (Head, 2014; Malm and Hornborg, 2014; Moore, 2014) I will in this chapter explore how various versions of the Anthropocene lend themselves differently to scrutinizing tourism as simultaneously a geophysical force (Gren and Huijbens, 2014), and as dependent on other geophysical forces. I argue that while the notion of the Anthropocene fruitfully enables retelling world history as a 'geostory' (Latour, 2014a) where 'humans are not an outside force perturbing an otherwise natural system but rather an integral and interacting part of the Earth System itself' (Steffen, 2007, 615), rendering it useful for tourism studies necessitates problematizing the actors and activities put at the centre of this (geo)story.

To facilitate this problematization I draw on Ollman's (2003, 2008) insistence on abstracting phenomena's level of generality. The act of abstracting should here be understood as the way analyses and accounts *by necessity* parcel out the world (*abstrahere*, Latin, 'to pull from'), 'distinguishing certain features and focusing on and organizing them in ways deemed appropriate' (Ollman, 2003, 60) to enable thinking about it and describing it. Stressing this inescapable element of analysis, in other words, allows illuminating what various accounts consider as parts worthy of focus. Stressing *levels of generality,* thereafter, signals how analyses treat phenomena as more unique or more universal. Accounts of the Anthropocene premiering 'mankind' or 'humanity', for instance, abstract analysis to emphasize planetary environmental transformation at a relatively high (i.e. more universal) level of generality, with mankind or humanity (and the earth) as entities in focus. Other accounts, as I will return to, abstract analysis to focus on much more unique or contingent phenomena.

The chapter proceeds as follows. First, I discuss various ways the Anthropocene has been conceptualized to emphasize how ambiguous its story can appear. In the following section I further illuminate this ambiguity by reconnecting to abstracting levels of generality as a crucial dimension of analysis. Thereafter I combine these reflections in exploring tourism, golf, Bro Hof Slott and TIGLS before, in the conclusion, returning to possible lessons for tourism studies. For Bro Hof Slott, fieldwork was conducted 2011–13, while fieldwork for TIGLS was conducted 2009–14. Combined, a total of 38 planners, politicians, activists, residents, and business representatives have been interviewed. I have, moreover, analysed planning material, marketing material, visited the sites repeatedly and drawn from the media coverage these facilities have received. Though I place these developments alongside each other, my ambition is strictly speaking not to compare them point by point. Their respective peculiarities should be respected, and it would be impossible to generalize findings from either of them to the nature(s) of more 'ordinary' golf developments, or to tourism at large. But it *is* possible to draw on these cases, using the 'force of example' (Flyvbjerg, 2006, 228), to underscore power-permeated environmental transformation as integral to tourism – and to thereby put more emphasis on conflicts and divergent interests than usually awarded when the Anthropocene is equated with 'the geology of mankind' (Crutzen, 2002).

Anthropocene ambiguities, in brief

Today, the Anthropocene appears as an attempt to tell a story of planetary environmental transformation. Though this story been criticized for a dualist leaning of viewing humans as '[o]verwhelming the Great Forces of Nature' (Steffen *et al.*, 2007; see Moore, 2014, for this critique), a key component might nonetheless, as Sayre (2012, 63) highlights, be that 'the ancient dichotomy of humans and nature is now empirically false at the global scale'. Environmental transformations have quite simply become too excessive to ignore, and facts of geology consequentially become components of social science inquiries (cf. Latour, 2014a). But, presented as a geological epoch we are quite simply entering (Zalasiewicz *et al.*, 2010), a consequentialist-biased argument (Moore, 2014), a narrative simplistically premiering humankind as one actor (Malm and Hornborg, 2014; Head, 2014), or a chance to productively rethink analytical presuppositions (Latour, 2014a; Chakrabarty, 2009), the Anthropocene is so much more than merely a novel conceptualization of environmental transformation. It is a conceptualization of current, past, and future, times that carries causal aspirations and that comes in a number of versions where the entanglements of humans and a changing earth are read in radically different ways. Not all these are equally productive for understanding tourism, or (upscale) golf, and the Anthropocene.

First put in print in an International Geosphere–Biosphere Programme newsletter (Crutzen and Stoermer, 2000), and further popularized through a short commentary in *Nature* (Crutzen, 2002), the Anthropocene as originally articulated underscored how '[u]nless there is a global catastrophe — a meteorite impact, a world war or a pandemic — mankind will remain a major environmental force for many millennia' (Crutzen, 2002, 23). The 'level of generality' (Ollman, 2003) abstracted in grasping the new geological epoch thereby initiated was primarily human society, mankind, as *one* 'major geological force' (Crutzen and Stoermer, 2000, 18). Mankind, not astronauts, had 'set foot on the moon'. Mankind, not travellers or commuters, were 'exhausting the fossil fuels'. Mankind, not emitters, 'releases many toxic substances in the environment' (all quotes from Crutzen and Stoermer, 2000, 17).

The Anthropocene as originally articulated, thus signalled an emphasis on how mankind, at large, had recently remade, and continuously remakes, the environment in ways that necessitated denoting a new geological epoch where we would be 'largely treading on *terra incognita*' (Crutzen, 2002, 23). Further underscoring such uncertainty, Steffen *et al.* (2011a, 747) call the Holocene, supposedly now supplanted by the Anthropocene, 'the only global environment that we are sure is "safe operating space" for the complex, extensive civilization that *Homo sapiens* has constructed'. In this version, as Head critically comments, 'we have conceptualized the Anthropocene with an undifferentiated human, ... contrary to the abundant evidence of spatial and temporal differences in influences below the species level' (Head, 2014, 114). The 'we' here notwithstanding, in what I will henceforth call the species-centred version, the Anthropocene not only operates with abstractions (humanity, *homo sapiens*, mankind) analytically unworkable for the social sciences, but moreover risks resulting in neo-Malthusian forms of technocratic management, such as when Crutzen (2006) advocates control of human population. If 'mankind' releases toxic substances, consumes resources, etc., surely 'mankind' should become the target of policies.

But, as evident from Head's objection, the species-centred version has been criticized recently, with several scholars accentuating how 'mankind' is perhaps not today's great geological force. On the one hand, the Anthropos is in these critiques regarded as 'a variable force in an assemblage with others' (Head, 2014, 114, see also Chakrabarty, 2009; Latour, 2014a; Moore, 2014). Environments are, in other words, co-produced by humans *and* non-humans. On the other hand, shifting focus to human action, the great environmental force might be production processes and specific parts of 'mankind's' consumption rather than 'mankind' as such (Malm and Hornborg, 2014; Moore, 2014). As Malm and Hornborg emphasize, '[d]epending on the circumstances in which a specimen of *Homo Sapiens* is born ... her imprint on the atmosphere may vary by a factor of more than 1000' (2014, 65). Here, the critique of a simplistic focus on mankind actually echoes an ambiguity inherent to how drivers are understood also among those advocating the Anthropocene as a useful notion. It is possible to identify a turn towards acknowledging the Anthropos as 'made of highly localised networks of some individual bodies whose responsibility is staggering' (Latour, 2014b, 6). While the Anthropocene geostory sometimes comes with a certain Malthusian flavour, emphasizing human *numbers* as key to understanding environmental impacts, most explanations at least open up for more multi-faceted stories. Such an opening can, for example, be discerned in how Zalasiewicz *et al.* (2010, 2228–9) answer their own question concerning how the actions of humans have altered the course of Earth's deep history:

> The answer boils down to the unprecedented rise in human numbers since the early nineteenth century – from under a billion then to over six billion now, set to be nine billion or more by midcentury. This population growth is intimately linked with massive expansion in the use of fossil fuels, which powered the Industrial Revolution, and allowed the mechanization of agriculture that enabled those additional billions to be fed.

In this passage a rather Malthusian emphasis on the sheer number of people alive is gradually coupled with an emphasis on the technologies sustaining these populations (i.e. historically contingent qualities). Merely an abstract 'mankind' could consequently never truly be at the heart of the Anthropocene as geostory.

This geostory is rather about 'humans and our societies', about humans with the 'technological or organizational capability to match or dominate the great forces of nature' (Steffen *et al.*, 2007, 614).

In underscoring the alleged role technology plays, presentations of the Anthropocene frequently highlight dramatic increases in a range of activities utilized as *indicators* for humankind's effects. Through scrutinizing these activities an opening appears for probing power, politics, political economy and a whole range of issues of interest to the rather heterogeneous community of scholars researching tourism. Steffen *et al.* (2011a, 742), for instance, speaking of a 'Great Acceleration' (or stage 2 of the Anthropocene) since the mid-20th century, emphasize the concomitant growth of population, total real GDP, Foreign Direct Investment, damming of rivers, water use, fertilizer consumption, urban population, paper consumption, McDonald restaurants, transport by motor vehicles, communication by telephones, and (yes) international tourism in a series of graphs underscoring how these phenomena have all increased more or less exponentially during this period. And indeed, bringing up McDonald restaurants or fertilizer consumption is something quite different than bringing up 'mankind' or 'humanity'. Here, the possibility of telling a more multi-faceted and historically contingent version of the Anthropocene appears.

While Steffen *et al.* (2007, 614) in a rather teleological vein had earlier emphasized human nature in how fire 'put us firmly on the long path towards the Anthropocene', Steffen *et al.* (2011a, 751) instead emphasized a 'growth-oriented economy based on neo-liberal economic principles and assumptions' as 'a value that has driven the Great Acceleration'. Steffen *et al.* (2011b), similarly, relate the 'Great Acceleration' to neo-classical economic thinking, Second World War destruction of pre-industrial European institutions, partnerships among government and academia, commodification of previously public goods, a growth imperative as core societal value, neoliberal economic principles, Bretton Woods institutions, and that the Second World War 'produced a cadre of scientists and technologists, as well as a spectrum of new technologies (most of which depended on the cheap energy provided by fossil fuels), that could then be turned towards the civil economy' (Steffen *et al.*, 2011b, 850). Unless one considers human beings hard-wired for neoliberalism or planetary warfare, the Anthropocene could consequentially not even among those whole-heartedly proposing this as a meaningful term be seen as fully deduced from human nature (i.e. from 'mankind' or humanity). Historical contingency supplants teleology, while a dizzying array of possible drivers to explore is offered.

It simultaneously bears mentioning that Crutzen (2002) already in his (perhaps therefore incorrectly named) account of *the geology of mankind* underscored that humans' effects on the global environment had 'largely been caused by only 25% of the world population' (Crutzen, 2002, 23), while Steffen *et al.* (2011a, 746) remark that 'the world's poorest countries, with a combined population of about 800 million, have contributed less than 1% of the cumulative emissions'. The vast differences between specimens of *homo sapiens* are thus just as impossible to ignore as the vast planetary transformation.

Acknowledging such particularities 'below the species-level' unveils the Anthropocene narrative (if this should even be called one coherent narrative) as riveted by ambiguities. As soon as specific activities and practices are brought up as indicators of environmental effects, it becomes possible (indeed, necessary) to stress who and what lies behind these activities. What Sayre (2012), in commenting on the Anthropocene, denotes as 'the politics of the anthropogenic' could here be brought up as a way to further accentuate such differences and historical contingency. This politics, Sayre (2012, 59) asserts, 'concerns who caused which changes, with what impacts on whom'. This, I believe, is precisely where one should begin to unravel processes if the Anthropocene notion is to be workable for tourism studies, where tourists as a relatively privileged *subset* of humans form the node.

Abstracting the Anthropocene's levels of generality

The ambiguities underlined above have much to do with earlier discussions on scaled analyses. Bro Hof Slott and TIGLS illuminate the entanglement of local transformations and globalizing processes (cf. McCarthy, 2008; Woods, 2007). Topographies are reshaped to resituate landscapes in relation to global flows of golf tourists, while the Anthropocene as geostory itself highlights *planetary* environmental transformation rather than 'merely' socio-ecological transformation. But while scale undoubtedly forms a crucial component of this story, I will in this section further elaborate on how ambiguities concerning alleged Anthropocene drivers can be further explored through drawing on Ollman's (2003, 2008) emphasis on abstracting levels of generality. Though tied to considerations of spatial and temporal scale, Ollman's framework (as I brought up in the introduction) simultaneously stress how analyses abstract phenomena as more unique or more universal, which in a sense adds one more layer. For example, to claim that something is 'human' is to appeal to another degree of universality than to claim that something is 'global'.

As a conscious way of 'subdividing the world' (2003, 61), the importance Ollman awards abstraction could hardly be overstated. Only through breaking reality down into manageable parts can the world be communicated and thought about (Ollman, 2003, 60). An analytical foundation is laid through determining studies' spatial and temporal extensions, and through setting up vantage points making it possible to view the parts one subdivides in relation to the bigger system they form part of (and thereby viewing the system through its parts). '[L]earning how to abstract', Ollman asserts, 'is the first step in learning how to think' (2003, 71). The crucial analytical task here becomes just how reality should be subdivided for grasping tourism and the Anthropocene. As I showed above, (hu)mankind, or humanity, is far from the self-evident central driver in this proposed geological epoch. Thus, accentuating the various levels of generality abstracted in versions of the Anthropocene provides an opportunity to explicitly emphasize just what analyses render invisible or put to the forefront, and thereby the often hidden presuppositions of influential accounts.

To regard 'humanity' or 'mankind' as the Anthropocene's main driver could, in light of this discussion, be likened to what Ollman calls a lazy abstraction, an analysis where inherited conceptual constructs are simply and uncritically deployed (Ollman, 2003, 61). Underscoring mankind's effects is easy, simply because so much thought, from Malthusian dystopians like Ehrlich (1971) to techno-optimists like Lomborg (2001), tends to centre on humankind as the key unit of analysis. Consequentially, this version of the Anthropocene

> makes for an easy story ... because it does not challenge the naturalized inequalities, alienation, and violence inscribed in modernity's strategic relations of power and production. It is an easy story to tell because it does not ask us to think about these relations *at all*. The mosaic of human activity in the web of life is reduced to an abstract humanity as homogenous acting unit.
>
> (Moore, 2014, 2)

But though easily deployed, 'an abstract humanity' is much too coarse for understanding tourism and the Anthropocene. Key in grasping just what kind of geophysical force tourism is might instead be to analytically embrace the particularities of specific processes of environmental transformations. To enable this embrace, abstracting levels of generality offers a handy heuristic device.

Let me illustrate; with recourse to Marx Ollman notes how he distinguished production in capitalist society from production in general, and 'production as a whole' in capitalism from 'production as a specific branch of industry' (Ollman, 2003, 86–8). Dependent on the level of generality abstracted production could thus be understood as a universal trait of all societies (say tool-making), as forms of capitalist production (commodity production to accumulate capital) or as the production of specific things (boats, boots, or baths) whose dynamic is irreducible to production in general or capitalist production. Likewise, while tourism is, as Britton (1991, 475) famously remarked, 'predominantly capitalistically organised', tourism is organized around selling specific kinds of embodied, immediately consumed, experiences (Gibson, 2009). This production of experiences is irreducible to capitalism in general, even though tourism would most likely be inconceivable outside the dialectically interrelated technological, economic and political developments of capitalist globalization (cf. Bianchi, 2009, 2011; Gibson, 2009; Rojek, 1985, 2013).

In his elaboration on Marxian dialectics, Ollman (2003) identified seven major levels of generality on which Marx abstracted issues. These are also the levels of generality I primarily utilize to analyse tourism, golf and two upscale golf developments. Ranging from (1) the unique nature of a situation or person, the 'here and now, or however long what is unique lasts' (Ollman, 2003, 88) (2) 'what is general to people, their activities, and products because they exist and function within modern capitalism, understood as the last twenty to fifty years' (Ollman, 2003, 88), (3) capitalism as such, (4) class society, (5) human society, (6) the animal world and (7) material parts of nature, these cover everything from the most particular to the universal. Various levels, moreover, could never be disentangled. They shape and are shaped by each other. Capitalism (3), is for example simultaneously a specific form of class society (4), a form of human society (5) and a particular way of organizing material parts of nature (7) (cf. Chakrabarty, 2009; Moore, 2014). Capitalists, likewise, are not only economic agents but unique, nameable, persons (1), parts of humanity (6) and material parts of nature (7) (Donald Trump obeys the same laws of physics as a beggar, a piece of clay or a seagull.) Critique of the species-centred version of the Anthropocene could with these levels of generality in mind be regarded as attempts to shorten the story in order to stress particular groups and particular historical periods instead of a long march from the discovery of fire onwards (Malm and Hornborg, 2014). Relabelling the Anthropocene as the Capitalocene in Moore's (2014) account conversely signals an attempt to extend analysis back in time to acknowledge massive global environmental transformation predating the frequently adopted starting point with Watt's 1784 steam engine found in influential accounts of the Anthropocene (cf. Crutzen, 2002).

Reabstracting the problem, extending or shortening the focus, putting more particular historical processes at the centre, thus enables retelling new geostories. The Anthropocene now appears more of a level 2 or 3 problem than a level 5 problem. The Great Acceleration is for example evidently more about the shape of capitalism since the Second World War than about the mere existence of human societies. Meanwhile, tourism's contemporary chief characteristics are perhaps most visible at level 2, as phenomena of modern capitalism. It is certainly not naturally human, given how people once had to be *taught* how to become tourists (Franklin, 2004). The workings of the golf developments I study might become easiest to discern through abstracting the analysis on level 1 and 2, the 'here and now' as internalizing modern capitalism. This, crucially, does not mean that other levels of generality are irrelevant. Omitted qualities are 'equally real, and, for different kinds of problems, equally important' (Ollman, 2008, 16). Heuristic devices are really what abstracted levels are. As Ollman (2003, 88) remarks, '[o]ther maps of levels of generality could be drawn, and for other kinds of problems they might be very useful'. In relation to tourism, one could, for example, imagine a map with an additional level (say 2.5) between 'modern capitalism' and capitalism as such to emphasize the period since the 19th century during which forests, shorelines, mountains, etc. became regarded as desirable destinations to visit (cf. Corbin, 1994; Franklin, 2004; Löfgren, 1999).

Placing tourism, and golf

The year 2013 saw 1.087 billion international tourist arrivals worldwide, accompanied by an additional 5–6 billion domestic tourists (UNWTO, 2014). But while these numbers testify to a world criss-crossed by pleasure and business travellers, reading them as suggesting a world of tourists would be a grave mistake. Some individuals are responsible for several arrivals respectively, and a much smaller part of the global population than these figures suggest are thus tourists. Just as the 17th–19th-century Grand Tour of the Mediterranean was an elite activity (Löfgren, 1999), so is contemporary tourism (even if this global elite in absolute numbers has become massive).

Already emphasizing *tourism* and the Anthropocene thus accentuates the 'spatial and temporal differences in influences below the species level' Head (2014, 114) found wanting in many accounts of this proposed geological epoch. In comparison to the species-centred version already emphasizing tourism signifies a reabstraction. But, drawing on Ollman (2003), analysis could be further reabstracted to emphasize various tourist industries (cf. Cohen, 1979; Leiper, 2008). A two-day hike through the forests of Söderåsen in Southern Sweden and a two-week trip to an all-inclusive resort at Rhodos could both be regarded as parts of 'tourism as a geophysical force' (Gren and Huijbens, 2014). But the ways humans and non-humans intermingle on a hike or by the seashore differ, as do the possible planetary effects. Analysis could therefore profit from an emphasis on the nuanced particularities of *specific* forms of tourism and *specific* tourist developments.

A recent attempt by this book's editors to introduce tourism and the Anthropocene points precisely towards such a multi-faceted focus. Within the scope of a single article Gren and Huijbens (2014) shift between humans as a geophysical force, tourism as a geophysical force 'which has contributed to the reshaping of the Earth for human purposes and to climate change' (2014, 9), and a specific airline (Icelandair) as a geophysical force. Hence, a scalar dynamic of abstractions appear. Just as tourism is not the same as humanity, Icelandair is not the same as 'tourism'. As abstractions narrow, they simultaneously provide possibilities for putting clearer focus on the 'politics of the anthropogenic' (Sayre, 2012). Neither all humans, nor all Icelanders, are unequivocally responsible for the greenhouse gases emitted through Icelandair flights. Analysis can be much more specific. Focusing on actors, the geophysical 'culprits' would instead be those choosing to fly Icelandair. Focusing on structures, the creation of a subject in search of new travel experiences and a bundle of industries catering for this subject could instead be put to the forefront (cf. Franklin, 2004).

Much like for tourism, various abstractions can be explored also for golf. With tourism emphasized, golf disappears among all the activities gathered under this moniker. But, drawing on the critique of simplistically viewing tourism as one industry (Leiper, 2008), golf can be construed as one of *several* tourism-related industries important in their own right. Golf (seems to have) surfaced as 'Gouff' in 15th-century Scotland, where the first clubs were founded during the 18th century. Within Scotland golf courses spread partly dependent on how railroads were laid out during the 19th century (Price, 2002). Elsewhere, the sport instead initially spread concomitantly with the British Empire. In 1829 Royal Calcutta became the first club formed off the British Isles (Price, 2002). The entanglements of golf as leisure activity, technological developments and societal organization was thereby evident at an early stage. And such entanglements have been just as pronounced later on. As Perkins (2010, 315–16) asserts;

> The development of turf science after the Second World War allowed courses
> to become much more controlled environments, often now relying on regular

application of fertilizers and pesticides and a carefully automated mowing regime. ... The systematic use of earthmoving equipment instead of hand labor allowed courses to be imposed onto environments, rather than matched to landforms, and the golf buggy led to an inexorable spread of cart paths across what were formerly grassy fairways.

New technological developments, in other words, amplified the extent to which golf courses could transform environments. Just like the geostory of the Anthropocene might really be a story of political economy and ever more powerful technologies, so is golf's geostory. Perkins's illustration simultaneously suggests a reading of golf as about the appropriation and transformation of particular topographies. Golf is, as Lowerson (1994) remarks, 'the most territorially hungry of sports'. Today, approximately 35,000 golf developments cover up to 3.5m ha globally, while golf courses alone cover 1.4–2.1m ha (cf. Briassoulis, 2007; Gössling, 2002; Saito, 2010). Such vast areas of greenery, in total almost the size of Taiwan, are sustained through continuous investments, often labour-intensive maintenance efforts, and flows of water, pesticide, fungicide, fertilizers, etc. As leisure activity, then, golf is intimately intertwined in environmental transformation. It is a geophysical force.

Already a decade ago the Worldwatch Institute (2004) estimated that irrigating the world's golf courses consumed 9,500,000m³ of water per day. Meanwhile, a single Mediterranean golf course can consume up to 10,000m³ of water per hectare per year, the equivalent of the average annual water consumption of 12,000 people (Briassoulis, 2007). Water use, undoubtedly, is not merely an abstract part of the Great Acceleration (cf. Steffen *et al.*, 2011a), but about how particular actors use particular creeks, rivers, groundwater sources, etc. for particular groups' benefit. Returning to Sayre's (2012, 59) politics of the anthropogenic as about 'who caused which changes, with what impacts on whom' golf's (geo)story could thus be expressed as one where golf operators turn landscapes green for the benefit of golfers, but with the production of such landscapes risking lessening water availability for others.

Various kinds of golf developments do however not entail the same environmental transformations, with courses beneficial or degrading depending on the kind of inherited landscape transformed (Colding and Folke, 2009). The 'here and now' (Ollman, 2003) matters. The characteristic of golf has varied *both* over time and between various kinds of courses. Ceron-Ayana (2010) claims that golf 'gentrified' when regularized courses rather than public land became the site where golf was played. Adams and Rooney (1985) conversely claim that US golf during the latter half of the 20th century underwent popularization and democratization (see also Perkins, 2010). Rather than signalling a contradiction, this points to the importance of acknowledging differences also *within* this specific kind of tourist industry. Bro Hof Slott and TIGLS, importantly, are not merely golf facilities. They are *upscale* golf facilities, and this is reflected in the ways they transform the landscapes. Emphasizing this entails yet another reabstraction, now from an industry close-up to a close-up on what Ollman (2003) calls the first level of generality, the 'unique situation'.

On the socio-ecological entanglements of Bro Hof Slott and TIGLS

I will now turn to my two high-end golf developments as unique situations entangled in processes at higher levels of generality. This, I hope, allows centring on aspects easily lost when 'tourism' or, much worse, 'mankind' becomes the agent at a story's centre. But just what are these developments? Perhaps most notably, and as I started this chapter by stating, both Bro Hof Slott Golf Club, and TIGLS created what their respective owners regarded as optimal golfing landscapes through fundamentally transforming pre-existing landscapes. At Bro Hof Slott, producing the aforementioned Stadium Course and a second course inland (the Castle Course, opened 2010) together entailed removing 3 million m³ of soil, blasting 18,000m³ of rocks to optimize lake views, and covering each course with 70,000 tons of sand. Turning a former manorial landscape into upscale golfing grounds furthermore entailed installing an intricate drainage system, as well as extensive renovations to both manor house and pre-existing outbuildings repurposed for the golf facility's demands.

TIGLS, established at the Menie Estate, also meant that a manorial landscape was radically reshaped. A dynamic dune system, previously offering rare habitats for birds and plants, was supplanted by a stabilized golf landscape. The Menie House (renamed MacLeod house to honor Trump's Scottish-born mother) now offers dining and accommodation, '[g]uaranteeing unsurpassed luxury, comfort and service' (see TIGLS, n.d.). Such emphasis on 'luxury' permeates the developer's rhetoric throughout, with TIGLS to bring in 'wealthy Americans, wealthy Chinese, wealthy Europeans to come and play golf' (Neil Hobday, then TIGLS Project Director, cited in Jönsson and Baeten, 2014). Bro Hof Slott is likewise quite evidently an elite landscape, something to which the marble-covered bunkers, astonishingly smooth lawns made possible by a labour-intensive lawn-moving regime, the menu at the club house restaurant, and the thoroughly transformed shoreline topography testify. Thus, both developments accentuate not only this particular form of leisure as a particular form of environmental transformation, but how this environmental transformation was for the benefit of a specific clientele. TIGLS's £145–215 (€169–251) high season green fees or Bro Hof Slott's SEK1150–1850 (€122–196) senior green fees price these developments far above virtually all other golf developments in their respective countries. Hence, they necessitate acknowledging differences both between tourists and non-tourists, and between groups of tourists, in grasping 'tourism as a geophysical force' (Gren and Huijbens, 2014). These environments were not produced by 'tourists' or 'tourism', but by specific golf-tourist-industry actors aiming to attract wealthy consumers.

In both Aberdeenshire and in Upplands-Bro, the production of upscale golfing grounds was, furthermore, entangled in planning mediations concerning what rural landscapes could be rendered politically acceptable. Establishing TIGLS hinged on rendering land not zoned for development into land deemed suitable for a golf resort 'of a scale not previously seen in the United Kingdom' (Johnston

Carmichael, cited in DPEA, 2008, 77). Already this planning-political re-evaluation of the countryside was considered controversial, but even more so was how TIGLS managed to render the Foveran Links Site of Special Scientific Interest developable. While the Infrastructure Services Committee (formally deciding the development's fate) turned the resort application down, this merely resulted in an unprecedented planning-political overhaul that saw TIGLS approved by Scottish ministers following a public inquiry (Jönsson, 2014). For the first time, Scottish ministers used their powers to rescale a planning proposal to the national scale on a proposal otherwise refused. (The 250 proposals previously called in through such means were all for developments *approved* at lower scales of governance.) Similarly, Bro Hof Slott required extensive planning-political mediations, primarily because the developer regarded immediate water contact as an absolute necessity for the facility's flagship course. While the developer managed to get an exemption from shoreline protection legislation to fulfil this desire, a 75ha land and 175ha water municipal nature reserve maintained by the developer was established concomitantly to compensate for the golf resort's impacts on the shores (see Upplands-Bro, 2004).

And what can this then say about the particular forms of 'modern capitalism' (Ollman, 2003) that these developments function within? At TIGLS, granting the developer the possibility to transform an erstwhile protected stretch of land was intimately intertwined in a certain kind of normalized 'neoliberal mindset' (Keil, 2009). Among proponents, the sheer possibility of attracting wealthy tourists to Aberdeenshire was framed as a 'once-in-a-lifetime opportunity' (then Aberdeenshire Council Leader Anne Robertson, cited in the *Scotsman*, 2007) to be exploited, seemingly regardless of what established plans and environmental protection suggested. Thus, 'planning was remade in ways that rendered "planning" increasingly useless as a concept. Trump's entrepreneurial instincts – rather than negotiated long-term strategies – came to set the agenda for the transformation of the Aberdeenshire countryside' (Jönsson and Baeten, 2014, 66). Like some assert that the Anthropocene earth is (cf. Steffen *et al.*, 2011a), this landscape too could be considered a material manifestation of neoliberalism (cf. Tasan-Kok and Baeten, 2012). Though 'neoliberalism' is not the word Ollman (2003) uses, this offers an apt illustration of the entanglement of the 'here and now' in a modern capitalism which, undoubtedly, is not the *same* modern capitalism as the one from Marx's 19th-century abstractions.

Also Bro Hof Slott as 'unique situation' (Ollman, 2003) clearly functions as it does because it functions within 'modern capitalism'. This includes the normalization of inter-suburban competition evident in the explicit desire among municipal decision-makers to have Upplands-Bro known as a potential golfing destination (and thereby distinguishable from other municipalities surrounding Stockholm). The municipal vision was for leisure to form the backbone of Upplands-Bro's identity. But Bro Hof Slott as entangled in modern capitalism also includes how construction costs were funded through owner Björn Örås investing over SEK400m (€44m) of his own wealth. This wealth was primarily made through Örås-owned Poolia, a staffing agency started as Ekonompoolen in

1989 (Jönsson, forthcoming a). The fortunes of this company, and thereby the possibility of Bro Hof Slott, came to rest on shifts in labour-political regulation, which removed earlier partial bans on these kinds of businesses – thus enabling a remarkable expansion of staffing agencies since the mid-1990s (Johnson, 2010). Thereby, what could easily risk being regarded a separate phenomenon, the temporalization of employment so characteristic of modern capitalism (cf. Standing, 2011), comes to permeate the leisure landscape. Bro Hof Slott exists in its current form because the Swedish labour market functions as it does.

Tracing processes need however not end at this level of generality. As tourist developments produced through appropriating and selectively reshaping *manorial* landscapes, analysis could be reabstracted to illuminate class society (Ollman's level 4) beyond its capitalist iteration (cf. Jönsson, forthcoming b). Archaeological evaluations and excavations in the vicinity of Bro Hof Slott moreover unveil a history of human settlements far beyond the history of the manor (Upplands-Bro, 2004). The landscape can be viewed *vis-à-vis* a longer history of human societies; Ollman's fifth level. It bears repeating that levels of generality are about analytical abstraction, not about whether other levels exist (cf. Ollman, 2008). But abstracting analysis at such a high level of generality erases the historically contingent processes that lead to the landscape eventually becoming a high-end, high-profile, golf development. For my problem, grasping upscale golf developments as environmental transformations, this abstraction does not work well.

Telling two non-teleological transformation-stories

As Head (2014) asserts, a problem with how the Anthropocene is presented might be how the 'emerging narrative tends to present human history in a linear, deterministic and teleological frame at odds with both scientific and social scientific understandings of evolutionary and historical contingency' (Head, 2014, 114). Such a teleological frame overlooks the indeterminacy and instability of actual processes. Neither the grounds now occupied by Bro Hof Slott, nor those occupied by TIGLS, were somehow predetermined to become golf developments. The inherent indeterminacy of their trajectories should be acknowledged, and can be further explored through accounting for unfinished facets of the two developments together with the conflicts the developments have become entangled in.

At Bro Hof Slott, unrealized plans involve both a 70-room conference/hotel development, and a whisky distillery intended to become a regional tourist attraction drawing 30,000 visitors each year (see Upplands-Bro, 2004, 8). Controversies regarding where the area earmarked for golf development ends and the adjacent nature reserve begins has led to the developer not yet completing the detailed development plan. Unsurprising, given the descriptions of TIGLS as en route to becoming the biggest resort in the UK, visions also here went far beyond the current development. A 2010 master plan outlined, among other things, an additional golf course, a 450-room hotel, 600 holiday home units, 200 apartments, 186 golf villas and 500 residential units, in total spanning about 470 ha. Nothing of this has however materialized to date, with Trump stating the erection of a wind turbine park south-east of the development as rationale for discontinuing resort construction. Cleaner energy production did not combine well with the undisturbed seaside vistas Trump desired. Incompatible visions for what landscapes should be produced here seem a fundamental part of the differences below the species level.

Though I have stressed local environmental transformations, it should, furthermore, not be forgotten that both developments remain entwined with the global transformations frequently accentuated in accounts of the Anthropocene. The very reason for radically reorganizing these landscapes was after all to attract golfers from elsewhere. As these developments were to be added to the list of courses players must play before they die or get dead tired of the game, they were to result in an increase of air miles travelled. Protests against the TIGLS development have consequentially coupled the ongoing transformation of the North Sea coast, from dynamic sand dunes to golf course, with the air traffic-induced environmental impacts a large-scale golf development could generate. As activists from the group Plane Stupid in 2009 occupied a taxiway at Aberdeen's Dyce Airport, they hung a banner stating 'Nae Trump Games with Climate Change' (Jönsson and Baeten, 2014). The same fears over atmospheric change fuelling much concern over the Anthropocene thus became remarked in what could easily be construed as 'merely' a local planning-political conflict. At Bro Hof Slott climate change has instead been reimagined as business opportunity, with course architect Robert Trent Jones Jr commenting in marketing material that 'climatic changes have made the latitudes in height with and north of St Andrews increasingly attractive, at least during the summer'. In sharp contrast with how this issue is usually understood among those proposing the Anthropocene as a meaningful conceptualization, climate change is here construed less as leading towards a scary *terra incognita*, and more as merely turning the north into a top golf destination. The hopes that some have expressed, that we are entering an Anthropocene stage 3 characterized by growing awareness of environmental impact and attempts to form global governance system (Steffen *et al.*, 2007, 2011b), might thus be somewhat premature. Indeed, the revelation that far from all regard current levels of environmental transformation as problematic might in itself be the scariest part of entering an already scary *terra incognita*.

But finally, with both Bro Hof Slott and TIGLS existing in a stunted form due to conflicts, these developments are bound to attract less tourists than they otherwise would have. Their impact is not as significant as it perhaps could have been. To the extent that they would have caused people to travel the world more frequently, luring golfers to visit rural landscape as world-famous attractions, the conflicts outlined above would thus lessen the power of 'tourism as a geophysical force' (Gren and Huijbens, 2014). Though the reductions in tourists such conflicts result in hardly make a dent in the overall pattern, I believe that this argument retains its pertinence. Again, this is a way of accentuating the manifold indeterminate, specific, environmental transformations, and particular processes, that together result in what has been labelled 'the new world of the Anthropocene' (Zalasiewicz *et al.*, 2010). Reabstracting analysis to highlight such transformations does, decidedly, not mean downplaying concerns over environmental transformation's possible effects and the direction the world seems to be heading. Both Ollman (2003, 92), and Chakrabarthy (2009, 220–2), though taking historical contingencies into account, acknowledge that ecosystem collapse *can* have species-wide consequences. But it is none the less still possible to justifiably de-emphasize aggregates in analysis of what led to the brink of possible collapse, for the benefit of all the particular activities and processes that *together* constitute aggregates. The problem is certainly not that it would be factually incorrect to state that '[o]ver the past 50 years, humans have changed the world's ecosystems more rapidly and extensively than in any other comparable period in human history' (Steffen *et al.*, 2007, 617), or that 'no previous migrations of organisms ... have rivalled the human-caused introductions of alien species' (Zalasiewicz *et al.*, 2010, 2230). The problem is that, to actually grasp tourism's role and stake in such transformation, analysis must acknowledge the 'politics of the anthropogenic' (Sayre, 2012), and how the Anthropos is (again) 'made of highly localised networks of some individual bodies whose responsibility is staggering' (Latour, 2014b, 6). To this end, abstractions directing our eyes too much towards aggregates rather than particularities offer little guidance.

Conclusions

And where does this then leave tourism studies? My chapter has been an attempt to utilize two high-end golf developments to tell a non-monolithic, and non-teleological, story of a specific kind of tourism and the Anthropocene. The effects and entanglements of Bro Hof Slott and TIGLS could not be understood by abstracting analysis to emphasize an abstract 'humanity', a grand phenomenon called 'tourism' or even generic 'golf developments'. Rather, these developments are unique cases shaped by and shaping processes and relations with longer temporal duration and/or greater spatial extent. Through this shift in focus considerations concerning responsibility in the Anthropocene can perhaps also be scaled down. Conflicts are now seen as less about 'planetary stewardship' (Steffen *et al.*, 2011a), than about the shape and reshaping of particular environments (even if, as campaigns against TIGLS illustrate, they can connect this transformation to planetary issues).

But the shift in focus advocated throughout this chapter perhaps above all offers an opportunity to analyse radically remade environments *without* losing grip of the particular, power-permeated, processes shaping these environments. Here, the actions of the Scottish state in rendering TIGLS possible, or the ways Upplands-Bro's politicians hoped that Bro Hof Slott could render the municipality distinguishable from other locales surrounding Sweden's capital, are not mere elaborations on a more important story of mankind through the millennia. They are the story. Thus, new issues to explore are added to the already long list of Anthropocene drivers. Inter-suburban competition, neoliberal rural planning and the temporalization of labour are now foregrounded as drivers of environmental transformation – and consequentially as issues worthy of focus in order to grasp forms of tourism and the Anthropocene.

If such particularities in environmental transformation can be productively explored, the Anthropocene notion could potentially mainstream environmental considerations in tourism studies. Forms of tourism are now understood as forms of environmental change. Focus shifts, as Gren and Huijbens (2014) express this, from tourism as geography-ing force to tourism as geophysical force. The abstract earth of the 'space cadets' (cf. Koelsch, 2001, 265–6) is thus supplanted by a mesh of interacting, living, forces that matter. The world tourism studies encounters is a world in constant transformation as it is, and under yet more transformation pressures because of a myriad of activities, tourist-related and not.

For Gren and Huijbens (2014, 13), reflections on tourism and the Anthropocene signal a call to 'further develop the cross-border traffic also to the natural sciences rather than confirming its place as a social science (post)discipline'. And, while I fully agree with the necessity of involving all disciplines able to illuminate aspects of the often extensive environmental transformations through which tourism is made possible, one reservation seems crucial. In fostering such cross-border traffic tourism studies *must* hold on to one fundamental facet of the social sciences. Tourism studies must retain an analysis of the power relations and historically contingent processes that reflect and/or produce the differences making the species-centred version of the Anthropocene so problematic. To this end, the Anthropos of the Anthropocene could be read just like the Anthropos of anthropology, a discipline for which Latour (2014b) has recently called the Anthropocene an 'amazing gift'. For anthropology, focusing on human lives means precisely what I advocate in this chapter. It means a focus on the particular, perpetually power-permeated, ways particular practices are structured rather than a focus on *a* kind of human actor or humankind as *one* actor. Here, an attention to analyses' levels of generality and the abstractions utilized should prove fruitful.

Theorizing tourism in relation to vast local and global environmental changes thereby comes to require theorizing inequalities and power relations inherent to tourism. Trump exerts another geophysical influence than those employed to mow lawns at his resorts, who in turn exhibit another kind of geophysical influence to those travelling to play these courses (who in turn exhibit another kind of influence than those playing other courses elsewhere). Though such a remark might seem obvious, it remains pertinent given both (certain forms of) tourism studies (cf. Bianchi, 2009; Hall, 2011), and (certain conceptualizations of) the Anthropocene's (Head, 2014) well-documented difficulties with acknowledging (class) differences and the concomitant differences concerning greenhouse gas emissions, resource use, etc.

Yet, finally, whether we actually inhabit 'the new world of the Anthropocene' (Zalasiewicz *et al.*, 2010) might be less important than whether the Anthropocene has become an influential concept for locating ourselves. With the 2015 Royal Geographical Society with the Institute of British Geographers' conference recently centring on the 'Geographies of the Anthropocene', and with articles proposing and debating the Anthropocene as label for the present repeatedly cited, the latter question seems only possible to answer affirmatively. If we are indeed increasingly *regarded* as inhabiting the Anthropocene this almost automatically becomes a notion of interest, especially at a juncture where accounts of the Anthropocene remain so ambiguous. Engaging with this geostory seems crucial to ensure that 'we' (as tourism studies scholars) do not find ourselves faced with an influential concept stabilized with presuppositions problematic for grasping the particularities of various forms of tourism and the ways these transform environments. This engagement, undoubtedly, includes continuously reabstracting and reformulating the problem at hand, to find a version of the Anthropocene apt for understanding tourism, local- and planetary environmental transformation.

References

Adams, R.L.A., and Rooney, J.F. 1985. Evolution of American golf facilities. *Geographical Review*, 75(4), 419–38.

Bianchi, R.V. 2009. The 'critical turn' in tourist studies: A radical critique. *Tourism Geographies*, 11(4), 484–504.

Bianchi, R.V. 2011. Tourism and Marxist political economy. In J. Mosedale (ed.), *Political Economy of Tourism: A Critical Perspective*. London: Routledge, 17–38.

Briassoulis, H. 2007. Golf-centered development in coastal Mediterranean Europe: A soft sustainability test. *Journal of Sustainable Tourism*, 15(5), 441–61.

Britton, S. 1991. Tourism, capital, and place: Towards a critical geography of tourism. *Environment and Planning D*, 9(4), 451–78.

Ceron-Anaya, H. 2010. An approach to the history of golf: Business, symbolic capital, and technologies of the self. *Journal of Sport and Social Issues*, 34(3), 339–58.

Chakrabarty, D. 2009. The climate of history: Four theses. *Critical Inquiry*, 35, 197–222.

Cohen, E. 1979. Rethinking the sociology of tourism. *Annals of Tourism Research*, 6(1), 18–35.

Colding J., and Folke, C. 2009. The role of golf courses in biodiversity conservation and ecosystem management. *Ecosystems*, 12(2), 191–206.

Corbin, A. 1994. *The Lure of the Sea: The Discovery of the Seaside in the Western World 1750–1840*. Cambridge: Polity Press.

Crutzen, P. 2002. Geology of mankind. *Nature*, 415, 23.

Crutzen, P. 2006. The Anthropocene. In E. Ehlers and T. Krafft (eds), *Earth System Science in the Anthropocene*. Berlin: Springer, 13–19.

Crutzen, P., and Stoermer, E. 2000. The 'Anthropocene'. *Global Change Newsletter*, 41, 17–18.

DPEA, Directorate for Planning and Environmental Appeals. 2008. *Report to the Scottish Ministers Directorate for Planning and Environmental Appeals*. <www. scotland.gov. uk/Resource/Doc/212607/0067709.pdf> [accessed Oct. 2014].

Ehrlich, P. 1971. *The Population Bomb*. New York: Ballantine Books.

Flyvbjerg, B. 2006. Five misunderstandings about case-study research. *Qualitative Inquiry*, 12(2), 219–45.

Franklin, A. 2004. Tourism as an ordering: Towards a new ontology of tourism. *Tourist Studies*, 4(3), 277–301.

Gibson, C. 2009. Geographies of tourism: Critical research on capitalism and local livelihoods. *Progress in Human Geography*, 33(4), 527–34.

Gössling, S. 2002. Global environmental consequences of tourism. *Global Environmental Change*, 12(4), 283–302.

Gren, M., and Huijbens, E.H. 2014. Tourism and the Anthropocene. *Scandinavian Journal of Hospitality and Tourism,* 14(1), 6–22.

Hall, C.M. 2011. Yes, Virginia, there is a tourism class. In J. Mosedale (ed.), *Political Economy of Tourism: A Critical Perspective.* London: Routledge, 111–25.

Head, L. 2014. Contingencies of the Anthropocene: Lessons from the 'Neolithic'. *The Anthropocene Review,* 1(2), 113–25.

Johnson, A. 2010. *Hyrt går hem: Historien om den Svenska bemanningsbranschen.* Stockholm: Informationsförlaget Heimdahls.

Jönsson, E. 2014. Contested expectations: Trump International Golf Links Scotland, polarised visions, and the making of the Menie Estate landscape as resource. *Geoforum,* 52, 226–35.

Jönsson, E. forthcoming a. The Nature of an Upscale Nature: Bro Hof Slott Golf Club and the political ecology of high-end golf. *Tourist Studies.*

Jönsson, E. forthcoming b. Brogård backwards: The high-end golf landscape, and the morphology of manorial space. *Geografiska Annaler Series B: Human Geography.*

Jönsson, E., and Baeten, G. 2014. 'Because I am who I am and my mother is Scottish': Neoliberal planning and entrepreneurial instincts at Trump International Golf Links Scotland. *Space and Polity,* 18(1), 54–69.

Keil, R. 2009. The urban politics of roll-with-it neoliberalization. *City,* 13(2–3), 230–45.

Koelsch, W.R. 2001. Academic geography, American style: An institutional perspective. In G.S. Dunbar (ed.), *Geography: Discipline, Profession and Subject since 1870: An International Survey.* Dordrecht: Kluwer Academic Publishing, 245–80.

Latour, B. 2014a. Agency at the time of the Anthropocene. *New Literary History* 45(1), 1–18.

Latour, B. 2014b. Anthropology at the time of the Anthropocene – a personal view of what is to be studied. <http://www.bruno-latour.fr/sites/default/files/139-AAA-Washington. pdf> [accessed Jan. 2015].

Leiper, N. 2008. Why 'the tourism industry' is misleading as a generic expression: The case for the plural variation, 'tourism industries'. *Tourism Management,* 29(2), 237–51.

Löfgren, O. 1999. *On Holiday: A History of Vacationing.* Berkeley-Los Angeles, CA: University of California Press.

Lomborg, B. 2001. *The Skeptical Environmentalist: Measuring the Real State of the World.* Cambridge: Cambridge University Press.

Lowerson, J. 1994. Golf for all? The problem of municipal provision. In A Cochran and M. Farrally (eds), *Science and Golf II: Proceedings of the 1994 World Scientific Congress on Golf.* London; Routledge, 602–10.

McCarthy, J. 2008. Rural geography: Globalizing the countryside. *Progress in Human Geography,* 32(1), 129–37.

Malm. A., and Hornborg, A. 2014. The geology of mankind? A critique of the Anthropocene narrative. *The Anthropocene Review,* 1(1), 62–9.

Moore, J.W. 2014. The Capitalocene, part I: On the nature and origins of our ecological crisis. Unpublished manuscript.

Ollman, B. 2003. *Dance of the Dialectic: Steps in Marx's Method.* Chicago, IL: University of Illinois Press.

Ollman, B. 2008. Why dialectics? Why now? In B. Ollman and T. Smith (eds), *Dialectics for the New Century.* Houndmills and New York: Palgrave Macmillan, 8–26.

Perkins, C. 2010. The performance of golf: Landscape, place, and practice in north west England. *Journal of Sport and Social Issues,* 34(3), 312–38.

Price, R. 2002. *Scotland's Golf Courses.* Edinburgh: Meercat Press.

Rojek, C. 1985. *Capitalism and Leisure Theory.* London: Tavistock.

Rojek, C. 2013. Is Marx still relevant to the study of leisure? *Leisure Studies,* 32(1), 19–33.

Saito, O. 2010. Measuring the lifecycle carbon footprint of a golf course and greening the golf industry in Japan. Paper presented at the 4th International Conference on Sustainability Engineering and Science, 30 Nov.–3 Dec., Auckland.

Sayre, N. 2012. The politics of the anthropogenic. *Annual Review of Anthropology,* 41, 57–70.

Scotsman. 2007. It's a tremendous victory, insists Trump – but controversy deepens. 21 Nov. <http://www.scotsman.com/news/scotland/top-stories/it-s-a-tremendous-victory-insists-trump-but-controversy-deepens-1-700855> [accessed Oct. 2014].

Standing, G. 2011. *The Precariat: The New Dangerous Class.* London: Bloomsbury.

Steffen, W., Crutzen, P.J., and Mcneill, J.R. 2007. The Anthropocene: Are humans now overwhelming the great forces of nature? *Ambio,* 36(8), 614–20.

Steffen, W., *et al.* 2011a. The Anthropocene: From global change to planetary stewardship. *Ambio,* 40, 739–61.

Steffen, W., Grinewald, J., Crutzen, P., and McNeill, J. 2011b. The Anthropocene: Conceptual and historical perspectives. *Philosophical Transactions of the Royal Society A,* 368(1938), 842–67.

Taşan-Kok, T., and Baeten, G. (eds) 2012. *Contradictions of Neoliberal Planning.* Berlin: Springer.

TIGLS (n.d.) MacLeod House and Lodge Hotel. <http://www.trumpgolfscotland.com/5-starHotel> [accessed Jan. 2015].

UNWTO, World Tourism Organisation 2014. *UNWTO Tourism Highlights,* 2014 edn. <http://dtxtq4w60xqpw.cloudfront.net/sites/all/files/pdf/unwto_highlights14_en.pdf> [accessed Oct. 2014].

Upplands-Bro. 2004. *Detaljplan för Brogård.* Upplands-Bro: Upplands-Bro Kommun.

Woods, M. 2007. Engaging the global countryside: Globalization, hybridity and the reconstitution of rural place. *Progress in Human Geography,* 31(4), 485–507.

Worldwatch Institute. 2004. Matters of scale – planet golf. <www.worldwatch.org/node/797> [accessed Jan. 2015].

Zalasiewicz, J., *et al.* 2008. Are we now living in the Anthropocene? *GSA Today,* 18(2), 4–8.

Zalasiewicz, J., Williams, M., Steffen, W., and Crutzen, P. 2010. The new world of the Anthropocene. *Environmental Science and Technology,* 44(7), 2228–31.

10 Mapping the Anthropocene and tour-ism

Martin Gren

Introduction

The Anthropocene originates from natural science, but the concept has during a relatively short period of time managed to spread into other domains. As this volume shows, the time has now also come to the field of tourism studies. In my understanding, this evolving 'Anthropocene turn' across the sciences and the humanities is a set of mapping expeditions which have in common that they explore assumptions and consequences of earthly life and existence under the spell of geological forces, earthly boundaries and planetary limits. The quest for the map-maker is thus to decipher what the Anthropocene means, to which phenomena and state of affairs it refers, and to identify potential implications. The particular query to be addressed here is how tourism could enter and find a place in the grand Anthropocene and planetary scheme of things. Consequently, the exploratory aim of this chapter *is to tentatively map out some of the issues and challenges that the concept of the Anthropocene poses for the theorization of tourism.*

But before travelling into tourism as a phenomenal and conceptual domain, a word of caution is necessary. The map-maker is advised to keep in mind that the Anthropocene is still by and large a *terra incognita* full of blank spots, riddles and uncertainties. Although it 'is now the subject of extensive scientific investigation', when we trespass into Anthropocene territory we are doing so under the condition that 'almost no thought has yet been given to its larger meaning' (Hamilton, 2013, 190). The social sciences are here in demand, but specifically in relation to global sustainability and Earth system governance 'their input lacks well understood contours, strength, and assertiveness' (Biermann, 2014, 21). In other words, we are here and now all travelling on tourist visas into what is by and large uncharted Anthropocene territory. In fact, not even Paul Crutzen, who in conjunction with Eugene Stoermer coined and popularized the Anthropocene concept, has a map to offer us. In his own words: 'The Anthropocene, what is it, really? Nobody yet knows' (Schwägerl, 2014, 219).

What we do know already is that the Anthropocene above all calls for a reorientation towards the Earth and its relationship with humanity (the Anthropos). For tourism studies one overall theoretical challenge seems clear enough, and that is to develop some kind of Anthropocene understanding of tourism in which the braided geo-agencies of the Earth and the Anthropos are at the centre of concern. By and large this too is conceptual *terra incognita,* no ready-made conceptual maps are yet available in the domain of tourism theory. In fact, it is highly uncertain if one can rely upon modern theorizations of tourism and tourists for way-finding in the Anthropocene. What appears to be methodologically required is therefore a slow process of problematization. In times when our earthly undertakings end up at the planetary scale there is a need to travel bit by bit, and pay meticulous attention to the conceptual steps taken in a tourism theory placed under the geometer of the Anthropocene. One such small step consists of the theorization of tourism as a geo-force innately related to the planetary scale at which the Anthropos meets the new Earth of the Anthropocene (Gren and Huijbens, 2014).

Yet, whatever the value of such a theoretical project may be, in effect it could turn out to be little more than allocating tourism a small slot under the big canopy of the Anthropocene. Not much of a change, some may lament, since it risks continuing an uncanny marginalization of tourism in modern social science and social theory. Why not at this time take the opportunity of the Anthropocene, and at the same time consider another much more wide-ranging option with the potential of upgrading tourism in the hierarchy of social science phenomena? *Indeed, why not try to place the whole gamut of tourism at the very core of the Anthropocene itself?* Indeed a bold endeavour, but, of course, as modest in execution as that little hyphen to be found in the title of the chapter: 'tour-ism'.

With this cliff-hanger dangling it is high time for drawing the map of the chapter. The first section addresses the cartographic issue of mapping the Anthropocene in social science, specifically in relation to the reference plane of the social. The second section considers the Anthropos in terms of its geo-forces and non-human agencies which are ushered in by the Anthropocene. The third section investigates the lacunae of the Earth in social theory and the emergence of the new Earth of the Anthropocene, particularly in relation to the cardinal co-ordinates of Society and Nature. The fourth section examines some issues of the Anthropocene in relation to the political. The fifth section places tourism at the heart of the Anthropocene, and offers 'tour-ism' as a descriptive and analytical concept for engagements with the Anthropocene in tourism studies. The sixth section is the final destination of concluding remarks, to be followed by a short coda that just had to be included.

The Anthropocene and the reference plane of the social

In the current attempts to map the Anthropocene, the intertwined relationship between the geo-forces of the Anthropos and the Earth at planetary scale is at the centre of concern. The implications and challenges will eventually play out also in social science where tourism studies and tourism theory is housed. This raises the fundamental cartographical issue about the reference plane used in social science, and how it relates to the Anthropocene which comes dressed with an Earth and an Anthropos filled with geo-forces and earthly non-human agencies.

In order to map phenomena in social science one has to prepare the reference plane so that it foremost privileges and captures that which is being theorized as *social*. An example would be Luhmann's systems theory in which the social is defined as communication and nothing but communication (see e.g. Luhmann, 2012). Preparing the reference plane of the social thus involves an ontological cut which distinguishes the social from its other (or outside), particularly from the *natural* which is taken to be the reference plane of and for natural science. However, when engaging with the Anthropocene this ontological distillation of the social separated from the natural becomes highly problematic. As Rowan puts it:

> the most important aspect of the Anthropocene is that it allows the distinction between the social and the natural, the human and the inhuman to be muddied by way of their mutually constitutive intrusions.
>
> (Rowan in Johnson and Morehouse, 2014, 448–9)

The Anthropocene ushers in a fundamental problematization of the usage of the reference plane of the social conceptualized as a separate and somehow purified ontological realm *sui generis* distinct from the natural. For the purposes here, four interrelated and overlapping aspects and challenges for mapping the Anthropocene in relation to the reference plane of the social can be distinguished.

First, the Anthropocene brings forth a conceptualization of the Anthropos (also referred to in the literature as 'humanity', 'the human species', 'humankind', 'the human race' or 'humans') as an agency harbouring a geo-force, often signified as *geological*. Strictly speaking this geo-force of the Anthropos cannot be mapped on the reference plane of the social because in social theory it becomes distinguished as non-social. Secondly, in an 'Anthropocene understanding', the geo-force of the Anthropos is also related to another force not easily captured on a reference plane jaded with the social, that is, the Earth. Furthermore, when mapping the Earth in social science, it seems now to be increasingly difficult to simply put it on the reference plane of the natural. The new Earth of the Anthropocene appears to be much less purely natural than it used to be, and it does not simply translate as Nature. The geo-forces of the Earth are considered to be increasingly braided with the geo-forces of the Anthropos, even up to the point that the Earth of the Anthropocene is imbricated with the Anthropos. This implies, contrary to many prevalent mappings, that the Anthropocene is not to be conceived of as yet another rebottled and upscaled mixture of Nature and Society.

Thirdly, this imbrication suggests that the Anthropocene heralds another reference plane than the ones of the social and the natural. A requirement of such a reference plane is that it should be able to capture and adequately represent an Earth braided with an Anthropos and where both, as well as their coupling realm, include various geo-forces as fundamentals. As noted, most often these forces are referred to as 'geological', but they may well include also other like geo-biological, geo-physical and geo-chemical ones. Again, it becomes important to keep in mind that all these geo-forces blur the ontological boundaries between the social and the natural. As an illustration of such lines of reasoning, Yusoff suggests that the Anthropocene:

> might be understood quite simply as a revolution of the Earth: a moment of planetary change characterized by the realization of geomorphic power as a consequence of the social mobilization of fossil fuels.
>
> (Yusoff in Johnson and Morehouse, 2014, 452)

The Anthropocene coupling of 'geomorphic power' and 'social mobilization' elucidates the need for a reference plane beyond the social and the natural able to somehow simultaneously capture the entwining of the Anthropos and the Earth. For the lack of better terminology, it can here be named the reference plane of the 'GeoAnthropos System'. This geo-conjuncture leads directly to the fourth and final aspect to be mentioned here, which is the question of scale. In modern social theorizing scale has often been operationalized by the local and the global, but the Anthropocene now throws another scale into the game: the *planetary*. Important to note is that the planetary is not to be understood as merely another name for the global. Instead it designates quantitative and qualitative dimensions of the functioning of the Earth with or without the Anthropos. The invocation of the planetary scale then means that mapping in and of the Anthropocene will be concerned with tracing whatever happens here and there on Earth in relation to the functioning of the 'GeoAnthropos System'. One may still, and possibly have to, climb also the ladders of the local and the global, but in the Anthropocene both need to be placed in the translation function of the planetary.

So it is that the Anthropocene problematizes the reference plane of the social as clearly differentiated from the reference plane of the natural. At stake is also how the Anthropos of the Anthropocene, particularly as it appears in natural science-based accounts, is entering social theorizing.

Mapping the Anthropos of the Anthropocene

To place the Anthropos in a prominent position in geology and natural science may well be a radical move, but the situation is of course very different in social science. After all, what is the Anthropos in social science if not, in some form, its object of study? By necessity this raises questions about the conceptualization of the Anthropos as 'humanity' and as geo-force in relation to social theorizing.

One of the first procedures in theorizing the social is to problematize the unity of social subjects, be they individuals or collectives of some sort. Consequently, map-makers of the Anthropocene in social science have expressed concerns about how the Anthropos has been depicted in natural science accounts. Reservations and the criticisms have been particularly directed towards presentations of a unitary or universal Anthropos, which the usage of 'humanity', 'humankind', the 'human race' and the 'human species' readily evokes. As illustrated here by Malm:

The notion of the 'Anthropocene' glosses over these essential social facts of our epoch. It elevates the actions of a comparatively small subcategory of humanity to the species level.

(Malm in Hornborg *et al.*, 2012, 120)

It is true that the original Great Acceleration graphs, which have become an iconic symbol of the Anthropocene, did precisely treat 'humanity' as an aggregated whole (Steffen *et al.*, 2004). This is clearly at odds with mainstream theorizing in social science where it is difficult to assign the Anthropos a location and value as universal unity, like 'humanity', on a reference plane already saturated with social differentials. A common criticism has thus been that the usage of the Anthropocene obscures, naturalizes and de-politicizes what in reality is a non-unitary non-universal Anthropos permeated by geographical and anthropological differences together with all sorts of other social variances to be found in the human world.

One could here note that in a recent update of the Great Acceleration graphs it is now explicitly acknowledged that the original one ignored 'the fact that the Great Acceleration has, until very recently, been almost entirely driven by a small fraction of the human population, those in the developed countries' (Steffen *et al.*, 2015a, 11). Yes, but the social scientist may of course nevertheless continue to object. Not all of 'those in the developed countries' have been equally accelerated, nor are they to be understood or presented as equal drivers of the Great Acceleration.

Reasoning about the Anthropos also takes us further into the cartographic basecamp of social science where we find a human *social* subject who often becomes uncomfortable when being seated next to the natural. This means that the more the Anthropos of the Anthropocene is being filled with non-social geo-forces, the more it risks slipping through the fishing net devised for catching social subjects. Yet the *Anthropos* that natural science delivers comes precisely aligned with geo-forces which put question marks around the mapping of the Anthropos as a multitude of social subjects only. The Anthropocene turn then contributes to the critique of social constructivism within social science and reverberates with the material turn and recent movements which have in common an interest in mapping also various non-human agencies as part and co-constitutive also of the human social world. Consequently, one could find an emerging area of map-makings of the social that include an understanding in which inhuman geo-forces are incorporated. As exemplified by Yusoff:

The extension of the social into the strata inadvertently produces new modes of subjectification that are geologic, thereby rendering social forces (and the 'bodies politic' of society) as composed, at least in part, of inhuman forces.

(Yusoff in Johnson and Morehouse, 2014, 452)

The Anthropos of the Anthropocene here becomes, at least partly, a geological being of some kind who shares its distributed agency with the forces of the Earth.

For the map-maker who is dependent upon the modern tools of social theory this presents a cartographic problem. For whereas there are numerous opportunities to map the Anthropos as a multitude of social subjects, the conceptual and terminological toolbox for designating its 'inhuman forces' and earthly planetary existence is both limited and underdeveloped. Among the most frequently used name proposals so far are: 'Anthropoceans', 'Earthlings', 'Earthbound' and 'Gaians'. The search to name the earthliness of the Anthropos is actually rather ironic, given that the original etymological meaning of human (*homo*) is 'from humus, by analogy [hu]man from earth' (Olsson, 2007, 58).

As if adding a spoonful of etymological irony, 'humanity' (from the old French of *humanité*) may well translate as 'life on Earth'. However, for the Anthropos of the Anthropocene life does not only mean to live *on* the Earth, but also *of* and *through* its agency and forces. One challenge for social science therefore becomes not only to map the Anthropos in terms of its non-human agency and geo-force, but also how to theorize its symbiosis with the Earth as a co-constitutive agency. This does not mean that social markings of the Anthropos will wither away or become obsolete, but it does put question marks around a one-sided conceptualization of the Anthropos as a distilled social agency. Rephrased, the Anthropos of the Anthropocene is always less and more than the social.

Whatever the conceptual riddles may be for the map-maker in social science who is grappling with the Anthropos, there now remains what I understand to be the quintessential cartographic issue ushered in by the Anthropocene. What shall one do with the Earth, and what kind of Earth is it that we are called upon to face? Furthermore, what does such an Anthropocene earthly turn imply for a modern social theorizing in which Society and Nature often have functioned as cardinal co-ordinates?

The Earth and the cardinal co-ordinates of Society and Nature

'Back to Earth!' is the quest which continuously reappears in the Anthropocene literature. Most often there is little doubt that it also means serious business and far-reaching changes. Indeed, it may require nothing less than 'a full revolution in our relationship with Earth' (Rockström and Klum, 2012, 29). Calls to return to the Earth also seem to imply that it has somehow been strangely absent. If so, then one may wonder why?

One could say that in modern social theorizing the Earth has most often been taken for granted and merely served as a backdrop surface for the human social world. A principal reason for its lack of conceptual place in modern social theory is that the Earth has been buried under the cardinal coordinates of Society and Nature (Latour, 2013). According to conventional understanding Society consists of internal social relations among humans and has Nature and non-human agencies as an external outside. The crux of the matter for social theorizing is now that in the same moment as the Earth of the Anthropocene is introduced, the validity and reliability of the cardinal co-ordinates of Society and Nature are also unhinged. As Descola suggests, the great modern divide between Society and Nature may now be 'vanishing', for 'where does nature stop and culture begin in regard to global warming, in the thinning of the ozone layer, in the production of specialized cells from stem cells?' (Descola, 2013, 82). In as much as Nature and Society readily appear as mutually exclusive co-ordinates in social theory, they can also be considered to fall under the very same earthly vicinity. As Morton formulates it:

> Two things that seem distinct – human society and Nature – are two different angles of the same thing.
>
> (Morton, 2010, 133)

In the Anthropocene we are up against an Earth that *both precedes and succeeds* Society and Nature, understood both as co-ordinates and ontological realms. In other words, Nature and Society dissolve into an entangled web of all sorts of earthly agencies and existences that are ubiquitous relative to an all-embracing Earth in which the Anthropos itself is included. It is also here that the compass-needle of modern social theorizing begins to spin. Is the Earth of the Anthropocene, formerly known as Nature, now to be understood as produced also by Society? Is the Anthropos, formerly known as Social, now to be understood as constituted also by inhuman geo-forces and agencies exchanged with the Earth?

One of the most important map-makers of the Anthropocene, Bruno Latour, portrays the Anthropocene as an evolving 'terratory' of attachments which the moderns have no maps of, nor know how to navigate:

> An entirely new situation: behind us, attachments; ahead of us, ever more attachments. Suspension of the 'modernization front.' End of emancipation as the only possible destiny. And what is worse: 'we' no longer know *who* we are, nor of course *where* we are, we who had believed that we were modern. End of modernization. End of story. Time to start over.
>
> Is there another system of coordinates that can replace the one we have lost, now that the modernist parenthesis is closing?
>
> (Latour, 2013, 10)

One of the distinguishing cartographic problems for way-finding in the Anthropocene is thus that the coordinates of Society and Nature may no longer serve as fix-points, as they are being overlayered by the Anthropos and the Earth drawn into an orbit of mutual entanglements that meet up at planetary scale. A key cartographic challenge for navigating the Anthropocene is then to develop alternatives to a deprived modern system of co-ordinates. In turn, this raises the overarching question about what kind of Earth the Anthropocene ushers in, and what it means for the Anthropos to live with it.

To begin with, the Earth of the Anthropocene is not to be conceptualized merely as one element among others. Instead, it embraces all earthly existences at the same time as it offers not the singularity and unity which the former Nature was supposed to provide. The Earth of the Anthropocene is then not like the old terrestrial Earth, which appears as Nature stamped with Society on world maps, but a complex and dynamic system whose properties are far from known. In fact, this new Earth is most often not even called Earth, but 'Earth system' or 'Gaia' for that matter. Whatever its proper name and (in)definite descriptions may be, '[t]he Earth System is not "the landscape", it is not "ecosystems", and it is not "the environment"' (Hamilton 2015, 2), and hence it does not surrender as the former Earth of spatial extension to translations onto the flat surface of the map or a unified globe. Moreover, the Earth system (or Gaia) has also its map-makers inscribed in its own 'territory':

> Since humankind is an integral part and driver of Earth system dynamics we can only observe these dynamics from the inside; at least at the planetary level, the observer is always part of the system.
>
> (Glasier *et al.*, 2012, 197)

For the map-maker of the Anthropocene, who is obliged to take this Earth system into account, this presents new-fangled challenges. Although maps have long since been stripped from simple representationalism, the map-makers of the former Earth were at least not part of its territory. The Earth system of the Anthropocene has the Anthropos itself imbricated. Its geographies, temporalities and agencies are all entangled with the Earth system in a multiplicity of ways. So it also is that in the Anthropocene geography (literally 'earth-writing'), at last, becomes one with its own subject matter in a planetary embrace. For not only does the Anthropos write about the Earth, it also writes its Anthropos.

The Anthropocene and the political

The Anthropocene signals profound challenges and the map-makers are currently doing their best, faced as they are with 'the identification and articulation of a world whose social, political, and physical parameters are changing faster than our capacity to process and analyze them' (Johnson and Morehouse, 2014, 441). In addition, the map-makers also have to perform their cartographic undertakings on contested and disputed ground. At the agora of the political the Anthropocene may even be dismissed almost *tout court*:

> What is 'the Anthropocene' right now if not the masculinist obverse of the Earth Mother? Witness 'the Anthropocene' – a neo-patriarchal, equally inappropriate all-powerful geo-engineering father figure making Earth System Science safe for (hu)man-centeredness. Under the banner of 'the Anthropocene', Earth System Science bids to submerge the extra-human planetary cybernetics of Gaia – its proper object – under an all-too-human fantasy of control theory.
>
> (Clarke, 2014, 104)

The Anthropocene is, undoubtedly, also political. The naming itself is, of course, burdened with politics. Accepting the Anthropocene as a new geological epoch involves the risk of granting it an inevitable 'natural' condition and destiny of its own, with implications for its political appropriation. Rejecting it paves the road towards other political agendas. Whatever the particular takes, in the Anthropocene the terrain of the political enlarges for the Anthropos, as it becomes enclosed by an Earth system acting as a climate compressor and limiter of all planetary undertakings. The Earth of the Anthropocene which the Anthropos inhabit will henceforth also be an Earth system which is partly of their own making, and hence it inevitably becomes a real political matter.

The overall political matter in and of the Anthropocene would be concerned with composing the entangled and braided terratory held in common by both the Earth system and the Anthropos. A central political concern would be the possibilities for the Anthropos to maintain a habitable Earth for itself. Somewhat paradoxically this goal may well imply the development of a politics aimed at leaving the Anthropocene as quickly as possible. According to the 'planetary boundary' framework the anthropogenic perturbation levels of four of the nine Earth system processes now exceed the proposed boundaries for a 'safe operating space for humanity' (Steffen *et al.*, 2015b). This does not look like an invitation card to the politics of sustainable development, but rather as an urgent call for a hasty retreat from what is considered to be a highly risky and potentially very dangerous territory for the Anthropos. As one of the frequently repeated calls for political action reads: *We are the first generation to know this, we must act now!* (see e.g. Rockström and Klum, 2012, 31). So back to the Holocene, the epoch that we know for sure provided a habitable Earth for the Anthropos.

That planetary limits and boundaries should form the basis for Anthropocene politics, as proposed by Earth system governance (Biermann, 2014), or more generally the invocation of the Earth as a kind of key agent in politics, has not passed without reservations. Is that not old physiocratism and environmental determinism rebottled? Concerns have been expressed about the risk of turning the Anthropocene into a naturalized meta-dispatcher which short-cuts due political processes. There is nothing inevitable or natural in turning the Earth into an oyster for an ever expanding uneven geographical production and consumption, hence some may argue that the real issue that needs to be addressed is all about a socio-economic system. Consequently, one will find attempts to move Anthropocene politics to the historically and geographically specific conditions pertaining to capitalism as 'a more accurate genesis of global climate change than the activity of a singular universal humanity, or *Anthropos*' (Rowan in Johnson and Morehouse, 2014, 448). At the same time one could also say that in the Anthropocene the Earth becomes the real limit of capital and to capitalist sorcery.

Politics in and of the Anthropocene will continue to be realpolitik, or perhaps it evolves into a new form of geopolitics concerned with:

> what it means to cohabit with the Earth as an Earth force rather than just a social one, to share in the geologic, geophysical, atmospheric and oceanic forces with the Earth; in concert with Earth processes, times and matter (that have no single genesis).
>
> (Yusoff in Johnson and Morehouse, 2014, 455)

The geo-force of the Anthropos is the sum of the collective actions of billions of human beings; at the same time '[w]hat it means to live in the Anthropocene is different for everyone depending on each person's circumstances, priorities, environment and aims' (Schwägerl, 2014, 200). Adding a geological agency to the political domain does certainly not mean that politics will vanish in the Anthropocene, or that the Anthropos becomes a pre-constituted entity not open for political contestation and composing. Yet, the problematics around the political agency of the Anthropos as 'humanity', or at the species level, remains.

Chakrabarty has suggested that, 'in becoming a geophysical force on the planet, we have also developed a form of collective existence that has no ontological dimension' (2012, 13). This non-ontological mode of existence is simultaneously braided with a distinguishing political feature of the Anthropos, which means that 'there is no corresponding "humanity" that in its oneness can act as a political agent' (Chakrabarty, 2012, 14). In the words of Lovelock, the 'concepts of humanity or the human race sound good in political exhortations and sermons but are essentially beyond the perception of most of us' (Lovelock, 2014, 148). Paradoxically, as it were, this is also why an Anthropocene politics may become necessary at a species level:

> Humans today are not only the dominant species on the planet, they also collectively constitute a … a geological force that determines the climate of the planet much to the detriment of civilization itself. Today, it is precisely the 'survival of the species' on a 'world-wide scale' that is largely in question. All progressive political thought, including postcolonial criticism, will have to register this profound change in the human condition.
>
> (Chakrabarty, 2012, 15)

In spite of some political negotiations, a planetary politics of and for the Anthropocene has yet to emerge. The political formation of the Anthropos as some kind of a new demos and 'nomos of the Earth' (Schmitt, 2003) has barely begun. Nor has the political process of drawing a dividing line within the Anthropos that internally distinguishes friends from foes on the grounds of Anthropocene politics. In addition, there is unfortunately no reason to believe that politics in the Anthropocene will be less violent than before. Latour, for one, is clear enough:

> In becoming geological, human history will not become more peaceful; on the contrary, there is no evidence that Humans and the Earthbounds will be able to co-exist in peace.
>
> (Latour, 2014, unpaginated)

Tourism and tour-ism in the Anthropocene

It may seem like no easy task to provide a shelter for tourism under the panoply of the Anthropocene. With a history of being signified as a turn away from the duties and bondages of mundane everyday *social* life tourism runs the risk of being dismissed as a trivial and luxury pursuit performed for the main purposes of leisure and joy. Yes, of course, it is important that hotels recycle their bathrobes and that tourists travel and consume in more environmentally friendly ways. Yes, undoubtedly, like any other business tourism needs to become more 'green' and subscribe to the principles of sustainable development. However, as Lovelock notes:

> Taken literally, sustainable development simply means growth. No wonder the term is popular with economists who see the sustenance of growth as just what they need for economic stability.

> (Lovelock, 2014, 108)

So take up the challenges ahead, adapt and mitigate, if not for a higher cause then at least for the profitable sake of the business itself. After all, what is tourism if not a 'key driver for socio-economic progress' (World Tourism Organization, 2015)?

But then comes the Anthropocene, hovering in like a giant 'Geoviathan' over the bathing paraphernalia and the tourist's carbon footprints, placing its murky shrine on the (un)sustainability of tourism itself. Tourism, what have you really done to the Earth? As if that was not enough, what might the touristified Earth do with its Anthropos? It has been shown that tourism contributes to a quite considerable amount of all anthropogenic forcing, estimated to be 5.2–12.5 per cent in 2005 (Hall *et al.*, 2015; Gössling *et al.*, 2013). One may further note that today's tourism is commonly assessed to be 'objectively further from being sustainable than ever', and that it is even distinguished as 'a substantial contributor to the decline in the Earth's natural capital' (Hall *et al.*, 2015, 492–3).

In other words, before and after closer inspection, tourism is a deeply worrying and troublesome kind of business in the Anthropocene. Being a key driver for socio-economic progress paved by good old modern intentions is one thing, being a geo-force which eats away the planetary survival space for the Anthropos is something completely different. For after what in retrospect seems likely to be regarded as a modern parenthesis of green-washing by sustainable development comes the Anthropocene ledger of 'planetary boundaries' (Steffen *et al.*, 2015b) in which also the (un)sustainability of tourism will eventually have to find its location and meaning. According to one of the accompanying Anthropocene storylines the Anthropos has already transgressed planetary boundaries, and may no longer reside in the 'safe operating space for humanity'. Among the several dystopian harbingers that here could be added is the dramatic and serious loss of species, even though it 'does not yet qualify as a mass extinction in the palaeontological sense of the Big Five' (Barnovsky *et al.*, 2011, 51). Nevertheless, here is one calculated future of the Anthropocene in a planetary rub. Unfortunately it cannot be ruled out that the Anthropos has embarked on the cruise ship Anthropocene which is heading in a circular route towards the final destination of a sixth mass extinction, one in which tourists and non-tourists alike will go down with the ship designed for leisure purposes.

Although here admittedly grimly plotted in dark on a sketchy tourist map, the earthly potential future course of the Anthropos is something which any serious encounter with the Anthropocene necessarily will have to address. Also in the domains of tourism studies and tourism theory awaiting an Anthropocene a-tourism gaze. So what are tourism scholars really supposed to say and do about tourism in the Anthropocene? Should they continue as undercover travel agents in departmental disguise? Should they instead seek licence for providing palliative care for an Anthropos that might be touring itself to death?

Responding to the quest of the Anthropocene does certainly not mean that one should uncritically accept ready-made maps of a coming apocalypse, but these are not times for hiding behind smokescreen scepticism either (Hall *et al.*, 2015). Scientific and political controversies are of course as an inevitable part of tourism as they are imprinted on the enigma of the Anthropocene, but that does not erase the need for valid and reliable options for way-finding. Instead, all controversies around tourism in the Anthropocene should be mapped, scrutinized and made open as matters of concern as much as possible for the Anthropos, however defined and delineated. The big pattern on the map of the geo-conjuncture ushered in by the Anthropocene ought to by now be unequivocally clear in its overarching implications for the tourism research community. *If ever there was a time to think seriously about tourism, as thoroughly and critically as possible, this is the one.* Yes, if ever there was one time for tourism, the Anthropocene surely is.

A critical rethinking of tourism in the context of the Anthropocene would of course include travelling back to the Earth again, while provisionally keeping in mind that the 'last stage of the tourist endeavor is the return, which turns the tourists themselves into the attraction' (Enzensberger, 1996, 134). Tracing the roots of modern tourism leads to that Earth which the Europeans, a subspecies of the Anthropos eventually known for its extraordinary geo-powers, discovered in the 16th century. When that Earth was circumnavigated in the age of exploration America was completely unknown to the Europeans, and thus a not even suspected continent was discovered. Moreover:

> The discoveries were not invited. They were made without visas issued by the discovered peoples. The discoverers were Europeans, who appropriated, divided, and utilized the planet.
>
> (Schmitt, 2003, 352)

There are certainly other less neutral words available for describing a giant one-sided land-grab, but suffice to note here is that the 'discoverers have become tourists too' (Enzensberger, 1996, 127). With the blank spots of *terra incognita* eliminated, a cognitive space was opened up for a new modern and European 'cartographic reason' (Olsson, 1998; 2007; Abrahamsson and Gren, 2012), in which the Earth was to be successively transformed into a terrestrial globe for touring and later for tourism as the moderns have come to know and understand it. Transformed into tourists the former discoverers have continued to tour the Earth, and '[t]oday, everywhere on the face of the earth, there are patches of social reality growing out of the collective experiences of tourists' (MacCannell, 1999, 141). An astonishing earthly accomplishment, not to say miraculous.

Albeit not a miracle achieved by the Anthropos itself, nor solely by the powers of God and/or capitalism. Another miracle accompanied the geo-graphying forces, that is, the differentiation of the Anthropos into the subspecies of Anthropotourismicus, a still evolving modern touring creature whose travelling is driven by geo-power. As the etymology recognizes, travel involves earthly travails stemming from times where the notion of travel as pleasure was far away. Travel meant work, but it still does. The difference is that the work that enables modern tourism, corresponding to a semantic shift from traveller to tourist, has foremost been facilitated by the non-human geo-force of fossil fuel provided by the Earth. As this modern carbon-propelled tourism is still firmly locked in and sustained, it also elucidates tourism as a planetary environmental (un)sustainability issue fundamental in and of the Anthropocene. Contrary to tourism imaginings, the present and future impacts of the geo-force of tourism cannot be wished or green-washed away.

When all is said and done, tourism is an earthly business in both theory and on the ground (Gren and Huijbens, 2012). Especially so in the context of the Anthropocene, where it will be distinguished ever more in terms of its specific relation to the geo-capital of the Earth. In the language of tourism the Earth becomes the one and only destination, or the ultimate tourist attraction that conjunctively draws and binds the Anthropos and the Earth into an expanding (un)commons of mutual entanglements. In that earthly sense, 'one doesn't need to leave home to be a tourist' (MacCannell, 1999, 199). In the Anthropocene the scattered multitude of the Anthropos, tourists and non-tourists alike, can then join the formerly all exclusive choir and chant 'we are all tourists now!' No away to escape to, since all travelling and circumnavigating is on tourist visas on the one and only home of the Anthropos; destination Earth system. Or should Gaia be its proper name in tourism theory?

Of course, the usual reservation applies. Tourism has never been, and is still certainly not, an accessibility for all, not even for the many, and often only for the relatively few and wealthy. Tourism, also as a geo-force, is likely to continue to be utterly unevenly distributed among the Anthropos and its geographies. Yet, painting with a bigger brush, one can also note that a pervading driving force in and of modernity, if not longer, has all along been to have goods, objects, resources, information, humans, non-humans and the rest of earthly existences, to tour planet Earth. But whatever travels are always enabled movements by earthly geo-forces and agencies. So if I now were to tweak the conceptual knob of tourism just a little further, the meter may eventually stop at 'tour-ism', a signifier I propose for that ideology-and-practice of having earthly existences of all kinds touring the Earth. Although it has more recently been claimed that tourism is dead, or alternatively that it is now everywhere, this has so far primarily evoked calls for accrediting tourism as an integral and substantial part of a contemporary touristified society and thus far away from the harsh earthly and planetary conditions ushered in by the Anthropocene. As Enzensberger once put it: 'Originally conceived as something that redeemed its followers from society, tourism now brought society along' (Enzensberger, 1996, 131).

It may be that tourism 'is "real", then, as a constitutive force in the social world', and that it is 'a fundamental *social force* that assembles a broad array of social, political, economic, cultural, and material processes' (Minca and Oakes, 2012, 1). Yet, in as much as tour-ism is all too overarching in the planetary register to be reduced to tourism, so tourism in the Anthropocene can no longer be reduced to society or a social force. Tourism, in its modern variant appropriated and mediated by the ideology and practice of tour-ism, now instead appears as a fossil-fuel-driven mega-vessel for possessing the Earth, coordinated by the invisible fix-points of Society and Nature, and compelled by capitalism and economic growth. In the Anthropocene, on the other hand, economy will have to become planetarily upscaled to '*geo*conomy', where the social and spatial dissemination of scarce resources by household management transforms into the distributional requirements of the Earth system. As Latour remarks:

> The Economy is not the basis for the world finally revealed to everyone thanks to the benefits of globalization but a cancer whose metastases have gradually begun to infect the entire Earth.
>
> (Latour, 2013, 384)

The planetary household of the Earth of the Anthropocene thus encapsulates the away imprinted in the modern's understanding of tourism, while for the time being tour-ism will remain ubiquitous. Chips down, as if the rotundity of the Earth in the Anthropocene has finally returned all of the moderns' touring, leaving them with the terrifying revelation that they are about to meet the earthly consequences of their own tour-ism in advance. Welcome to the Anthropocene, we are all tourists now!

Concluding remarks

When embarking on a mapping expedition into the terratory of the Anthropocene it is highly uncertain as to how and to what extent one can really rely on old and familiar maps of the already known. Furthermore, in the Anthropocene map and territory become as braided as the Anthropos becomes entangled with its Earth. If one were to disobey the internal human circle of 'correlationism' (Meillassoux, 2008), one could even say that the Anthropocene is a signal of the Earth having contacted the Anthropos. An intra-terrestrial pointer in need of a map which can help the Anthropos to develop tools for way-finding not only *on* the Earth, but more crucially for living *with* the Earth system, or Gaia, on planetary scale. A gigantic challenge which for the map-maker of the Anthropocene becomes almost a wicked problem *par excellence*. As Rowan remarks:

> The Anthropocene is not a *problem* for which there can be a *solution*. Rather it names an emergent set of conditions that already fundamentally structure the horizon of human existence. It is thus not a new factor that can be accommodated within existing conceptual frameworks, including

those within which policy is developed, but signals a profound shift in the human relations to the planet that questions the very foundations of these frameworks themselves.

(Rowan in Johnson and Morehouse, 2014, 447)

The exploratory and tentative mapping here suggests that the Anthropocene cannot be easily accommodated within the existing conceptual frameworks of tourism theory. In the Anthropocene tourism is not to be read and placed only on the reference plane of the *social*, nor is it to be understood as a phenomenon which resides in the peripheral outskirts of modern society. Tourism is too important and significant to be understood in a narrow traditional sense, and thus needs to be aligned with the entangled geo-forces which have taken the Anthropos and the Earth into the Anthropocene.

Consequently, I have offered tour-ism as a concept for denoting a much wider ideology and practice of having things in general touring the Earth. This means that what has been depicted on the 'Great Acceleration' graph under the rubric of 'international travel' is only tourism in a narrow traditional sense and where tour-ism remains absent. Although tourism, as signifying a smaller portion of the *Anthropos* travelling for some kind of leisure purposes, will continue to be important, it is arguably *tour-ism* which by far is the most fundamental and pressing issue that the Anthropos has to address when facing the Earth of the Anthropocene, or Gaia. It follows also that in the context of the Anthropocene neither tour-ism nor tourism can be adequately placed only on the reference plane of the social which so far has often been privileged and taken-for-granted in tourism theory. Hereinafter, the minimum requirement of the theorization of tourism in the Anthropocene will be that it includes a conceptualization of tourism and tourists in terms of geo-forces that are only partly social in a modern purified sense.

In terms of hospitality the Anthropocene appears simultaneously as an uninvited earthly guest and as an unreliable terrestrial host who does not only 'give an unexpected twist to the social situation we live in', but more crucially to 'the human condition in general' (Veijola *et al.*, 2014, 2). Will the human condition survive the encounter with the Earth of the Anthropocene, or Gaia, the intruder which unasked for sends the Anthropos to travail the planetary scale of limits and boundaries? Will the moderns' understanding of tourism survive the encounter?

The revolutionary impulse that has elevated tourism into a world-wide phenomenon was too blind to understand its own dialectic, and too powerful to come to terms with its inevitable demise. Time and again tourism angrily attempts to escape the vicious circle of its inner logic and its confinement. And it fails every time.

(Enzensberger, 1996, 132)

Will tourism fail also in the time of the Anthropocene? Will tour-ism continue to prevail? The stakes are high, and the Anthropos cannot count on the Earth as its *justissima tellus*. As Hamilton puts it; 'Now in the Anthropocene, the era of Gaia's awakening, we can no longer think of the Earth as a patchwork of the natural and the unnatural, but only as a total system under attack' (Hamilton, 2014, 4).

In the meantime, it must be remembered that every map comes with its own destiny engraved by its taken-for-granted premises. The map always privileges certain kinds of understandings at the cost of excluding others. It is on this canvas of the present I sometimes stubbornly continue, in solitary vain, to advocate the 'Anthropo*geo*cene' as a more appropriate concept for the social sciences and the humanities. Yet well-intentioned attempts to fill in the blanks do seldom lead to definite descriptions, but to the abyss of Pandora's box. In one of its half-hidden closets I recognize another troubling lacuna in the concept of the Anthropocene. For the Anthropos the essential aspect of the Anthropocene condition is not geology. It's all about the Earth's capacity to provide the human earthlings with life. In other words, it's the 'biocene' that really matters. Hence, an even more awkward term can be proposed; the Anthropo*biogeo*cene. For some, a trivial pursuit in an empty game of neologism, for others a critical lesson in cartographic reason. For without maps, we do not know where we are, who we are, nor how to find our ways about. Lost in translation, lost in the Anthropocene.

Coda

Mapping the Anthropocene has taken its toll. Late nights, tears dripping. Too much extinction theory leaves little room for happy endings. The Anthropos may well be another phantom meta-dispatcher, but it also signifies the singularly dear loved ones in front of you. Caught by the geo-forces in between *zoe* and *bios*, there is so little a single earthling can do. Such is the atmosphere that moulded itself. Less to be interpreted as the golden spike of a dark acceptance of an Anthropocene apocalyptic epoch to come. More to be understood as a pointer to the beginning of what might very possibly be a long and torturous farewell to one of the onomatophores ('name-bearers') of the Anthropos known as the 'touring moderns' who stratified the Earth by their ideology and practice of tour-ism.

Acknowledgment

A bucket of thanks to George Moore for English guidance, in both content and form.

References

Abrahamsson, C., and Gren, M. (eds) 2012. *GO: On the Geographies of Gunnar Olsson*. Farnham: Ashgate.

Barnovsky, A.D., *et al.* 2011. Has the Earth's sixth mass extinction already arrived? *Nature*, 471(Mar.), 51–7.

Biermann, F. 2014. *Earth System Governance: World Politics in the Anthropocene*. Cambridge, MA: MIT Press.

Chakrabarty, D. 2012. Postcolonial studies and the challenge of climate change. *New Literary History*, 43(1), 1–18.

Clarke, B. 2014. 'The Anthropocene,' or, Gaia shrugs. *Journal of Contemporary Archeology*, 1(1), 101–4.

Descola, P. 2013. *The Ecology of Others*. Chicago, IL: Prickly Paradigm Press.

Enzensberger, H.M. 1996. A theory of tourism. *New German Critique*, 68, 117–35.

Glasier, M., Krause, G., Ratter, M.W., and Welp, M. (eds) 2012. *Human–Nature Interactions in the Anthropocene: Potentials of Social-Ecological Systems Analysis*. New York and London: Routledge.

Gren, M., and Huijbens, E.H. 2012. Tourism theory and the earth. *Annals of Tourism Research and Tourism*, 39(1), 155–70.

Gren, M., and Huijbens, E.H. 2014. Tourism and the Anthropocene. *Scandinavian Journal of Hospitality and Tourism*, 14(1), 6–22.

Gössling, S., Scott, D., and Hall, C.M. 2013. Challenges of tourism in a low-carbon economy. *WIRES Climate Change*, 4(6), 525–38.

Hall, C.M., *et al*. 2015. On climate change scepticism and denial in tourism. *Journal of Sustainable Tourism*, 23(1), 4–25.

Hall, C.M., Gössling, S., and Scott, D. (eds) 2015. *The Routledge Handbook of Tourism and Sustainability*. Abingdon, Oxon: Routledge.

Hamilton, C. 2013. *Earthmasters: The Dawn of the Age of Climate Engineering*. New Haven and New York: Yale University Press.

Hamilton, C. 2014. When earth juts through world. A contribution to 'The Situation Facing the Moderns After the Intrusion of Gaïa: A Philosophical Simulation', Sciences Po, Paris, 28–29 July.

Hamilton, C. 2015. Getting the Anthropocene so wrong. *The Anthropocene Review*, 2(2), 1–6.

Hornborg, A., Clark, B., and Hermele, K. (eds) 2012. *Ecology and Power: Struggles over Land and Material Resources in the Past, Present, and Future*. London and New York: Routledge.

Johnson, E., and Morehouse, H. 2014. After the Anthropocene: Politics and geographic inquiry for a new epoch. *Progress in Human Geography*, 38(3), 439–56.

Latour, B. 2013. *An Inquiry into Modes of Existence: An Anthropology of the Moderns*. Cambridge, MA: Harvard University Press.

Latour, B. 2014. The climate to come depends on the present time. <http://www.bruno-latour.fr/sites/default/files/downloads/14-11-ANTHROPO-transl-GB.pdf> [accessed Jan. 2015].

Lovelock, J. 2014. *A Rough Ride to the Future*. London: Allen Lane.

Luhmann, N. 2012. *Theory of Society*, vol. 1. Stanford, CA: Stanford University Press.

MacCannell, D. 1999. *The Tourist: A New Theory of the Leisure Class*. Berkeley, CA: University of California Press.

Meillassoux, Q. 2008. *After Finitude: An Essay on the Necessity of Contingency*. London: Bloomsbury.

Minca, C., and Oakes, T. (eds) 2012. *Real Tourism: Practice, Care, and Politics in Contemporary Travel Culture*. London and New York: Routledge.

Morton, T. 2010. *Ecological Thought*. Cambridge, MA, and London: Harvard University Press.

Olsson, G. 1998. Towards a critique of cartographical reason. *Ethics, Place and Environment*, 1(2), 145–55.

Olsson, G. 2007. *Abysmal: A Critique of Cartographical Reason.* Chicago, IL: University of Chicago Press.

Rockström, J., and Klum, M. 2012. *The Human Quest: Prospering within Planetary Boundaries.* Stockholm: Langenskiölds.

Schmitt, C. 2003. *The Nomos of the Earth in the International Law of the Jus Publicum Europaeum* (originally publ. in German, 1950). New York: Telos Press Publishing.

Schwägerl, C. 2014. *The Anthropocene: The Human Era and How it Shapes our Planet.* Santa Fe, NM, and London: Synergetic Press.

Steffen, W., Sanderson, A., Tyson, P.D., *et al.* 2004. *Global Change and the Earth System: A Planet under Pressure.* The IGBP Book Series. Berlin: Springer-Verlag.

Steffen, W., Broadgate, W., Deutsch, L., Gaffney, O., and Ludwig, C. 2015a. The trajectory of the Anthropocene: The great acceleration. *The Anthropocene Review*, 2(1), 1–18.

Steffen, W., *et al.* 2015b. Planetary boundaries: Guiding human development on a changing planet. *Science*, 347(6223), 1–10.

Veijola, S., Germann Molz, J., Pyyhtinen, O., Höckert, E., and Grit, A. 2014. *Disruptive Tourism and its Untidy Guests: Alternative Ontologies for Future Hospitalities.* Basingstoke: Palgrave Macmillan.

World Tourism Organization (UNWTO) 2015. Why tourism? <http://www2.unwto.org/content/why-tourism> [accessed Mar. 2015].

11   The Anthropocene and tourism destinations

Martin Gren and Edward H. Huijbens

Figure 11.1 Smeerenburg Glacier, South Smeerenburg Bay, Svalbard, July 2012 – A boat trip

©Tyrone Martinsson, published with permission

> The concept of the Anthropocene includes the spontaneous *minima moralia* of the current age. It implies concern regarding the cohabitation of the citizens of the Earth in human and non-human form. It calls upon us to cooperate in the network of simple and higher-level life circles, in which the actors of today's world generate their being in the modes of co-immunity.
>
> (Sloterdijk, in Klingan *et al.*, 2015, 271)

This book has explored some of the issues and challenges that the Anthropocene may pose for tourism, including how it might potentially reframe conceptual and empirical undertakings in tourism research. In this last chapter of the book we will draw together contributions from each of the chapters, and add some concluding reflections of our own.

Departures

In the first part of the book tourism evolved as co-extensive with the Earth, and tourists appeared as a subspecies of the Anthropos ever more on the move terrestrially. Animating the theme of planetary boundaries, and the needs of tourism policy from the local to the global, Eijgelaar, Amelung and Peeters sketched the contours of a climatically safe operating space for future tourism. One conclusion was unequivocal: we need to reduce the distances and frequency of travel and strive towards a modal shift in transportation practices. This shift requires a substantial structural and behavioural change which goes against the dominant tourisms' consumptive ethos of freedom, enjoyment and terrestrial commodification. In the Anthropocene there is little alternative for tourism politics, policy and planning other than to bring the geo-force of tourism and tourists into the foreground as a deeply problematic feature. It might well be that tourism, at least in its current fossil-fuel-driven consumptive guise and as one substantial driver of the Great Acceleration, needs to be abandoned. Huijbens, Costa and Gugger in their contribution make sense of the ways in which tourism can become co-extensive with the Earth through design, outlining the principles of a 'territorial constitution' created by students of the Laboratoire Bâle (studio laba) in Iceland in 2015. In making sense of Anthropos's geo-forces when it comes to constituting destinations and regions for tourism the key theme is responsibility towards the Earth and attuning to matter through concern.

The first part of the book was capped off by Hall who opened up the space between nature and tourism for consideration in the context of the Anthropocene, thereby adding scope to the planetary dimension of tourism's impact. Tourism is a major conduit not only for the commodification of nature for touristic purposes, but also for subsequent environmental losses that it may simultaneously bring along. Through tourism's potential detrimental impact on planetary biodiversity, we run the risk of 'loving nature to death'. As we are called to the gate of the Anthropocene we may thus no longer be able to rely on the modern itinerary of sustainable tourism development. In accordance with the contributions in the first part of the book, we might instead better prepare for a modal shift in tourism production and tourist consumption, towards planetary limits and boundaries, in order to preclude their devastating impacts on earth's life-supporting processes, if possible.

The second part of the book was glued together by issues of global sustainability and environmental ethics located at the border of the planetary. The geo-force of tourism was animated by Jóhannesson, Ren and van der Duim in their account of the earthly assembling of tourism in Lanzarote. By drawing on Actor-Network Theory (ANT) they brought forth the entanglements and the assembling of humans and more-than-humans involved in the geographical scaling of tourism practices. They also added an important value dimension to tourism orderings by considering *improvisation, value* and *care*. All three speak directly to ethical concerns bound to appear in the Anthropocene.

Ethics were pursued further by Kristofferson, Norum, and Kramvig in the context of whale encounters in the Arctic. They showed that human encounters with a particular non-human, the whale in Arctic waters, can give rise to a conflicted and unstable understanding of nature. Furthermore, these human–non-human relations may also enable the emergence of a companionable whale. The ethical frame thus shifts towards a reimagination of the whale as a companion species with rights and territories that enable humans to engage in new relationships attentive and hospitable to the non-human companion. Baruchello continued the ethical line of inquiry by maintaining that tourism is no vacation from personal responsibility. In a similar vein, in the Anthropocene we are increasingly required to include the planetary state of affairs when considering an individual's good life. As Baruchello argued, *homo viator*'s life-valuing onto-axiology should form the substance of a global Code of Ethics for Tourism. The second part of the book thus moved from considerations of the individual's perspective of the good life, through recognition of responsibility and hospitable attunement, to the entanglements and the assembling of humans and more-than-humans involved in the geographical production of tourism.

The third part of the book dealt with the ways in which tourism and tourists can cultivate earthly sensibilities and attune to the Earth of the Anthropocene. The first chapter by Svensson, Sörlin and Wormbs demonstrated how tourist practices need to be understood in their particular spatio-temporal settings in order to grasp what sustainable tourism practices could be under the terms of the Anthropocene, and how landscapes can be perceived and lived. Their study is indicative of the attunement necessary to make sense of tourism in the Anthropocene, wherein tourists become responsible not only for their impact on the destination but also for bringing something back, to let the destination have an impact on their everyday life. Jönsson followed up on this recognition of earthly sensibilities by locating golfing tourism in Sweden and Scotland in terms of its socio-ecological and political whereabouts. To him tourists and tourism appeared less as geophysical forces *per se* than as aggregates constituted through a wide variety of power-permeated geographically specific situations that internalize the political-economic particularities of modern capitalism. Outlining this patchwork of differentiated responsibilities in and for the current state of planetary affairs unmasks the political dimension of tourism in the Anthropocene. In the final contribution of part III, Gren provided a mapping of conceptual difficulties that arise when the geophysical understanding of the Anthropos and the Earth system of the Anthropocene meet a social science-based understanding where these are located outside of the social. Consequently, a core Anthropocene challenge for tourism theory was thus identified, that is, how the conceptualization of tourism as a social phenomenon can be aligned with tourism as a geo-force. Finally, Gren proposed the concept of 'tour-ism', the ideology and practice of having all sorts of existences tour the Earth, to be placed at the centre of the Anthropocene itself.

Between departure and arrival

In the introduction we sketched three broad tentative themes pertaining to tourism's encounter with the Anthropocene. We obviously used a broad brush, well aware that the Anthropocene may embody the greatest and most difficult of challenges for the Anthropos one could ever imagine, and where uncertainties abound. As the closing words of the recent update of the Great Acceleration graphs reads:

> Will the next 50 years bring the Great Decoupling or the Great Collapse? The latest 10 years of the Great Acceleration graphs show signs of both but cannot distinguish between these scenarios, or other possibilities. But 100 years on from the advent of the Great Acceleration, in 2050, we'll almost certainly know the answer.
>
> (Steffen *et al.* 2015a, 14)

As the timescales of geological and human history coalesce, '[w]ith the arrival of the Anthropocene we must now be suspicious of all ideas developed in the last 10,000 years' (Hamilton, 2014, 1). It is not difficult to add similar comments to the choir chanting the Anthropocene in big capitals. For example, Castree (2014a, 450) argues that the Anthropocene calls for:

> a far-reaching examination of virtually *every* aspect of 21st century life – from commodity production to transportations systems to energy systems to food consumption habits and beyond [emphasis in the original].

And we all know that every aspect mentioned above will be found in the heartlands of tourism. We know by now, too, that there are more to be found. Among those we have arrived at is an understanding and sense of the Anthropocene that precludes anthropocentrism, yet without being in any way reductionist, anti-humanist, or deterministic (Latour, 2014, 5). However 'geocentric' the Anthropocene may appear to be, in both conceptual and 'terratorial' sense it does certainly not preclude human agency. Yet, the 'geo-part' is, of course, absolutely essential. Especially important to note is that the Earth of the Anthropocene is not a fixed, already composed entity which resides in the background as a terrestrial surface for tourism. This Earth is instead a dynamic Earth system which has its Anthropos as part and parcel of its functioning. It is precisely this understanding of the Earth, as Earth system, which we believe forms the basis for rendering humans as a collective geo-force, that is, 'because we have changed the functioning of the Earth System' (Hamilton, 2015, 2). Rephrased in terms of tourism theory, the standard conceptualization of tourism as spatio-temporal mobility then corresponds to a one-sided and increasingly obsolete understanding of the Earth as merely a surface on which tourism takes place. Taking departure from the Earth of the Anthropocene, tourism would instead need to be conceptualized not only as a geo-force but also as a component in the very functioning of the Earth system itself.

Contrary to prevalent ideas of a humanity being on a collision course with nature, the Anthropocene suggests that we are beginning to realize that we are up against an Earth system of whose functioning we are part and parcel. According to the recent update of the planetary boundaries approach, four out of nine Earth system processes now exceed the proposed boundaries for a safe operating space (Steffen *et al.*, 2015b). Given tourism's considerable contribution to the amount of anthropogenic impact on the Earth system, it has undoubtedly an important and crucial role to play in the geo-juncture between the Anthropos and its safe operating space. For example, sustainable tourism on a global scale may then be understood as:

> the point in time when absolute resource use will begin to decline, despite a growing number of travellers, indicating not only dematerialization of the system, but development in recognition of the physical boundaries of the planetary system.
>
> (Gössling and Peeters, 2015, 655)

A recognition of the Anthropocene in tourism will eventually have to find its truth-value in terms of its usefulness also in negotiating and navigating tourism futures in practice. For example, Northcott (2014, 9) argues that the Anthropocene begs answers to three questions which take us into the realm of action. What kind of world do we have? What kind do we want? What can or must we do to get there? Addressing such questions is likely to demand a qualitative as well as a quantitative shift in how we understand the political. For example, climate change, debates around planetary boundaries, Earth system governance, planetary geoengineering, global sustainability, biosphere integrity, deforestation, acidification of the oceans, atmospheric carbon dioxide and other signifiers of the Anthropocene present political challenges at planetary scale, at the same time as they cannot remain there if due political process is to take place. As Latour (2014a, 4) points out: 'While it is impossible for people to grasp what it is to take up responsibility for the stewardship of the whole planet, it is much easier to see where one stands in relation to a critical zone of variable dimensions.'

In other words, there is a need to downscale the political in the Anthropocene. This is also, we believe, one area where tourism, as indeed 'a critical zone of variable dimensions', has substantial contributions to make. And what would the political of tourism in the Anthropocene be about, if not its role and agency in the composing of common 'Earth Worlds'? As for the Earth, it will increasingly become a matter of concern also for the political in the Anthropocene. Maybe it also needs to be rebaptized 'Gaia', a becoming entity which 'should not be considered an applied theory. Instead, it is a matter that vibrates in all sorts of different mediums' (Latour, 2014b, 69). Attuning is one key word here. We need to be attentive to Gaia's intrusive in-cisions and have these inform our de-cision (Zylinska, 2014, 98).

Destination Anthropocene and tourism destinies

Arriving at destination Anthropocene entails the prospect of facing profound changes in the global political, economic, environmental and social order, along with a wide range of possible consequences for individuals, also in the domain of tourism. Indeed, there is little that now suggests that the Anthropocene will be a place for tourism commodification of the terrestrial Earth as we have come to know it. As the clock of sustainable development is ticking towards the planetary scale, ever more aggressive and more forcefully sustained mitigation policies will be required also in tourism in order to curb the climatic trend, if possible at all (IPCC, 2014). Despite technological efficiency gains, transport-related greenhouse gas emissions are continuing to grow. Meanwhile, mitigation policies sit firmly askew the ideology and practice of tourism development on the ground, where in so many cases, particularly in the periphery, tourism stakeholders form a rather motley crew of loosely aligned solitary entrepreneurs often resistant to the absorption of new external knowledge which is the prerequisite for innovative change (see e.g. Hoarau *et al.*, 2014). Besides, whose local and geographically bounded tourism business would benefit from entrepreneuring which has planetary limits and boundaries as fixed points for action?

One may well argue that the Anthropocene can be 'immensely productive' on questions on how to relate to one another and to non-humans, and that the concept 'invite[s] such foresight at all geographical scales and in cognitive, moral and aesthetic registers' (Castree 2014b, 470). Yet, how destination entrepreneurs will fare in jointly developing innovations that contribute to easing the geo-force of the Anthropos, let alone the industry as a globalizing phenomenon, is difficult to envision within today's almost hegemonic frame of tourism operations. Nevertheless, dim prospects of overturning the tourism system *in toto* need to be counterbalanced by opening spaces for what can be done and achieved.

Destination Anthropocene comes with a multitude of potential tourism destinies that will have to be sustained by geo-ethical decisions. What we would like to highlight here is a nuanced 'geo-logisation' of hospitality ethics which transgresses issues of equity (e.g. of access and participation), professionalism or other human-centred ethics approaches (Fennell, 2006, 2012; Lovelock and Lovelock, 2013). The hospitality geo-ethics we envision would incorporate geo-resources at its core, their origins and usage, and their co-option into value creation in tourism as geo-ethical decisions about tourism activities in one 'Earth World'. The tentative tourism destinies in the Anthropocene we would like to offer in concluding this book are three. These could all transpire, or only one or none, but the number of future development trajectories of tourism is not the issue here. In the Anthropocene they might all be one.

Non-carbon tourism

The first potential development trajectory of a hospitality geo-ethics responsive to our earthly entanglements is what we term 'non-carbon tourism'. The burning of fossil fuels is at the heart of climate change and brings to the fore our collective embroilment with the Earth system through geo-forces. It is well recognized that to stem the pace of climate change, the burning of fossil fuels needs to be significantly reduced. This has led to speculation on the actual assets of the oil firms and ways we can boost the economy with new green technologies and jobs. On this trajectory the destiny of future tourism would ideally be paved by at least carbon-neutral practices, but in practice it still unfolds as business as usual with the ever increasing international tourism hitherto witnessed.

A geo-ethically concerned tourism to come would also be geo-political in ways that explicitly address the global inequality which affords travel opportunities to a limited but increasing share of an ever growing human population, and thus sustain the existing geo-powers of tourism which contribute to driving Earth system processes beyond safe operating space. At stake is whether the growth of international tourism, and aviation in particular, really can be sustained at all with non-carbon fuels and technology not yet in hand, and in many cases merely undergoing cognitive incubation. And can a green transition to renewable energy really solve the unsustainability of the tourism system, or does it imply that 'we would be rushing to hell in a handcart powered by a damaging excess of renewable energy' (Lovelock 2014, 16)? Perhaps the real geo-ethical and geo-political destiny of tourism in the Anthropocene points to home without an away, at least one reached by fossil fuels. This leads to our second trajectory.

Stay-home tourism

The second destiny for tourism in the Anthropocene is home, with the usual caveat that we are here referring to the affluent portion of the Anthropos who has both a home and the means to tour the Earth. Stay-home tourism is a possible trajectory of a geo-ethically informed hospitality which would be underpinned by a greater appreciation of the local and near at hand. In Levinas's (1971) words this recognition of home entails dwelling which is 'a recollection, a coming to oneself, a retreat home with oneself as in a land of refuge, which answers to a hospitality, an expectancy, a human welcome' (p. 156). As a way of addressing modern-day carbon-intensive travel practices, stay-home tourism development could bring destinations and places of interest closer to the former traveller. Fewer and shorter trips can make potential room for more sustainable tourism. An appreciation of home through a Heideggerian shift from travelling to dwelling can further alert us to geo-temporalities and geo-responsibilities to future generations. Dwelling is here about being grounded in the present moment, yet allowing for 'temporal mobility' as argued by Todres and Galvin (2010). Dwelling is indeed ontologically saturated with temporalities through tasks which 'are the constitutive acts of dwelling' (Ingold, 1993, 158). It behoves us to undertake these tasks and 'engage more strategically with a trenchant materiality that is us as it vies with us in agentic assemblages' (Bennett, 2010, 111). Including more earthlings closer to home, such as animals, vegetables and minerals, invites expectancy and allows for the proliferation of the possible existing in more than human registers. This can bring about a shift of perception from the individual's biological life course to that of species life, or even going as far as Yusoff (2013) immersing humanity in geologic time, through incorporating, for example, carbon as the fossilized mineral it is. We might here be looking at small-scale, slow, ecological tourism on a local or national scale, which could also have far-reaching positive effects on anthropogenic change in a planetary register, especially if combined with a 'turbulent material imagination' (Anderson, 2014, 138) and passions thereto (Thrift, 2008). Perhaps, then, tourism in the Anthropocene will eventually transform into a 'home-ism' which also has the Earth system included in its own fabrics?

Destination stewardship

The last of the three destinations for tourism in the Anthropocene has as another 'take home message' a twist on the notion of earthly stewardship, following Steffen *et al.*1 (2007). In its basic articulation their earthly stewardship revolves around three premises as outlined by Clark *et al.* (2005, 7):

> The scientific eye is re-directed from outer space to our 'living Earth' (Lovelock 2003), which operates as one single dynamical system far from thermodynamical equilibrium.
>
> The scientific ambition is re-qualified by fully acknowledging the limits of cognition as highlighted by the notorious uncertainties associated with nonlinearity, complexity, and irreproducibility (Schellnhuber 2002); if the Earth system is a clockwork at all, then it is an organismic one that baffles our best anticipatory capacities.
>
> The scientific ethos is re-balanced at last by accepting that knowledge generation is inextricably embedded in the cultural–historical context (Nowotny *et al.*, 2001) — there is nothing wrong with being particularly curious about the items and issues that matter most for society and with recognizing that the coveted borderlines between observing subjects and scrutinized objects have often been mere constructions of a preposterous reductionism. Thus the research community becomes part of their own riddles, the research specimens become part of their own explanations, and co-production becomes the (post)normal way of coping with the cognitive 'challenges of a changing Earth' (Steffen *et al.* 2002) (*references from the original*).

Steffen *et al.* (2007) claim that the period from 2016 onwards will be one characterized by Earth system stewardship, premised on the three refocused augmentations of the original Copernican revolution listed above. This suggests also that '[t]he human being-in-the-world of which the twentieth century spoke thus turns out to be a being-on-board a cosmic vehicle – call it Gaia or Terra or Sphaira or what you will – which is susceptible to malfunctioning' (Sloterdijk, in Klingan *et al.*, 2015, 268). A key thing to recognize in a science for planetary sustainability is that there 'is no engineer at work and thus the relations between elements cannot be that of the parts with a whole' (Latour, 2014a, 5). We argue, our stewardship cannot be towards the Earth as a whole, or a globe, but only slices thereof: in-cisions that inform de-cisions as Zylinska (2014) puts it. Therefore our vision of an earthly stewardship is one where geo-hospitality includes stories of our more-than-human entanglements. Stories that afford encounters with inorganic matter inform us of 'the spatio-temporal junctures at which one state or regime of an Earth system passes into another' (Clark, 2014, 31), and animate a geo-politics of the Anthropocene that holds on to a promise of tourism's transformative capacities. This 'geo-politics ... is a complex blend of sociopolitical and physico-material negotiations, in which either side of the confluence is as experimental or improvisational as the other' (Clark, 2014, 34). The earthly stewardship is thus one of a geo-ethically informed geo-hospitality, where we can become attentive, also in tourism, to the ways fossil fuels speak as a marker of the Anthropocene forming us as geological subjects, or to an Earth system which is also a tainted mirror of our own touring. And '[w]hile we wait for Gaia, it isn't the sense of the absurd that threatens us now, but rather our lack of adequate preparation for the civilization to come' (Latour, 2013, 486).

On a boat waiting for Gaia

From the port of Húsavík, at the edge of the Arctic Circle in the north of Iceland, the company North Sailing has operated whale-watching excursions in renovated Icelandic wooden fishing vessels since 1995 (Cunningham *et al.*, 2012). In recent years the company has acquired wooden schooners through relations established at the Norwegian Risør Trebåtfestival and as of 2015 one of the three schooners they own, *Opal*, has been fitted with a hybrid propulsion system that allows the boat to be run on renewable energy instead of fossil fuel in addition to the classic wind propulsion. With this schooner whale-watching trips are offered on the Skjálfandi Bay at Húsavík, but also to the east coast of Greenland where wind power recharges the electric engine originally charged with Icelandic hydropower. A diesel generator is on board but merely for fail safe.

Although the journey to Húsavík may have been by a fossil-fuel-driven mode of transportation, the trip itself from there holds potential. Lying in berth of the oaken two-masted schooner *Opal*, one can indeed get a sense of the forest's thoughts (Kohn, 2013) through the creaking of planks and rafters in the boat. The slowed-down travel experience affords an awareness of time passing during the passage of the journey itself, and via natural change such as light and dark, tides and weather (Varley and Medway, 2011, see also Morton, 2013, 69). These are openings in terms of life forces and their reproduction, as bodies and as the affects that bodies become affiliated to (Yusoff, 2013, 791). Not only is the journey a carbon-free one, it affords an attuning to the rhythms of the Earth and dimensions of temporality (Lefebvre, 2004), offering an opportunity for us to develop a sense of humility and perspective that is the prerequisite for any environmentally sound or sustainable tourism. The elemental exposure to the winds of the Arctic Ocean unravels the Anthropocene quandary of carbon-based travel, whilst sustaining some of the transformative powers of travel experiences. Through the exposure to the schooner's oaken beams, their smells and sounds, an appreciation of the near at hand emerges. Dimensions of temporality are unravelled through the schooner's history and building/maintenance practices culminating 1,000 years of ship-building in the North Atlantic. The emergent intergenerational responsibilities of the Anthropocene are here brought to the fore, but moreover how timescales can be shifted. Developing responsibilities and attuning to more than human rhythms of life *with* the Earth are thus afforded to those undertaking the schooner's journey. These affordances and encounters with the earthly elements inform story-telling which allows for a minimal geo-ethics for the Anthropocene (Zylinska, 2014).

And as we return to the port of Húsavík, we sit quietly on the deck for a while before disembarking. 'We have to slow down, re-localize, re-think, compose' (Latour, 2014b, 70) new geo-imaginations of tourism in and of the Anthropocene.

References

Anderson, B. 2014. *Encountering Affect: Capacities, Apparatuses, Conditions*. Farnham: Ashgate Publishing.

Bennett, J. 2010. *Vibrant Matter: A Political Ecology of Things*. Durham, NC: Duke University Press.

Castree, N. 2014a. The Anthropocene and geography II: Current contributions. *Geography Compass*, 8(7), 450–63.

Castree, N. 2014b. The Anthropocene and geography III: Future directions. *Geography Compass*, 8(7), 464–76.

Clark, N. 2014. Geo-politics and the disaster of the Anthropocene. *Sociological Review*, 62: S1, 19–37.

Clark, W.C., Crutzen, P.J. and Schellnhuber, H.J. 2005. *Science for Global Sustainability: Toward a New Paradigm*. CID Working Paper, 120. Cambridge, MA: Science, Environment and Development Group, Center for International Development, Harvard University.

Cunningham, P. Huijbens, E., and Wearing, S. 2012. Whaling or watching: Twisting the sustainability rhetoric and possible outcomes. *Journal of Sustainable Tourism*, 20(1), 143–61.

Fennell, D.A. 2006. *Tourism Ethics*. Clevedon: Channel View Publications.

Fennell, D.A. 2012. *Tourism and Animal Ethics*. London: Routledge.

Gössling, S., and Peeters, P. 2015. Assessing tourism´s global environmental impact 1900–2050. *Journal of Sustainable Tourism*, 23(5), 639–59.

Hamilton, C. 2014. When Earth juts through world. A contribution to 'The Situation Facing the Moderns After the Intrusion of Gaïa: A Philosophical Simulation', Sciences Po, Paris, 28–29 July.

Hamilton, C. 2015. Getting the Anthropocene so wrong. *The Anthropocene Review*, 1–6. doi: 10.1177/2053019615584974.

Hoarau, H. Wigger, K., and Bystrowska, M. 2014. Innovation and climate change: The role of network relations and the attitudes of tourism actors on Svalbard. In G.A. Alsos, D. Eide and E.L. Madsen (eds), *Handbook of Research and Innovation in Tourism Industries*. Cheltenham: Edward Elgar, 303–24.

Ingold, T. 1993. The temporality of the landscape. *World Archaeology*, 25(2), 152–74.

IPCC 2014. *Climate Change 2014. Impacts, Adaption, and Vulnerability.* New York: Cambridge University Press.

Klingan, K., Sepahvand, A., Rosol, C. and Scherer, B.M. (eds) 2015. *Textures of the Anthropocene: Ray.* Cambridge, MA: MIT Press.

Kohn, E. 2013. *How Forests Think: Toward an Anthropology beyond the Human.* Berkeley, CA: University of California Press.

Latour, B. 2013. *An Inquiry into Modes of Existence: An Anthropology of the Moderns.* Cambridge, MA: Harvard University Press.

Latour, B. 2014. On selves, forms, and forces. *Journal of Ethnographic Theory*, 4(2), 1–6.

Latour, B. 2014a. Some advantages of the notion of 'critical zone' for geopolitics. *Procedia Earth and Planetary Science*, 10, 3–6.

Latour, B. 2014b. Bruno Latour. Interview with Camila Marambio. *Miami Rail* (Winter), 68–71.

Lefebvre, H. 2004. *Rhythmanalysis: Space, Time and Everyday Life.* London: Continuum.

Levinas, E. 1971. *Totality and Infinity: An Essay on Exteriority.* The Hague: Martinus Nijhoff.

Lovelock, J. 2014. *A Rough Ride to the Future.* London: Allen Lane.

Lovelock, B.A., and Lovelock, K. 2013. *The Ethics of Tourism: Critical and Applied Perspectives.* London: Routledge.

Morton, T. 2013. *Hyperobjects: Philosophy and Ecology After the End of the World.* Minneapolis, MN, and London: University of Minnesota Press.

Northcott, M.S. 2014. *A Political Theology of Climate Change.* London: Society for Promoting Christian Knowledge.

Steffen, W., Crutzen, P., and McNeill, J. 2007. The Anthropocene: Are humans now overwhelming the great forces of nature? *Ambio*, 36(8), 614–21.

Steffen, W., Broadgate, W., Deutsch, L., Gaffney, O., and Ludwig, C. 2015a. The trajectory of the Anthropocene: The great acceleration. *The Anthropocene Review*, (2)1, 1–18.

Steffen, W., *et al.* 2015b. Planetary boundaries: Guiding human development on a changing planet. *Science*, 347(6223), 1–10.

Thrift, N. 2008. *Non-Representational Theory. Space, Politics, Affect.* London: Routledge.

Todres, L., and Galvin, K. 2010. 'Dwelling-mobility': An existential theory of well-being. *International Journal of Qualitative Studies on Health and Well-Being*, 5(3). doi: 10.3402/qhw.v5i3.5444.

Varley, P., and Medway, D. 2011. Ecosophy and tourism: Rethinking a mountain resort. *Tourism Management*, 32(4), 902–11.

Yusoff, K. 2013. Geologic life: Prehistory, climate, futures in the Anthropocene. *Environment and Planning D: Society and Space*, 31, 779–95.

Zylinska, J. 2014. *Minimal Ethics for the Anthropocene.* Ann Arbor, MI: Open Humanities Press.

Index